Country music is like no other music—a proud music reflecting what's best in America.

But while country music is different from other art forms, its creators, unfortunately, are not much different from artists in other fields. For years, rock and roll has had the reputation for being the home of self-destructive rowdies. For even longer, Hollywood, with its casting couch and coke parties, was widely regarded as *the* hotbed of sin. But the truth is, these two arenas have nothing on country when it comes to sex, drugs, drink, and disaster.

This book is about that dark side of country music. It's about country singers who have survived great personal and professional trials; those who did not; and those who were victims of circumstances beyond their control. Unlike their music, their stories won't leave you tapping your feet and humming along, though they are, tragically, every bit as real and every bit as moving.

And unlike many of them, their music lives on to remind us of why they lived—and often, why they died . . . .

COUNTRY MUSIC BABYLON

Other Books by Jeff Rovin

COUNTRY MUSIC BABYLON

JEFF ROVIN

ST. MARTIN'S PAPERBACKS

COUNTRY MUSIC BABYLON

Copyright © 1993 by Jeff Rovin.

Cover photograph by Katherine Allen/Stock South.

ISBN: 0-312-95027-6

Printed in the United States of America

St. Martin's Paperbacks edition/May 1993

10 9 8 7 6 5 4 3 2 1

Contents

Introduction

"It is as fundamental as sunshine and rain, snow and wind and the light of the moon peeping through the trees. Some folks like it and some dislike it very much, but it'll be there long after you and I have passed out of this picture for the next one."

—Original *Grand Ole Opry* host George Hay on country music

It'll come as a surprise to no one that country music originated in the country—though not *this* country. The roots of country music are in Europe: in England, Scotland, Ireland, Germany, and France, where farmers and laborers would sing (and still do, in fact) about their lives, needs, loves and hardships, songs like "Soldier, Soldier, Won't You Marry Me?" or "Robin Adair," or spirit-lifting ditties like "Frog Went a-Courtin' " or "O, Sweet Molly Malone." They passed these songs to their children and also brought them along when they came to these shores. Sea shanties were generally just country music carried offshore by sailors and sung as they swabbed the decks or hoisted the sails.

The tradition of singing during and after work lived most strongly in the south and portions of the midwest, where people labored in the fields. Sometimes they'd sing a cappella as they worked; often, they'd relax after a long day by singing and accompanying themselves on the banjo or guitar. From somewhere inside they'd also find the energy to dance—especially the Irish immigrants—usually to a fierce fiddle tempo.

Distinctly different kinds of "country" music developed over the years, most notably bluegrass, with its fiddle and banjo-driven melodies; Dixieland Jazz, which added horns and woodwinds to create a smart or smouldering mix; western swing, which was essentially a blend of the two; and Cajun, the folk music of France that makes contagious use of the accordion, fiddle, triangle, and washboard.

In time, other kinds of music influenced these traditional forms—such as gospel, with its rich harmonies—creating more wonderful hybrids; still, the music of the country was seldom heard beyond the fields and hills, barns and community halls of the south.

Many things changed in music when Thomas Edison invented the phonograph in 1878. Though it took some thirty years for the technology to become fully workable —and, just as importantly, widely affordable—phonographs brought music and artists to people who never before had access to them, from classical music to Broadway shows to popular singers and musicians to regional phenomena like jazz and country music.

In 1922, a pair of fiddlers, Uncle Eck Robertson and Henry Gilliand, made the first country recordings, "Sally Goodin'" and "Arkansaw Traveller." And while the recording companies didn't call it country music back then—they sold it as "hillbilly music" or "old-time southern songs" or "mountain ballads"—whatever name they used, the music was a hit, speaking to a huge audience of working men and women.

For the most part, there were several reasons the music caught on with the record buying public. For one thing, it had energy, as Okeh Records pointed out in a catalogue from 1925:

"Hear, folks, the music of the Hill Billies! These here mountaineers sure have a way of fetching music out of the banjo, fiddle, and guitar that surprises listeners, old and young, into feeling skittish. Theirs is a spirited entertainment and one you will warm to."

It was toe-tapping music.

For another thing, those simple melodies got in people's minds and stayed there. There was nothing complex about them: you just listened and hummed away.

Finally, its appeal was also due to the honesty of the songwriters and the singers. During the Depression in particular, country music addressed the dreams and fears of the people. While Al Jolson was taking a hopeful swing at things—sitting on top of the world or enjoying the rainbow 'round his shoulder—country musicians were singing about lost love, lost farms, and lost dreams.

The genre's first superstar, blind guitarist Riley Puckett, cut his first record in 1924. Puckett's velvety baritone and innovative guitar work—along with his famous yodel, which had novelty value in the north—kept him on top for years and paved the way for the likes of Jimmie Rodgers, the Carter Family and, most importantly, the "barn dance" radio shows that brought country to homes that didn't own phonographs. One station, the month-old WSM in Nashville, began its hour-long *Barn Dance* on November 28, 1925 and featured the immortal strains of "Tennessee Waggoner" courtesy of white-whiskered, eighty-two-year-old fiddler Uncle Jimmy Thompson, a Civil War veteran. Two years later, emcee George Dewey Hay nicknamed the show the *Grand Ole Opry*, and on December 10, 1927, the name of the popular now three-hour show was officially changed. The show was so popular, in fact, that in 1939, in an effort to limit the crowds that wanted to see the show as it was broadcast, the managers were reluctantly forced to charge admission.

Country music found an even wider audience thanks

to the popular singing cowboys of the movies. In 1934, Gene Autry—a former saxophonist who also admired and imitated Jimmie Rodgers—was in the right place at the right time when Hollywood came calling, looking for someone who would appeal to the same audience that listened to the barn dance shows on the radio. The movies made him a multi-media superstar, and later did the same for Roy Rogers and Tex Ritter.

During the 1930s and 1940s, other broadcast and recording artists like Tex Williams, Merle Travis, and especially the great Hank Williams helped country break from its regional bonds. The two World Wars helped as well, as soldiers from the south brought their country music around the world, an open door that certainly helped Hank Williams gain even greater fame in the late 1940s and early 1950s than he had before the war.

But while there were crossover hits onto the pop charts over the years—such as Johnny Horton's classic "The Battle of New Orleans," which was the biggest song of *any* kind in 1959—these incursions into the mainstream were few and relatively far between. Often, country stars topped the charts only when they "abandoned" their roots, for example, Gene Autry when he recorded the Christmas songs "Rudolph the Rednosed Reindeer" and "Here Comes Santa Claus" in 1949, and Dolly Parton with "9 to 5" from her hit film in 1981. Not that Dolly didn't take flak for "selling out": even Bill Clinton got into the act of music criticism. While still a candidate for the presidency, he was asked who, ideally, he would like to have perform at his inaugural ball. He said, "Dolly Parton," then added, "to sing some of her early music."

The truth was, Dolly wasn't alone: over the years, Glen Campbell, Johnny Cash, Crystal Gayle, and others had crossed over. Often, it wasn't even calculated. In the 1960s, Nashville grew like Hollywood had in the 1920s:

it became the mecca for mass entertainment of its kind. Not surprisingly, many country artists responded militantly to the increasingly mainstream Nashville "sound." Artists like Waylon Jennings and Willie Nelson felt that country had abandoned its heart, that it had become Muzak, a heartless distillation of what music buyers around the world perceived it to be: traditional hillbilly music. Music Gomer Pyle listened to on TV. Music they played on *Hee Haw*.

Resenting the stereotype that Nashville itself seemed to be perpetuating for a buck, these men became "Outlaws," mixing country with rock and more traditional blues and other styles, giving it a harder edge than it had had for years. They developed new forms, such as countrypolitan and progressive—much to the chagrin of the Nashville traditionalists. Many artists moved to the "new Nashville," Austin, Texas, while others relocated to Los Angeles and other non-country sites.

Back in the mainstream of country music, the need for artists to abandon country in order to hit the pop charts began to change in a big way in the late 1980s. Artists like Reba McEntire helped get country back to its roots at a time when mainstream America was ready for them. Garth Brooks did likewise. So did Alan Jackson, George Strait, and others. By the 1990s, country stars weren't just *on* the pop charts, they owned them. Stars like Brooks and newcomer Billy Ray Cyrus flew high while the likes of Michael Jackson, Bruce Springsteen, and Bon Jovi posted shockingly low record sales. (It was embarrassing to see Springsteen, who used to be Mr. Taciturn, suddenly showing up everywhere from MTV to *Rolling Stone* to *Saturday Night Live* to get publicity. It was equally embarrassing to watch the media, like lapdogs, lining up to give him a forum, though it didn't help record sales a bit. There *is* justice in the world.)

Just *how* big has country become? Consider: in 1980,

there were 1,500 country music stations in the U.S. Today, there are over 2,500. In 1985, sixteen country albums went gold (sold a half-million copies); in 1991, thirty-five albums went platinum (sold one million copies). By the end of 1992, country was outselling every other form of music by almost two-to-one over "traditional" pop. The Judds pulled more viewers on a cable pay-per-view TV special than the Rolling Stones and the New Kids on the Block.

Different people attribute the boom to different things. Many pundits say that country owes its popularity to the current economic climate. Just as country music spoke for the masses during the Depression, hard times today have left everyone identifying with the sad, lonely balladeer.

While there's certainly some truth to that, especially where country's popularity on radio is concerned, it doesn't account for the staggering record sales. People with disposable income are buying records in the tens of millions.

Actor John Ritter, Tex's son—and, not surprisingly, a huge country music fan—is convinced that the seeds of the country phenomenon were planted in the 1960s when the folksy Bob Dylan brought country to the Baby Boomers.

"It's kept building like a tidal wave since Dylan started recording in Nashville in the middle 1960s, and did that wonderful duet with Johnny Cash ("Girl From North Country"). By the end of the decade, the industry was calling what he did 'country rock,' but that was like when they coined the term rockabilly to describe what Elvis and his contemporaries did, that mix of country with rhythm and blues. It was still, at heart, country music."

Dylan helped bring attention to country, but the majority of music industry observers—this one included—

attribute the sudden, mammoth appeal of country music to a lack of competition. This isn't the back-handed compliment it appears to be, for if folks don't like what they hear, they won't come back. There wouldn't have been four Garth Brooks albums in the top thirty pop charts at one time in the closing weeks of 1992—with close to twenty-five million in sales between them. But the truth is, middle class, raised-on-pop adults have no or, at best, marginal interest in heavy metal and rap, so they've turned to country. Pam Tillis, the hot young country star and daughter of Mel Tillis, says, "In the 1960s and 1970s . . . it seemed like country was ashamed of itself, like it was apologetic and wanted to be pop. But now it's the last bastion of song, with melodies and lack of artifice."

Very true. Wreckx-N-Effect's "Rump Shaker" just wasn't a ditty middle America was prepared to sing in the shower. Wynonna's "No One Else On Earth" was.

David Letterman's bandleader, Paul Shaffer, puts it more concisely: "Country," he says, "is soul music for white people."

It's also a musical form in which women can talk directly to women—or men, letting us eavesdrop and leaving us to dwell on our flaws—and also to teenagers and families. Reba McEntire says, "Liking country is suddenly hip. The younger generation will be our audience for the next ten years. They can relate to what I sing about—it's something that happens to them every day."

While country music is different from other art forms, its creators, unfortunately, are not much different from artists in other fields. For the last thirty years, rock and roll has had the reputation for being the home of self-destructive rowdies. For over twice as long as that, Hollywood, with its casting couch and coke parties, was widely regarded as *the* hotbed of sin. But the truth is, these two arenas have *nothing* on country when it comes to sex, drugs, drink, and disaster.

This book is about that dark side of country music. It's about country singers who have survived great personal and professional trials; those who did not; and those who were victims of circumstances beyond their control. Unlike their music, their stories won't leave you tapping your feet and humming along, though they are, tragically, every bit as real and every bit as moving.

And unlike many of them, at least their music lives on to remind us of why they lived—and, often, why they died.

Hank Williams

ELVIS may be the undisputed King. Clapton may be God to many. And Bruce was once the Boss.

But Hank was something more: he was Everyman, someone whose music transcends his own suffering, makes you smile whatever your mood, exists on a plane of its own, untouched by any popular singer, country or otherwise, who has come since.

In one of the very rare interviews he gave during his short life—the singer was twenty-nine when he died—Hank Williams was asked to define country music. Without hesitation, he answered that he could do that in one word: "Sincerity."

Williams had that. He knew the pain about which he sang, and he knew other people who had suffered it. As he told one interviewer, "You got to know a lot about hard work. You got to have smelled a lot of mule manure before you can sing like a hillbilly."

When he sang, the high, slightly nasal voice with its painful catch or triumphant yodel was that of a man who had lived a great deal, who had known joy and sorrow, who had succumbed to temptation and was able to sing about all of it directly to each member of the audience.

When he sang, it was truth as country music had never known it before, or since.

Born September 17, 1923, just outside Georgiana, Alabama, Hiriam "Hank" Williams (Hiram was misspelled on his birth certificate) was born with spina bifida, an incomplete formation and fusion of the spinal canal, which allows the nerves and cord itself to protude and lie just beneath the skin. The defect would cause him enormous pain in his youth and, later, would lead to an addiction to pain killers. He started out with a good understanding of what it was to suffer; life just added salt to the wound.

Hank's father Elonzo ("Lonnie") was a poor lumber company employee and World War I vet who ended up in a Veteran's Administration hospital in Alexandria, Louisiana when Hank was just seven—the residual effects of shell-shock, gas, and mostly having been beaten unconscious by a fellow soldier who'd been in love with the same French ma'm'selle.

Hank's mother Lilly was left alone to raise Hank and his one-year-older sister Irene. In a way, the tough, six-foot-tall woman was happier, never having had much regard for Lonnie and his lack of ambition . . . while more than one friend of the family speculated that Lonnie, too, was happier where he was now, in the arms of the VA. (He and Lilly were divorced in 1942; five years later, she would marry William Wallace Stone.)

After Lonnie left, the three Williamses moved into Georgiana proper where their shack burned down, leaving them with nothing. The next day, in an effort to earn money, Irene roasted a pound of peanuts, which Hank bagged and took to town to sell in the streets. He earned thirty cents and promptly expanded his business to shining shoes and, later, to selling packets of seeds. Most of what the young boy learned about life and people he learned on that street corner.

Meanwhile, Lilly was doing all right herself. She'd found an empty old home that she turned into a boarding house. One of her borders was a girl cousin, who had come to Georgiana to finish high school. Since the girl's parents had no money, Lilly agreed to take her if they would take Hank for a year. So it was off to the country again for Hank where on Saturday nights, with absolutely nothing else to do, the eleven-year-old would sneak off and hang out with loggers and farmers, listening to their music, learning the rudiments of guitar-playing and, unfortunately, acquiring a taste for liquor. Unlike the relatively well-to-do kids who had looked down at him in Georgiana, Hank found acceptance among the men who liked having a little mascot, a kid they could make a man in their own image.

When Hank returned to Georgiana, his mother moved the family to a different boarding house in Greenville, and Hank—bright-eyed and always singing to himself, now—went back to the streets, selling peanuts and shining shoes. There, he had met a small, scruffy black street singer named Rufus Payne who called himself Tee-Tot and strummed a guitar and sang for pennies. Hank was fascinated by the man and his music and hung out with him, much to his mother's chagrin—though she agreed, after relentless badgering, to buy her son a used guitar.

For two years, Hank and Tee-Tot were inseparable, singing and drinking together, the experienced performer teaching the boy how to work a crowd, how to sell a song, how to look a man or especially a woman straight in the eye when he sang. Hank ate it up. His schoolwork suffered, and he spent a great deal of his spare time in Greenville listening to hillbilly songs on their banged-up old radio. But Hank told his mother it didn't matter: he was going to become a hillbilly singer.

That was all Mamma Williams needed to hear. Unhappy with how things had been going in Greenville anyway, she up-and-moved the family to Montgomery, where the schools were better and the men were of a higher class for her daughter. But if Lilly thought the move would dull Hank's enthusiasm for music, she was mistaken. Montgomery was the home of "his" stations, WSFA and WCOV. To Hank, Montgomery, Alabama was music city.

He continued not to do his schoolwork, though he had learned not to tell his mother that. Instead, he wrote songs, practiced diligently, and when the Empire Theater sponsored a talent contest, Hank entered, sang his own song "WPA Blues," and won the fifteen dollar first prize. His win earned him an audition at WSFA and, impressing the management, he earned a spot performing on the station's *Saturday Night Jamboree*. The fourteen-year-old went from there to a twice-a-week gig on WCOV, then returned to WSFA to star on Dad Crysell's show as "The Singing Kid": when he began getting fan mail from listeners in Greenville and Georgiana, he knew he had arrived. He'd found his calling.

Meanwhile, his grades in school went from bad to disastrous. Because he worked late and drank hard, he ended up sleeping through most of his classes. Finally, when he was nineteen years old and still in the ninth grade, he decided he'd had enough of this kind of education. Hank decided to pursue music full-time.

Even before deciding to leave school, he had organized local talent into the Drifting Cowboys. They performed at dances and at local bars, where the clientele was rough-and-tumble and where Hank became as adept at fighting as he was at singing and drinking. He took to carrying a blackjack, brass knuckles, and finally a .38 after one enraged customer bit off a big chunk of his forehead.

In 1942, the singer fell in love with drugstore employee Audrey Mae Sheppard Guy, who was married at the time to a G.I. fighting abroad. An aspiring singer, Audrey pulled a Dear John, divorcing her husband and marrying Hank in December of 1944.

As it turns out, Audrey had bigger plans for Hank than Hank did. He just wanted to sing; she wanted him to be wealthy and famous. Her thinking was more than a little self-serving: if he hit it big, and she were singing backup for him—despite the fact that she hadn't much of a voice —then she, too, would be rich and famous.

But Hank constantly thwarted her ambitions and his own best interests because of his drinking. On occasion, she managed to keep him from drinking until after a show—but nearly as often, he was too drunk to go on. For although he and the bottle were very good friends, he couldn't hold his liquor: four drinks and he was obliterated. Thus, despite Hank's talent and growing fame in Alabama, and despite glowing recommendations from *Grand Ole Opry* stars Roy Acuff and Ernest Tubb, his reputation for drunkenness and unreliability kept him from being offered a place on the program. He continued to be in demand locally, though big time fame eluded him. Or rather, he eluded it.

Two years passed, and Audrey'd finally had enough of mucking around in the sticks. In the summer of 1946, at her prodding—and with her in tow—Hank headed for Nashville. Upon arriving, they walked unannounced into the offices of Acuff-Rose, the industry's pre-eminent management and publishing firm. After listening to some of Hank's songs, songwriter Fred Rose took a chance and gave him a publishing contract. He also began sending him out on tour in order to give his compositions exposure.

Six months later, with Hank's reputation building, Rose landed him a recording deal with the minor Sterling label. His recordings sold well enough for bigtime

MGM to take a chance on him. His first MGM record, "Move It On Over"—sung to a hound, and the best of the man-in-a-doghouse songs—was a decent-sized hit in 1947. Rose scored a major coup when he got his budding star onto Shreveport, Louisiana's popular radio show *Louisiana Hayride* in May of 1948, and that's when the ball really started to roll for the singer.

Hank was on his best behavior down in Shreveport. He realized (and if he forgot, Audrey reminded him) how important *Louisiana Hayride* was to his career . . . and to his marriage. Despite her ambition, Audrey had become increasingly unhappy with things on the home front. Hank was not only drinking heavily, but his longtime fondness for collecting (and pointing) guns increased, and there were bitter and violent arguments. By February, fearing for her life and despairing that Hank was never going to make it big, Audrey had filed for divorce complaining, in her papers, that Hank "has committed actual violence on her person attended with danger to her life or health."

Then Shreveport beckoned, and Audrey agreed to go (for whose benefit? one wonders), but only if Hank didn't drink. He swore he wouldn't, and for months he lived up to his pledge. The couple's domestic life was relatively blissful; Audrey became pregnant, and in May of 1949, Randall Hank Williams was born. Professionally, things were also going Hank's way. He was a hit on the show and on the "Folk Record Charts," his "Lovesick Blues" outselling releases by the likes of bigshots George Morgan and Eddy Arnold.

Finally, the *Grand Ole Opry* could no longer ignore his rising star, and on June 11, 1949, he appeared on the show. It was an amazing coming-together of the ultimate artist and *the* most demanding audience, the latter being so dazzled by the singer that it brought him back for an unprecedented six encores. Famed Opry announcer Grant Turner remembers, "How he *worked* that audience! He focused his attention on the audience, drawing it close to him, becoming a part of it and the audience becoming a part of him."

Grand Ole Opry legend Minnie Pearl recalls, "He had real animal magnetism. He destroyed the women in the audience."

Tee-Tot had taught him well, but Hank sure knew how to use what he had!

With the boost the *Grand Ole Opry* gave him, Hank quickly become the biggest-selling country artist in the business, with hits like "You're Gonna Change" and "Wedding Bells" in 1949, "Long Gone Lonesome Blues," "Why Don't You Love Me?" and "I Just Don't Like This Kind of Livin' " in 1950, and an incredible seven top-ten hits the following year. He grew richer than he (or Audrey or, for that matter, Lilly) had ever imagined possible, but he could never shake the demons that had taken hold of him back around the campfire with those loggers and farmers. And then there was his back pain, which worsened the older he got and the more he traveled.

He'd started drinking again when he clicked at the *Grand Ole Opry*. He needed a release from the pressure, which is also why he started taking mistresses—some of them as young as fifteen years old. He didn't want to drink *and* be criticized, and that wouldn't happen with a one-night-stand.

His absences caused Audrey to jump on him when he came home, triggering awful fights. He reportedly beat her severely on several occasions, which caused him to feel guilty and drink even more. Inebriation started another vicious circle going, having to rely on Benzedrine to get up for gigs, then downers and more booze so he could sleep afterwards. He started missing dates again, even at the *Grand Ole Opry*. Star Faron Young ("The

Singing Sheriff") told *Opry* historian Chet Hagan (author of the superlative book *Grand Ole Opry*), "The Opry people gave him plenty of chances. You know, they run him off for a while and he'd come back and be drunk all over again."

Indeed, they gave him unprecedented chances, even convincing him to spend some time at Vanderbilt Hospital in an effort to get on the wagon. WSM radio station executive Irving Waugh says that Hank did indeed sober up during his stay, and that his mother was hopeful when she went to the hospital to pick him up.

"Well," says Waugh, "they got to about the second red light and he jumped out, leaving her there on the street with the car. And he disappeared for another three weeks."

Drinking, whoring, and sleeping off both.

When he returned to the realm of the living, Hank felt repentant enough to try and keep up his road schedule, though he regularly got into fights at restaurants when he was asked to remove his hat, which he refused to do because he was balding and extremely self-conscious of same. He would pitch a fit at hotels when managers asked him to quiet down in the rooms and hall, where Hank the Kid was known to shoot at paintings for recreation or when guests or housekeepers disturbed him. Once, he was so startled by a maid who walked in unannounced that he pulled out a gun and shot at *her*. Fortunately, the weapon misfired, and the housekeeper was able to scoop up a lamp and knock him unconscious. Another time, he reportedly blew a movie deal with MGM because he walked into a top executive's office, put his feet on the man's desk and, of course, refused to take off his hat. To say that he was in a tripwire emotional state due to drink and the pressures of fame is an understatement.

As if things weren't bad enough for Hank, he was

thrown from his horse while hunting in the fall of 1951, rupturing several discs in his back and forcing doctors to operate. The spinal fusion was supposed to take care of most of his back problems, pre-existing and otherwise. But he became addicted to the painkillers, which frequently left him dazed and/or hostile. Even more hostile than usual.

But however he was offstage, when he managed to get on-stage, the pain was only in the voice and in his eyes. He still had the magic, *was* magic, and no one escaped his spell.

Except for Audrey. Hank's concerts and recordings were earning him a great deal of money, and Audrey was finally having her day in the sun. She spent money freely, adding rooms to the house they'd bought, picking up furniture and furs and jewelry and everything else that struck her fancy, including Cadillacs and cattle for the farm they also owned. The marriage was a marriage in name only. When he wasn't throwing punches at Audrey, he was busy throwing her expensive new belongings onto the front lawn because he was drunk, pissed, or both. She was seeing other men, and he was seeing other women; he even got one of them, pretty, blonde Bobbie Jett, pregnant.

In January of 1952, after Hank picked up a gun at a New Year's Party and fired several shots at Audrey and two female friends, Audrey had had enough. Hank moved out of the house, and the divorce became official in May.

In October of 1952, the singer signed a contract with Bobbie Jett in which he agreed to cover the hospital expenses, as well as $100 per month payable in the middle of each month as long as the child lives. The contract also stipulated that the child would be turned over to Hank's mother. A daughter was born in January. (See chapter on Hank Williams, Jr. and Jett Williams.)

Throughout 1952, drink and drugs made Hank's behavior more erratic than it had ever been. At a concert in Richmond, Virginia, on January 29, he was so out of it that he forgot the words to the songs. When the sell-out crowd booed him, he told them he had a right to be discombobulated and began stripping to show them the surgical scar on his back. A bandmate stopped him, and realizing what he'd done, Hank tried to regain some of his dignity by singing. But the songs he sang were those he'd already performed and, to more boos, he left the stage.

In San Francisco, he spent the morning with a reporter, giving him a lengthy interview; by the time of the concert that evening, Hank was so bombed that he didn't recognize the man or remember even having met him.

To top things off, in the fall, *Grand Ole Opry* management reluctantly decided that they were better off without the biggest country star in the world. Though he was never officially fired, he wasn't asked to perform, either.

"Everyone," says Irving Waugh, "was just waiting for him to straighten himself out."

Waiting and praying. But it never happened, even though the number one hits kept coming: the infectious "Jambalaya," "Honky Tonk Blues," and others.

Friends and fans alike hoped things would turn around for Hank when he met a woman, stunning nineteen-year-old Billie Jean Jones Eshlimar, a divorcée who lived in Nashville and worked for the phone company. He fell in love and was so dazzled by her devotion to him that he wrote a song about the recently departed Audrey that expressed his disappointment with her: "Your Cheatin' Heart." It became the song for which Hank Williams is best remembered, and in its painful honesty and memorable melody may well be the greatest country song of them all.

Hank married Billie Jean on October 18, 1952, against the wishes of his mother—who had finally cozied up to Audrey, even though Lilly knew what a golddigger she was. The newlyweds set up housekeeping at Lilly's boarding house, in what was supposed to be a temporary arrangement—that is, until Hank's post-divorce finances had a chance to recover and they could find a place of their own.

But while Hank initially had a great deal of enthusiasm for the relationship, drink and drugs soon overwhelmed him and cooled his love. Audrey long maintained that he told her he wanted to get back together with her, but those sentiments—if he really did express them—have to be considered in the context of Hank's mental state. Though he went back on the road, supporting records that kept on selling, he was a mess— and getting worse.

The devoted Billie Jean accompanied Hank at first, but his chronic abuse of drugs and drink had resulted in increasingly less control over his bladder and bowels and she quickly tired of waking up in his waste. On December 11, after nearly two solid months on the road, Billie Jean and her brother Sonny brought Hank to Shreveport's North Louisiana Sanitarium in an effort to clean him up.

He complained of chest pains and of difficulty he had breathing. He was given Demerol, but his resistance to the sedative was amazing (or not, considering what he was used to putting in his system). The day he checked in, he managed to leave. Packing a gun, he went wandering around the streets, a poor, staggering, pathetic figure. Hank was arrested, jailed, and returned to the sanitarium, where doctors put him on the more potent sodium amytal. *That* calmed his temper and curbed his appetite for drink.

Two days later, doped and repentant, he was back on

the road, trying to fulfill his commitments. But it was rare that he gave the kind of show that had made him famous. Onstage, he went through the songs without heart, or he'd get snippy with the audience, refusing to sing hits that they requested and ending up in shouting matches with fans. Backstage, he'd get into fights with people who wanted autographs, with bandmates, or with theater managers. One such fight got so far out of hand that it ended only when Hank was brought down with a hard kick to the groin. If those closest to Hank couldn't always prevent the fights, at least they made sure that he wasn't within arm's reach of a gun.

In the closing weeks of 1952, Hank was on the road without his wife. He was almost constantly on *something* —morphine was the drug he favored at the time—and since she couldn't control his habits, she felt it would be best if she stayed away from him, not appear to judge him or criticize him, not add to his distress or shame.

The family had a pleasant time together over the holidays, giving Billie Jean hope that things would be better when Hank returned. They parted on good terms, even though she and Lilly did *not* get along. Rather than stay at the boarding house, she went to her parents' home nearby.

On December 30, Hank found himself stranded in Knoxville due to bad weather, so he checked into a hotel, phoned his mother, and told her to send a driver from Montgomery with his powder blue Cadillac convertible so he could get to Charleston for the next night's performance. Then, thanks to forged prescriptions, Hank was able to get himself morphine and the powerful sedative chloral hydrate. He took the drugs, drank some tequila, and passed out. (Musician Jerry Rivers said that Hank was *never* a recreational drug user, but that his philosophy was, "If it helps to take one pill every four hours, it must be even better to take four pills every one hour.")

The next day, seventeen-year-old Charles Carr arrived with the Cadillac. He went up to Hank's room and found the singer barely conscious. Phoning Hank's handlers, he reported that he didn't think Hank would be fit to do a show that night. They agreed and told him to head instead for Canton, Ohio, where the singer was booked for a New Year's performance. Carr was instructed to try and keep Hank sober, if possible.

Hank came around and, deciding he'd rather fly than drive, went to the airport for a three-thirty flight. But within two hours bad weather had forced them back, and the duo returned to the hotel. Hank complained of back pain, and Dr. P.H. Cardwell came and gave him two injections of morphine and B-12. Hank slipped quickly into unconsciousness, and Carr ordered room service. After eating, he had porters carry Hank to the car for the long drive to Ohio. It was ten forty-five.

Just before midnight, outside Blaine, Tennessee, highway patrolman Swann Kitts stopped Carr after the young man tried to pass another vehicle and nearly plowed head-on into the patrol car. After approaching the car, the officer shined his flashlight on Hank, who was sprawled in the back seat, and said that he looked dead. Carr assured him that Mr. Williams was all right, just sedated. Carr paid the fine and continued on. But Officer Kitts had his doubts.

So do many Williams buffs and music historians, who maintain that Williams was already dead. This belief has been reinforced by Kitts's report, which has surfaced after twenty-nine years. It reads, in part:

> "After investigating this matter, I think that Williams was dead when he was dressed and carried out of the hotel. Since he was drunk and was given the injections and could have taken some capsules

earlier, with all this he couldn't have lasted over an hour and a half or two hours.

"Taking all this into consideration, he must have died in Knoxville at the hotel."

But there are two facts which contradict this conclusion.

Sometime during the ride, Hank woke up. He took a pencil and paper from his pocket and wrote several sad lines that may have been lyrics to a new song. We'll never know. The paper was found in his hand five and a half hours later. Carr didn't forge his handwriting and put it there. It's likely that he woke up, wrote this final composition, then popped a chloral hydrate pill, poured some vodka down after it, and went back to sleep.

The second fact which contradicts this finding is that at one point during the morning, several eyewitnesses report that Hank himself walked into a diner in Bluefield, West Virginia and hired a driver, cabbie Don Surface, to ride as a backup in case Carr became too tired to drive. Though Surface hasn't surfaced again since that fateful night, he was seen by several people leaving with Williams.

No, the singer was alive as the men continued on, Hank sleeping in the back seat, Surface dozing in the front.

Shortly before dawn on New Year's Day, fifty miles to the north in Oak Hill, Carr got lost. Surface was no help, so the teenager parked on Main Street, intending to go into the Pure Oil gas station across the street to ask directions.

When he got out, he noticed that the blanket Hank had been lying under had fallen off. He opened the door, went to spread it over the singer, and noticed that he was unnaturally still. He lifted the man's hand; it was cold.

Carr ran to the service station, and the owner called

the police. Officer Howard Jamey arrived within minutes, opened the door, bent over Hank, and felt for a pulse. Jamey straightened and looked at Carr.

"This man is dead."

Leaving Carr and Surface at the gas station, Jamey slipped behind the wheel of the Cadillac and headed to the Oak Hill Hospital, where Williams was pronounced dead. Word spread quickly through the town, and fans rushed to the hospital, managing to strip the car of mementoes while Jamey was inside the hospital and Carr was on the phone, reporting the bad news to Lilly.

Mrs. Williams notified Audrey—who, bizarrely, had become her closer-than-ever pal due to their mutual resentment of Billie Jean—and the two women flew to West Virginia. Upon claiming her son's remains, Lilly demanded an autopsy; the coroner attributed the twenty-nine-year-old singer's death to heart failure brought on by excessive drinking.

Lilly phoned Billie Jean, who went to pieces. Not only did she receive no consolation from Lilly and Audrey, but the two women took it upon themselves to organize the funeral without consulting the widow. Later, they made life miserable for Billie Jean by declaring themselves Hank's only real family and, of course, legal heirs. Even Bobbie Jett would receive better treatment from Mrs. Williams . . . more on which, later.

Lilly contacted Hank's father and invited him to come; though she had no respect for Lonnie, he *was* the dead man's father. Besides, though Hank had chosen to have little contact with Lonnie over the years, the elder Williams *had* made several attempts to reconcile with his boy. He deserved to see Hank off.

Worldwide, fans and colleagues had more important things on their minds: their incomparable loss. Years later, June Carter would sum it up for the music industry when she said, "We loved him, we had lost him, and we still miss him."

Up north, in the Canton Memorial Auditorium where Hank had been headed, a spotlight shone on an empty stage while a record player turned and Hank's music filled the room. Fans had not returned their tickets for a refund; instead, they came to the theater to share their grief. And on Sunday, January 4, the day of the funeral, nearly twenty-five thousand people turned out in the streets of Montgomery, Alabama, to pay their respects to their fallen hero. For days after his death, country stations around the nation played his music in tribute, often nonstop. Just *how* important Hank was to people was made even clearer when the family and local authorities realized that his burial plot wasn't big enough for the monolithic memorial they planned. The solution? Get out the shovels and move the bodies surrounding dear Hank.

For Hank, the suffering was over. For his fans, at least they still had what they always had—his music. For his family, though, the sorrow and tragedy did not yet end.

There was no will, no insurance, and squabbling over the estate began almost at once. Billie Jean removed herself from it, gratefully, by accepting thirty thousand dollars from Lilly—though she later went back to court to fight Audrey over the question of who really *was* Hank's widow and, thus, entitled to certain royalties. Audrey had had another reason for insisting, in print, that Hank had intended to divorce Billie Jean and remarry her in February of 1953; she was planning a singing career (again!) with her group the Drifting Cowgirls and would have benefitted from being the real, final, no-doubt-about-it Mrs. Hank Williams. To the surprise of no one but Audrey, the courts found in Billie Jean's favor.

The year after Hank's death, Lilly authorized MGM to make a movie about Hank. *Your Cheatin' Heart* was finally made in 1964 and starred George Hamilton. But Lilly didn't do much more administering after that: she died of heart failure just two years after her son, on February 26, at the age of fifty-six.

Lonnie died in 1970 at the age of seventy-eight.

The off-key Audrey did as she'd threatened to do: sing. She toured and did some recording, but her show business career was a bust. In a failed effort to recoup her losses, she published Hank Williams scrapbooks. She ended up owing the IRS a bundle, lost her house, reportedly became hooked on sleeping pills, sold off possessions to fans to earn money, and died in 1975 at the age of fifty-three.

Billie Jean also pursued a singing career billed as the real Mrs. Hank Williams, met up-and-coming star Johnny Horton (see p. 33) in 1954, and married him. After his death, she married an insurance executive, started frequenting revival meetings, and found religion. Who can blame her?

Hank's sister Irene had become a realtor in Texas, but switched to smuggling cocaine because the hours and pay were better. She was caught and sentenced to eight years in prison.

Both of Hank's children had their share of strife as well (see p. 109).

It would be wrong, of course, to call Hank Williams a lucky man. He suffered too much and died too young. But if there's any consolation in his sad tale, it's the fact that he left behind his heart, his "sincerity." And that makes all of us, at least, that much richer.

Roy Rogers

"**W**HEN my time comes," says Roy Rogers, "just skin me and put me right up there on Trigger, just as if nothing had ever changed."

It's a fitting if ironic statement from one of the great singing cowboys since, for many years, there was nothing *but* change in the life of Leonard Slye. Change and tragedy, the kind that would have seen most of us trading in our buckskins for a straightjacket.

Born in Cincinnati, Ohio, on November 5, 1911, the son of a guitar-maker, Leonard grew knowing, loving, and performing music. While working as a fruit picker, he formed the International Cowboys with his cousin, briefly changed his name to Dick Weston (as in the nearly homonymic "western"), established the Pioneer Trio (later the famous Sons of the Pioneers), and was featured in the movie serial *The Phantom Empire* (1934), which starred Gene Autry.

In 1938, Rogers was given a film of his own, *Under Western Skies*, but it wasn't until Autry went off to fight in World War II that Rogers and his palomino Trigger rode uncontested to box office prominence in wholesome, action-crammed films like *Don't Fence Me In*

(1945), *Helldorado* (1946), and *Springtime in the Sierras* (1947). When box office receipts dried up, Roy was one of the first film actors to move into TV, starring in the popular *Roy Rogers Show* from 1951 to 1957. Thanks to acting, singing, and shrewd business investments, he was worth over one hundred million dollars by the middle 1970s—quite a change from his fruit picking days!

But Roy got to know heartbreak as well as triumph. His son Roy, Jr. was born by Caesarian section, on October 30, 1946, the third child for Roy and his wife of ten years, Arlene. They already had two daughters, Cheryl, six, and Linda Lou, three.

A week after the delivery, the thirty-two-year-old Arlene was still in the hospital. On November 4, Roy was in Chicago, appearing in a rodeo. He and Arlene had a long phone conversation that morning, while she had breakfast, and Arlene was in very high spirits. However, at 9:00 A.M. she began bleeding internally; an hour later, she was dead.

Roy rushed home, devastated of course, but consoled somewhat by the fact that he had Roy, Jr. to remember Arlene by.

A year after the loss, Roy married his divorced co-star, Frances Octavia Smith—better known as Dale Evans—although he didn't leave tragedy behind.

In 1952, Roy and Dale lost their two-year-old daughter Robin, who had been born with Downs Syndrome.

On August 17, 1964, their twelve-year-old daughter Deborah Lee—Korean-born and adopted six years before—was one of a busload of children returning from Tijuana, Mexico, where they had brought food and clothing to an orphanage. As they were crossing the San Onofre Creek bridge along an undivided stretch of Highway 101, just outside of San Clemente, one of the front tires blew. While the driver struggled to regain control of the swerving bus, it swung onto the other side of the road, sideswiped two cars, crashed head-on into a station wagon, plowed ahead into four other cars, and finally struck a palm tree, which was all that prevented the bus from plunging down a forty-foot cliff. California Highway Patrol Lieutenant Walter Pudinski later said that had the bus missed it and gone over, dozens would have perished.

As it was, not everyone survived.

Because the tree had crushed in the door of the bus, it took rescue workers eighty minutes to get inside and assess the cost.

Four children and four adults were killed in the crash; sixty other people were injured, some seriously. Deborah had been standing in front of the bus, chatting with the driver; she was one of the dead.

Roy was in the hospital at the time, undergoing neck surgery, and Dale took the call at home, informing her of the crash.

"I can't accept it," she said. "I just can't." Shortly thereafter, medics went to the Rogers home and Dale was placed under sedation.

Fifteen months later, an awful and bizarre tragedy struck involving Roy's soldier son John David ("Sandy"). While serving in the military in Helmhausen, Germany, eighteen-year-old Private First Class Rogers felt ill after dinner and was taken to the dispensary. He was left alone and regurgitated at some point during the night; no one heard him and, too ill to help himself, Sandy died of "asphyxia due to aspiration of vomitus"—in other words, he choked to death on his own vomit.

Though that was the end of the devastating losses, there were still problems ahead.

There were six other children in the Rogers clan— including one from Dale's previous marriage to pianist Dale Butts—but Roy, Jr., was the standard-bearer of his father's famous name and, whether he liked it or not, the pressure was always on to do what was good and right and responsible. Realizing a bit late the onus the name placed on the boy, Roy took to calling him Dusty, a name that Roy, Jr. uses to this day.

In contrast to their easygoing screen images—the kind of mom and dad any kid would have loved to belong to —Roy, Sr. and Dale were not always easygoing parents.

Dusty told *People* magazine that he recalled one day when he and Sandy were being particularly rowdy and ignored Dale's shouts to settle down. Without losing her cool, Mrs. Rogers went and got the gun she used in personal appearances, aimed at the ceiling, and fired. As the shot reverberated through the house, the kids gave Dale their full and immediate attention.

As she stood there, an NRA poster-mom, her hip cocked like Annie Oakley's, her expression stern, she repeated softly, "I said it's time to stop."

They did. Fast.

Dusty adds that his father was not above more traditional forms of attention-getting, such as spanking; Roy defends his actions by saying, "If you spend time to teach kids right and wrong when they're little . . . it shows you love 'em."

Yet the wedge that came between father and son was not discipline. It was that rare case of a father who *didn't* want his son to go into the family business.

When Dusty graduated from high school, he had his heart set on becoming a singer/actor like his father— though he wanted it not because he was trying to emulate his dad, but because he genuinely loved performing. For his part, Roy had done everything possible to keep his kids out of the spotlight, going so far as to move his family from Hollywood to the more wholesome Chatsworth, and he kept on moving farther away as the filmtypes spread out.

Dusty recalls, "He wanted his kids raised on a ranch,

where they could have horses and pigs and chickens and cows."

Roy didn't want his son to be an entertainer because he knew how carnivorous the industry was, even more so in the 1960s than it had been in the 1940s and 1950s. He also knew what show business could do to families. That was why he kept moving.

Roy wanted Dusty to get himself a responsible, full-time job, and initially, Dusty tried hard to please his father. He took a job in a plant where, he says, his "main task was to test the seams in napalm bombs."

After just two weeks, Dusty realized that a nine-to-five job, especially this one, wasn't for him. He quit, and says, "That really angered Dad."

Roy made no effort to contain his rage, and though it might have been his intention to bully Dusty back to work, it had the opposite effect. Instead of knuckling down, Dusty pulled an *Easy Rider*, he and a group of friends driving off to "find themselves."

Roy was heartbroken but unyielding. "You can't always control your kids," he says. "All you can do is hope you've raised them with a set of values that will see them through a blow."

As for Dusty, he ended up in Ohio where, ironically, he got himself a good job in the construction industry while he did some singing on a local TV show. He also got married, had three children, and decided he wanted to raise them somewhere clean and quiet—a place like Apple Valley in San Bernadino, where Roy and Dale lived.

Dusty was twenty-seven at the time; and when he wasn't out building homes, he was out singing country music wherever he could find a stage or microphone. In the meantime, Roy had given up entertainment and added to his fortune by lending his name and likeness to a chain of highly successful fast food restaurants. (He stayed retired until 1992, when he teamed with his old studio, Republic Pictures, to do a wholesome, animated Roy Rogers TV series.)

Though father and son were living in the same town, they were not instantly reconciled. Dusty was anxious to be so, but Roy still had problems with what the young man had done. They inched closer together until, eight years later, Dusty happened to be going through his father's scrapbooks. He says he saw "all the things he's done, the children's hospitals he's visited," and he realized that "this is the man I had spent my whole life with and never really gotten to know."

All those years, Roy wasn't just being a strict father. The rules he'd established weren't just whim: he really wanted to bring some measure of grace and dignity to the world. Dusty resolved to get closer to Roy as soon as possible.

He suggested the two of them go for a ride in a pickup and, after a few minutes, with tears in his eyes, Dusty told his father how much he loved him, how he'd never really understood him until now.

Roy shot him a glance, pulled the pickup off the road, and then, Dusty says, "[we] hugged and kissed each other and cried." Walking through a field afterwards, he says they "had a long good talk about all the stuff that bothered us through the years." It all seemed so silly now. Roy trying to stop a kid from finding himself, doing what he wanted. Dusty rebelling because he was immature and, hey, it was the sixties, man.

Father and son admitted they'd both been wrong and, as a result, had lost more years than they cared to think about. But at least there was the future.

Since then, Dusty has been there for the Rogers clan, helping to see both Roy and Dale through serious heart attacks. And Roy and Dale have been loving parents and devoted grandparents.

And so everyone managed to ride off into the sunset singing "Happy Trails To You." Once in a rare while, it does happen.

Once in a *very* rare while.

Johnny Horton

THERE are crossover artists and then there are crossover phenomena.

Johnny Horton was one of the latter.

With a voice that could cry, croon, rock, or wail, and with movie star good-looks, chances are very good that he'd have become one of the biggest country artists of all-time. But like far too many brilliant stars in the country firmament, he never got the opportunity. That bane called "the road" kept him from reaching the sky.

Born on April 3, 1929, in Los Angeles, Johnny was still a young boy when his family moved to Tyler, Texas, where Horton enjoyed a normal childhood. He was close to his father, and his mother who taught him to play guitar—albeit, Johnny once said, just "three chords in two keys." (Which put him in good company: that was about all Elvis knew.)

He achieved excellent grades in Gallatin High School, and was also a star athlete; over two dozen schools offered him basketball scholarships. But he decided to skip the big time schools and stick close to home, attending Lon Morris Junior College in Jacksonville where (only in the fifties!) he was voted "most handsome student."

Transferring to Kilgore Junior College and then to

Baylor University and Seattle University, Johnny majored in geology, intending to become an engineer for the oil industry. He also started composing country-flavored tunes in college with which to entertain the ladies, though he never considered singing or songwriting as a full-time career (songs like "Bess, You're the Bes'" certainly didn't give any indication that the guy would make it in the pros).

Johnny was an avid fisherman—he once hosted a radio show for anglers in East Texas—and during school breaks, he worked part-time in the fishing industry up and down the coast, singing for his supper in seaside clubs during layovers. After completing one particularly rugged journey that took him way up north, to Alaska, Johnny found himself in Los Angeles, where some of his shipmates dared him to enter a singing contest that was being held at Harmony Park Corral in Anaheim.

After slugging his way through the rough seas of Alaska, this was a day at the beach. Guitar in hand, Johnny went on stage and won Anaheim over; the audience refusing to let the singer leave until he'd gone through all of the thirteen country songs that he knew. More important than his first prize victory, Johnny impressed a record producer who was in the audience, who was curious to see how the itinerant balladeer would play among the faithful.

Very well, as it turned out. Billed as the Singing Fisherman, Johnny performed on *Home Town Jamboree*, which broadcast from El Monte, just east of L.A. He was a hit and was asked to appear on *Louisiana Hayride* in Shreveport—Hank Williams's old stomping grounds.

Quickly achieving star status, Johnny recorded briefly for Mercury, then Dot, and was finally signed by the mighty Columbia. In 1956 his singles "Honky Tonk Man" and "I'm A One-Woman Man" were top ten hits. Horton's fifth single, "When It's Springtime in

Alaska," went to number one in 1959, but later that year it was a juggernaut called "The Battle of New Orleans," written by Jimmy Driftwood (based on an old standard called "The 8th of January") that launched him to superstardom. The song was number one on both the country and pop charts, selling over two million copies and becoming the biggest single of the year.

Johnny followed that smash with other million sellers, like "Sink the Bismarck," which was inspired by (but not sung in) the film of the same name, and "North to Alaska," from the John Wayne film (which *was* sung in the film).

Topping both the country and pop charts regularly, Johnny had it made. His home life was also going great: in September of 1953, he married Billie Jean Williams, widow of Hank, and six years later the two were settled in Shreveport, still very much in love and the parents of two daughters. Billie Jean certainly deserved this happiness after all that she had been through.

On November 4, 1960, Johnny went to Austin, Texas, which was soon to become a home for the Outlaw artists and other Nashville expatriates. After singing at the Skyline Club, he decided not to stay the night. Instead, Johnny and his guitarist, Herald Tomlinson, and his manager, Tillman Franks, climbed into the singer's white Cadillac. Johnny was at the wheel.

Elsewhere, a nineteen-year-old student at Texas A & M, climbed into his 1958 Ford. On the passenger's seat were two bottles of beer and a bottle of liquor.

Just outside of Milano, Texas, a few minutes past one-thirty in the morning, Davis's Ranchero plowed into the Cadillac. The student, guitarist Tomlinson, and Tillman Franks were rushed to St. Edward's Hospital in nearby Cameron with serious injuries. Johnny Horton was dead.

Good friend Johnny Cash delivered Horton's eulogy, and later said of the singer, "He was a fine singer, but just as important, he was a fine man. Maybe I should have started wearing black when we lost John."

Johnny remained on the charts for years after his death, in part because of Billie Jean's efforts. He had recorded literally hundreds of tracks in his home studio, and Billie Jean employed musicians to play backup and to flesh them out, Columbia releasing the completed recordings.

There's no telling where Johnny Horton's talent would have taken him. To continued success on the charts, most definitely. To the movies, almost certainly. He was also keenly interested in nurturing new talent, and one can imagine how many artists the young and vigorous star would have encouraged.

Unfortunately, one can *only* imagine.

And, sadly, country wasn't through burying its bright young stars.

Patsy Cline

AT the time of her death, upstart Patsy Cline was closing in on long-reigning Nashville-born superstar Kitty Wells as the most popular female vocalist in country music.

That was no mean feat. The classy, beloved Wells had had a big head start, singing on WXIX's "Dixie Early Birds" when Patsy was still a babe-in-tap-shoes. But Patsy had grit, youth, and one of the most appealing and versatile voices country music has ever heard. As Barbara Mandrell put it, she had "a voice like an angel's trumpet . . . and the diction of a cafe singer." One of Patsy's best friends, Loretta Lynn, says, "She was really like Hank Williams, the way she got this throb in her voice and really touched people's emotions."

Patsy also had some of the best songs in country music at the time, which helped earn her a slew of crossover hits. And she had friends (many say lovers) in high places —but Cline did not sleep her way to the top, as some have suggested. She got there on talent and drive.

But, like Johnny Horton, she died at the height of her fame, and we'll never know what the future held for this remarkable young woman.

Born Virginia Patterson Hensley on September 8,

1932, in Winchester, Virginia, Patsy was raised by her mother after her father, Sam, abandoned the family. As a little girl, she got her first taste of show business when she entered and won a tap dancing contest at the age of four. Realizing then that she wanted to be an entertainer, she also studied piano and typically could be heard singing while she played.

At the age of sixteen, Patsy dropped out of school in order to go to work and help pay the bills. She earned money by working days in Gaunt's Drug Store in their small town, and singing at night and on days off in local clubs, at square dances, and even on street corners. She once said, "My mother would pick me up at the drug store after work, and would take me wherever I could get a job. We'd usually get home about three in the morning and a few hours later I was up again getting ready to go to work in the drug store. And you know something? I loved every minute of it."

Believe it. Patsy was a workaholic before anyone knew what that was.

In 1948, Wally Fowler's Oak Ridge Quartet—regulars on Roy Acuff's *Dinner Bell* radio show—entertained in Winchester, and Patsy managed to wangle an audition with Fowler. He was so impressed by Patsy's voice that he encouraged her to go to Nashville, where he promised her an audition with Acuff himself.

Patsy went—spending the night before in a park because she didn't have enough money for a hotel—and dazzled Acuff as she had Fowler. He offered her a job on the show, but the salary wouldn't have been enough for Patsy to make ends meet, and she reluctantly and very courteously declined. However, she now knew that she had the talent to make it. All she needed was a different kind of break.

Back in Winchester, Patsy continued to work at the drug store, doing any solo gigs she could get, and she also began singing with Bill Peer and the Melody Playboys. In 1953, her marriage to Gerald Cline provided her with a bit of a financial cushion, and she was able to devote more time to music. She managed to land bookings on the *Louisiana Hayride*, the *Ozark Jubilee*, and other shows, and in 1955 she was signed by Four Star Records (which was distributed by powerful Decca), though her recordings there were undistinguished.

Two years later, Patsy got her big break when she was asked to appear on Arthur Godfrey's *Talent Scouts*. She sang "Walkin' After Midnight," which brought down the house and convinced Decca itself to record and release the song. It sold over one million copies and went to number three on the country charts.

Though Patsy's career had suddenly taken off, things were sputtering on the home front. Gerald was as bland a man as ever walked the earth, and the outgoing Patsy found herself drawn to another man: Charlie Dick, an equally outgoing Korean War veteran who worked as a printer for the local newspaper and was, as he himself admits, "a ladies' man"—though he swears "that stopped when I met Patsy."

Charlie remembers his inamorata as "a determined woman. She was what you'd call a career gal today. Patsy said to me before we got married, 'Someday I'm gonna be a famous singer, and if you want to be beside me, let's do it.'"

They did. Patsy divorced Gerald, and in September of 1957, she married Charlie. A year later, their daughter Julie was born; three-years after that, son Randy came along. (Charlie says, "Patsy was so determined to sing that she worked the *Opry* one night and gave birth to Randy the next.")

That determination paid off as the hits kept coming. "I Fall To Pieces" went to number one. "Crazy" by Willie Nelson, "Who Can I Count On?," "She's Got You,"

"When I Get Through With You" and others were also huge hits, and she became a star at the Opry. And not just through talent. Patsy may have been fringed cowgirl costumes and big smiles onstage, but offstage she was demanding and both a staunch friend and enemy. According to *Opry* historian Chet Hagen, when newcomer Jan Howard performed without genuflecting before Patsy, the star went to her backstage and snapped, "Well, you're a conceited little sonofabitch! . . . You don't say hello, kiss my ass, or nothin' else." Patsy was serious, but when Jan said she had no intention of kissing anyone's ass, Patsy smiled and backed down. She liked brass in a person.

Conversely, she could be the most supportive friend on earth. Loretta Lynn reports that when several top female singers decided they didn't want up-and-coming Lynn on the *Opry*, they called a meeting to plan her ouster and invited Patsy to attend. Patsy showed up all right, but with her good friend Loretta in tow.

End of attempted blacklist.

Patsy was equally demanding with Charlie. Singer Dottie West recalls, "She was strong and that was sometimes rough on a tough guy like Charlie." He drank and they fought, sometimes violently. West suggests, "Maybe Charlie turned to drinking because of her assertiveness."

As if smacking her weren't bad enough, Charlie once landed in jail for a night for having beat her. He says today, without apology, "We were just livin'. We made up as hard as we fought. We had a lot of fun making up." No doubt. At least then Patsy knew where his hands would be.

Patsy's career was briefly sidelined—and her life was very nearly ended—on June 14, 1961. She had gone to the local general store to pick up some hamburger rolls, when a car in the oncoming lane tried to pass the vehicle in front of it. The driver hadn't bothered to see if there were enough room: there wasn't, and the car plowed head-first into Patsy's. A woman died in the other car; Patsy suffered facial lacerations, a dislocated hip, and several broken ribs.

Patsy was in the hospital for over a month, and spent several months after that in a wheelchair. But her injuries didn't keep her from the *Opry* any longer than was absolutely necessary. Dolly Parton recalls, "She came out on crutches and sang. I was still a kid, but that was one of the big thrills of my life." She also went back to recording, though for a while she had to stay away from songs with high notes, since the broken ribs prevented her from hitting them.

She recovered. Her career remained in high-gear, and she was very much in demand on the concert circuit. On Saturday, March 2, 1963, Patsy played two sold-out concerts in Birmingham. The next day, she headed to Kansas City to play in a benefit for the family of country music disc jockey Cactus Jack McCall, who had been killed in a car accident. Also on the bill were Roy Acuff, Billy Walker, Wilma Lee and Stoney Cooper, Cowboy Copas, and Hawkshaw Hawkins.

After the concert—which raised just over three thousand dollars for the family—the Coopers got into their car and headed for their next gig. Acuff drove back to Nashville, and Walker took a commercial flight. The forty-nine-year-old *Opry* veteran Copas, forty-three-year-old Hawkins, and Patsy all chose to stay over until Tuesday and return in the Commanche piloted by Patsy's thirty-five-year-old manager Randy Hughes, who was also Copas's son-in-law.

There were rumors that Hughes and Patsy were closer than just manager/client, and that the chance to spend some time alone was one reason they stayed over an extra day. That was never proven, though, and the question soon became moot.

The plane took off at 2:00 P.M. on the fifth and landed in Dyersburg, Tennessee three hours later. While it was being refueled, the passengers went to the airport cafe for a snack, and Hughes went to check on weather conditions en route to Nashville. He was advised that there were strong winds and rain ahead, and that it would probably be a good idea to sit the storm out in Dyersburg, a suggestion which Hughes inexplicably ignored.

The pilot called his wife to tell her they'd be home by eight. Hawkins did likewise: his wife was expecting a baby in less than a month, and he wanted to make sure she was okay.

The plane spent just over an hour on the ground, and then was airborne once more.

Twenty minutes later, at around 6:30 P.M., residents of rain-soaked Camden, Tennessee, some eighty-five miles west of Nashville, heard a plane overhead. That wasn't uncommon, but they paid attention to this plane because the engine seemed to growl, then go silent, growl, then grow quiet. A few thought they heard a muffled thud, but it could have been a car backfiring in the distance or a gunshot. No one paid it much heed, and they went on with their business.

Hours passed—anxious hours in Nashville—because the plane was overdue and the weather was lousy. If they'd landed at another field, one of the passengers would have called. Something wasn't right.

At eleven, authorities decided to organize a search party to backtrack over the flight path and see what might have happened. Local help was recruited between Nashville and Dyersburg.

Because of the wide area being covered, and the difficulty of working in darkness and rain, it wasn't until 6 A.M. on March 6 that farmer W.J. Hollingsworth found the wreckage. It was strewn across sixty yards of wooded hill, in a section known as Fatty Bottom, five miles west of Camden. He didn't find any survivors; he didn't even find any bodies still in one piece.

Authorities converged on the spot and found the plane, crumpled and twisted on the ground amidst scraped and broken oak trees. It had come straight down, the force of the passage through the trees and subsequent impact against one—the "pop" that several people had heard—not only demolished the yellow plane and strewed the contents of the luggage all over, but destroyed the bodies as well. Discovered over two hundred feet from the crushed aircraft, where they'd been tossed on impact, the remains of the passengers were so badly broken and dismembered that only their wallets enabled searchers to tell who was who.

Search party member C.B. Uthman says today, "The whole thing looked like it'd gone through a meat grinder. You don't want to remember people lookin' like they did. You really don't. 'Cause it's with you every day of your life."

The deaths plunged Nashville into deep, deep mourning. More members of the family were gone too soon. Loretta Lynn says that she couldn't believe it when Patsy's booking agent called and gave her the news.

"Baloney," Lynn said. "Her and me is going shopping." She says she didn't believe it until she heard it on the radio, and then she fell apart. "When she died, I just about gave up. I thought this was the end for me, too." Patsy, she says, "was my friend, my mentor, my strength."

But Loretta went on. Nashville went on. "There is," said Loretta, "nothing else to do."

Four maroon hearses brought the caskets to their final resting places. Patsy's records continued to reach the top of the charts, songs like "Sweet Dreams"—which she had recorded in February of that year—"Faded Love," "He Called Me Baby," and "When You Need a Laugh." And her records *continue* to sell, to the tune of 75,000 a year—including, in 1981, one of the most morbid albums in history, electronically processed duets with Jim Reeves, who died in 1964 (see next chapter). She was the subject of a 1985 film, *Sweet Dreams*, with Jessica Lange lip-synching the original songs.

But all of this attention did not come just because she went to play with Hank and Johnny at the age of twenty-nine. Dottie West says, "Patsy is still around because she is what we all want to be—a real star. And people can't get enough of a real star."

Sadly, the Grim Reaper decided to stay in Nashville and work a little overtime: on March 7, Opry star Jack Anglin, of Johnny and Jack, was headed to a memorial service for Patsy when he was killed in a car crash. But the show went on in Nashville, as two days later, *Opry* manager Ott Devine went on stage before the performance and said to the sober house, "It is impossible to put into words our thoughts, our feelings, our love for Patsy, Hawk, Cope, Jack, and Randy. And so we ask that you in our audience please stand and join us for a moment of silent prayer in tribute to them."

They did, and after thanking the dead singers, Devine concluded, "They would want us to keep smiling, and to recall the happier occasions. I feel that I can speak for all of them when I say—let's continue in the tradition of the *Grand Ole Opry*."

They did, but the Grim Reaper wasn't quite finished on this costly pass through Music City.

Jim Reeves

TO his fans and colleagues he was "Gentleman" Jim Reeves—a dapper, always well-groomed (albeit toupeed) singer. His rich, honest voice and innovative orchestrations not only helped to shape the sound of modern country music but also picked up where Johnny Horton had left off, making country a regular and formidable presence on the pop charts both here and abroad.

He was also a gentle man, one who never forgot his roots or his fans, one who continued to tour when he could have rested on his laurels (and on his considerable bankbook). Instead, he kept entertaining right to the end —which, once again, came much too early.

Reeves was born in Galloway, Texas, on August 20, 1924, the son of a poor farmer. Although he'd always loved music as a boy, he loved baseball more and pursued a career on the diamond, eventually being signed by the St. Louis Cardinals. However, an injury forced him out of the game (some team veterans recall it as an arm injury, others as a leg injury, and one said it was both), and he took to disc jockeying for KGRI in Henderson, Texas.

In 1952, Jim cut two singles for Macy's, whose Queen of Hits platters were sold exclusively through the chain's stores in the south and southwest. The records did moderately well, and Reeves began to wonder if he might have a career in the recording end of music.

But it was still disc jockeying that paid the bills, and later in the year, he moved to Shreveport, Louisiana with his new bride, Mary White, to work as an announcer for the *Louisiana Hayride*. In a scenario straight out of *A Star Is Born*, Hank Williams failed to show one night, and desperate for an act, station executives tapped Reeves to fill in. Fabor Robinson, owner of Abbott Records, heard Reeves sing and signed him to a recording contract.

Though their first release, "Wagon of Love," got stuck in a rut, their second single, "Mexican Joe," sold over a million copies in 1953. Ditto their third recording, the memorable "Bimbo."

Reeves became a regular on *Louisiana Hayride*, and in 1955 mighty RCA came calling, buying Reeves's contract from Robinson along with the masters of the thirty-six tracks he'd cut. The singer quickly became a regular fixture on the country charts and, within a year, was asked to join the *Grand Ole Opry*.

But Jim was a restless, inquisitive man, and in 1957 he decided to try a slightly different style. His ballad "Four Walls" had an electric bass as well as a more intimate, less nasal singing style, which he'd worked on with his producer, Chet Atkins. The song was a country smash and went to number two on the pop charts; it was also a hit in Europe, especially in Great Britain, Norway, and Germany, and also in South Africa.

Hit followed hit: "A Touch of Velvet," "Guilty," "Blue Canadian Rockies," "Golden Memories and Silver Tears," "Billy Bayou," "He'll Have To Go," "I'm Getting Better," "Adios Amigo," and many more. "He'll Have To Go" alone sold over three million copies in 1960. Many folks in the country establishment looked down their noses at the singer they referred to as Mr. Velvet, a proponent of what was snidely called the "smooth school." But that didn't stop Reeves from recording or the records from selling and making inroads on stations and in stores where country had never been a powerful force.

Reeves toured overseas in 1957 and 1959 and was particularly taken with South Africa: not only did he record songs in the native Afrikaans, learning the lyrics phonetically, but he starred in the song-filled 1963 film *Kimberley Jim*, about a pair of gamblers who win a diamond mine in a crooked poker game. Though the thin "road picture" clone barely played the U.S. when it finally reached these shores two years later, it was a smash in its native land and a sequel was immediately put in the works. Jim felt so welcomed there and was so drawn to the country's wide-open spaces that he actively planned to buy a spread in South Africa.

Reeves spent nearly three hundred days of every year on the road with his band, the Blue Boys, and early in 1964 they did their most extensive European tour yet, hitting the United Kingdom, Austria, Germany, Scandinavia, Holland, and Italy. Beatlemania? Forget it. Everywhere Reeves went he drew huge and fanatic crowds, and his TV appearance in England earned a huge audience.

While Reeves was on the road, his wife helped oversee his many business ventures, which included considerable real estate holdings, a vast music publishing empire, and a company that arranged tours for himself and other artists. Upon returning from the lengthy European visit, Jim decided to spend at least a part of the summertime wading through these sundry ventures and concentrating on strengthening his interests outside of music.

So that he could get from gig to gig and also check in on his various holdings, Reeves had learned to fly. On

Friday, July 31, Reeves and his thirty-year-old pianist/
manager Dean Manuel flew some four hundred miles to
Batesville, Arkansas, to conclude a property deal. Since
Reeves had promised to appear on the *Grand Ole Opry*
the next night, the men finished their business, then
turned around in their rented single-engine Beechcraft
Debonair and headed home.

The bulk of the return trip was uneventful, until some
twenty miles from Beery Field when Reeves ran into a
heavy rainstorm. At ten miles out, he contacted air traffic controllers and reported that he was encountering
heavy turbulence, could they tell him how deep the
storm was and which way it was headed? Before anyone
could respond, the radio went dead.

Fearing the worst, local authorities immediately organized a search party some seven hundred people strong,
including many of Reeves's music buddies, such as Atkins, Marty Robbins, Ernest Tubb, Stonewall Jackson,
and Eddy Arnold.

Despite the driving rain, they spread out in the twenty
square miles of thick woods which Reeves had been passing over and found nothing. During the daylight hours,
military, state, and private aircraft combed the area from
above.

The party traipsed through the woods and hills all day
Saturday, though they were finally able to narrow their
search when a man told police that he'd heard an airplane engine cough and die practically overhead.

The searchers then concentrated on a thick section of
woods on a hill known as Old Baldy; on Sunday, they
found what they were looking for—what they were hoping they wouldn't find.

The plane was located just a quarter of a mile from
where the search had begun on Friday, on the other side
of U.S. 31 from the main search area, just a few hundred
feet from the home of the man who'd heard the crash.

The site was hidden by a fence, and the impact had reduced the plane to countless small pieces, most of which had buried themselves beneath the thick underbrush. In an eerie replay of the Patsy Cline crash, both of the passengers were dead and badly mangled; the only way searchers were able to identify Reeves was by his driver's license.

The star's death made headlines the world over, and his interment in Carthage, Texas, was well-attended by friends, fans, and family.

But the singer's music did not die. For the next three years he continued to have number one hits; he charted high in the 1970s and even the 1980s, albeit with more contemporary instrumentation and vocals backing him up. And thanks to the miracle of electronics, there was that ghastly pre-Natalie Cole duet with Patsy Cline.

Mary Reeves helped to perpetuate the cult by doing her best to make sure that only good stories about her husband appeared in print, and music historian Bryan Chalker has reported that, in deference to her, stories about her husband's fondness for Jack Daniels were not reported by the press. (Even so, he never went on rampages like Hank Williams or Johnny Cash. Even when he drank, Reeves tried to be that gentle man.)

Though many country purists disavowed Reeves during his life because of his melding of popular and country styles, his greatest legacy is that he brought more new fans into the fold than any artist in history. And he did it at a time when country stars were having to fight hard for consumer dollars against the surging rock 'n' roll.

Other crossover artists have been able to capitalize on the trails he blazed, and many of them sell more records, but this century will not see another crossover artist as important or influential as Jim Reeves.

Roy Acuff

THE scythe continued to fall.

On June 20, 1965, forty-year-old Ira Louvin of the harmonizing Louvin Brothers was killed in a car crash when an oncoming driver swerved into his lane. The loss devastated both his surviving brother Charlie and the *Grand Ole Opry* of which they were a beloved part. Nashville was still grieving when the King of Country Music, superstar Roy Acuff, gave them something else to worry about.

Born on a tenant farm in Maynardsville, Tennessee on September 15, 1903, the son of a lawyer/minister/fiddler, Roy originally wanted to be a ballplayer. When he was still a teenager, he was accepted to the New York Yankees summer camp, but suffered from sunstroke and had to retire.

Without much education, Roy had only music to fall back on. After traveling with medicine shows, he put together a band and, in 1933, began appearing on various regional radio programs. A record contract with the American Record Company (later Columbia) followed three years later, and he had smash hits with "Great Speckled Bird" and "Wabash Cannon Ball." Asked to audition for the *Grand Ole Opry* in February 1938, he forgot the words to "Great Speckled Bird" but was invited to join just the same. With his Crazy Tennesseans (previously called Tennessee Crackerjacks, then the Smoky Mountain Boys), he became one of the institution's greatest stars.

In 1942, Roy and singer/songwriter/manager Fred Rose were among the first country artists to take complete control of their fates by founding Acuff-Rose Publications, which was bankrolled by Acuff and became one of the most successful publishing companies in the history of Music City. They were responsible for beginning countless careers, not the least of which was that of Hank Williams. Roy also answered the call of Hollywood—albeit with somewhat less distinction—acting in films like *My Darling Clementine* (1943) and *Night Train to Memphis* (1946). And, paving the way for future actors-turned-politicians, Roy even made a bid for the governorship of Tennessee in 1948. The entertainer ran as a Republican in the heavily Democratic state, and it was a tribute to Acuff's popularity that he did as well as he did.

There were better singers and, God knows, better actors, but nobody did it *all* like Acuff did it. That was one of the reasons he became the first living member ever elected to the Country Music Hall of Fame. But his illustrious career—along with his life—almost came to an end on a rainy morning outside of Sparta, Tennessee.

It was seven-thirty in the morning on July 10 when Roy and his companions piled into two cars and headed out from Nashville for a gig in Terrell, North Carolina, some three hundred miles away. Roy was in the lead, driving his Chrysler Imperial with guitarist Shot Jackson in the passenger's seat and singer June Stearns lying in the back. Though the car was equipped with those new-fangled seatbelts, no one bothered to buckle up.

The rain had gotten heavier since they left, and by ten-thirty they were driving along Highway 26 in a downpour. Roy was behind a vehicle that was taking the two-lane highway *verrrrry* slowly, and the singer was in no mood to dawdle.

He put on his directional and eased into the left lane, speeding up as he did so. The wipers were slashing furiously, and once Acuff had made his move he saw just why the car in front of him had been going so slowly: there was another car up ahead. And in the moment it took him to notice that, he saw the headlights of an oncoming Ford spearing toward him over a rise.

Acuff applied the brakes, intending to get back into his lane, but his Imperial skidded on the wet roadway. He turned in the direction of the skid to try and regain control: he knew he wouldn't be able to get back into the right lane—the slow moving cars were still there, with his boys' wagon bringing up the rear—but he was hoping he could reach the ditch that lay along the left side of the road.

He never made it. He'd barely gotten control of the car when the Ford plowed into the Imperial's side, and both vehicles came to a sickening stop.

Behind Roy, driver Onie Wheeler was the only one awake in the band's station wagon.

"Roy's had a wreck!" he screamed. Bandmembers Jimmy Riddle, Oswald Kirby and Jimmy Fox woke quickly and sat up.

Wheeler pulled over and Riddle ran into the rain. He dashed to the car, and peered through the broken window. The bloodied Roy looked up at him.

"Help . . . Shot," he wheezed.

Riddle looked to where Shot Jackson was seated, covered in blood and writhing in pain. Riddle glanced quickly into the back seat and saw June pinned in the wreckage, awake but relatively unhurt.

Riddle tried the door, then ran around the vehicle to open the door on the driver's side. By now, Fox had arrived, along with other motorists who had stopped and were trying to get in. None of the doors would open. Several people also went to check on Edward Blish, the lone occupant of the Ford. His face was badly bloodied from being thrown against the windshield, and he was dazed; but miraculously, he didn't appear to be hurt apart from that.

Finally, led by Jimmy Fox, people started kicking and punching at the windows, clearing them of glass so they could try to crawl in. But their efforts were in vain; the metal was just too twisted to admit anyone. One of the witnesses had gone on to Sparta for help, and there was nothing to do but wait.

Kirby remembers standing beside the front passenger's side, trying to console Shot.

"Time and time again," he says, "Shot grabbed me and tried to pull me down to him as he was looking up at me and screaming . . . The most terrible thing that can happen to a man is to look in a person's eyes like that and not be able to do anything. We just couldn't get into the car."

Ambulances and a rescue crew arrived within minutes, and it took just over a quarter of an hour for them to get into the twisted wreckage.

At the hospital, doctors determined that Shot Jackson had suffered the most serious injuries: he had a fractured skull, a broken jaw, a punctured lung, eighteen broken ribs, and a badly bruised kidney. It would be over a year before he was back to anything remotely resembling good health.

June had broken her ankle, and Blish had broken his
jaw and lost several teeth.

Roy's injuries came close to rivaling those of Jackson.
He'd broken his pelvis in two places, shattered his collarbone, and had busted several ribs. Incredibly, though,
he had suffered no serious internal injuries.

Still hurting, the singer went back to the *Grand Ole
Opry* on August 28, limping onstage to a standing ovation. Except for that night, however, and a USO tour in
December and January, which went to Vietnam, Korea,
and other spots in the far east, Roy just didn't feel up to
performing that year. He took it easy, recovering and
stopping to smell roses other than Acuff-Rose. He
stopped touring altogether in 1972.

Years later, when asked what he learned from the experience, Roy replied, "I come very near killin' one of
my very best friends, and I like to have killed myself.
And it taught me just how quick your life can be taken
away from you."

It also taught him something else.

One of the last songs Roy had recorded before hitting
the road that fateful morning was a tune called "The
Wreck on the Highway." As he looked back on the accident, he said, "You know that (*part of the*) song . . .
that says nobody was prayin'? Well, that song is wrong,
'cause there was somebody prayin'—it was me."

In spite of the accident, the death of his dear wife
Mildred in 1981, and a heart attack that slowed him
down in the early 1980s, Roy kept praying—and moving
and shaking and entertaining until congestive heart failure finally claimed his long, full life in Nashville's Baptist Hospital on November 22, 1992.

"I won't say anything about my musical ability," he
once said, when asked how he wanted to be remembered. "That's a matter of taste, isn't it? What I *do* want
people to say is that I was stubborn and opinionated in

everything else, from business to politics. Because if you aren't, you got no vision and who needs you?"

Roy Acuff had vision *and* he had musical ability. A world full of fans mourn his passing but are glad to have had him for as long as they did.

Stringbean

I T was one of the most heinous crimes in the history of
country music, its victims beloved by locals and audiences nationwide.

Stringbean.

You had to love him from the name alone. Just looking
at him made people smile. Born on June 17, 1915, in
Annville, Kentucky, David Akeman was the son of a top-
notch banjo picker. David built himself his own banjo
when he was a boy and the tall, lanky lad began playing
professionally when he was eighteen. In 1935, he joined
Cy Rogers' Lonesome Pine Fiddlers, who entertained
on WLAP in Lexington; he broke out by doing comedy
and billed himself as "Stringbean, the Kentucky Wonder," a name he got when an announcer at WLAP in
Lexington, Kentucky, simply couldn't remember his
name and said, "Come on out and play for us, stringbean." Though it wasn't commonly known, Akeman
used the name less as an epithet about his skinny six-
foot-two-inch self than as a comment on his ability to
play a variety of stringed instruments.

Stringbean moved on in 1938, playing with Charlie
Monroe's Kentucky Partners on WBIG in Greenville,
North Carolina, then heading to Nashville in 1941 and

joining Bill Monroe on the *Grand Ole Opry*. In 1945, he formed his own group called (what else?) Stringbean and his Kentucky Wonders and was a popular act at the *Opry* and on the road, touring with acts like Flatt & Scruggs and Porter Wagoner. He recorded a number of albums over the years, including *Old Time Banjo Picking and Singing* and *Back in the Hills of Kentucky*. Among his best-known tunes were "Mountain Dew," "Moonshine in Them Old Kentucky Hills," and "Barn Yard Banjo Picking."

In 1969, Stringbean gained his greatest fame as one of the original stars of the hit CBS variety series *Hee Haw*, which was hosted by country legends Buck Owens and Roy Clark (who was arguably Stringbean's better on the banjo). Stringbean enjoyed doing the TV show, and audiences loved him and his hangdog look, brooding out from above the long, long shirt that was tucked into pants worn belted below the hips. When CBS decided to drop the series in 1971, all-new episodes were produced for syndication, where it has remained a popular fixture.

Without poor Stringbean.

It was fairly well-known around Nashville that the entertainer and his fifty-nine-year-old wife, Estelle, kept large sums of money on their persons and, reportedly, had some twenty thousand dollars in cash stashed in their unassuming little home, which was located off the beaten track near Ridgetop, Tennessee.

Opry and *Hee Haw* star Archie Campbell recalls, "The word got out that he wore overalls and he carried lots of money in them. And he did. He was warned about it different times. I know (*singer*) Bill Carlisle went up to him one time and said, 'Somebody's gonna knock you on the head.' "

It's a damn shame someone didn't. What happened was far worse.

Two men who had heard these rumors were twenty-

four-year-old John Brown and his twenty-three-year-old
cousin Doug—trash, the two of them, though John was
unquestionably the scummier, a sadistic jerk who used to
pass the time by disfiguring animals.

On Saturday, November 10, 1973, while Stringbean
was performing at the *Opry*, the men went to the house,
broke the window of the back door, and let themselves
in to search the place.

When they found nothing of value, they were pissed.
Then, realizing that no one would hear anything out
here in the woods, they decided to wait and get the
money from Stringbean himself when he returned
home.

Lighting cigarettes and taking beers from the refriger-
ator, they made themselves comfortable and waited,
passing the time by listening to their "host's" *Opry* performance on the radio.

At roughly ten-thirty, after the second show, Stringbean got out of his costume; grabbed the duffel bag he
always carried, where he kept one of his many guns; took
his wife's arm; and headed from the auditorium. They
stopped to chat with singer/guitarist Louis "Grandpa"
Jones and his wife Ramona, and Jones and Stringbean
made plans to go fishing the next day. After a bit more
chitchat, the couple climbed into their new Cadillac. As
usual, Estelle was at the wheel: she loved driving almost
as much as Stringbean hated it.

A half-hour later they were home, and Stringbean
opened the front door while his wife turned off the car
and collected her things.

No sooner had Stringbean stepped inside and turned
on the light than Doug Brown stepped in front of him.
The entertainer didn't need to hear his demands to
know what the youth had come for.

Stringbean told him to leave. Doug snickered and refused. Figuring it was one-on-one, the gangly singer

reached into his duffel bag and pulled out his gun, then John stepped from the shadows, pointed a gun at Stringbean, and shot him in the chest. Stringbean fell forward, dead.

Outside, Estelle heard the shooting and didn't bother to investigate. She was unarmed and did the sensible thing: she ran.

John Brown burst from the house in pursuit, gun in hand. Estelle stumbled and fell, and Brown had no trouble catching up to her. He stood over her, watching as she climbed to her knees and pleaded with him not to hurt her. Then he put three bullets into her head.

The killers fled with a few items, having overlooked the $3,180 in Stringbean's pants and the $2,150 folded into Estelle's bra.

The next morning, shortly before 7:00 A.M., Grandpa Jones arrived for his outing with Stringbean. As he pulled up, he saw Estelle's body lying facedown on the front lawn, some forty yards from the house. Leaving the car, he ran over, saw the blood on her head and on the grass, then ran to the house. He found Stringbean sprawled on the floor, one arm outstretched, the other tucked beneath him.

Trembling, Grandpa called the police.

Detectives turned the city upside down looking for clues and, in a matter of a few months, they found their perpetrators, men with Stringbean's chainsaw and some of his guns in their possession.

Tennesseans wanted blood, no one more than the politically active Roy Acuff, who used his influence in a doomed effort to get the death penalty reinstated. He and other outraged friends of the Akemans had to settle for something less. On November 9, 1974, just four days after the trial began, the cousins were found guilty of two counts of first degree murder and were sentenced to life imprisonment.

Big deal, scoffed Acuff. For years, it pained the singer and many of his colleagues to know that those two were still alive. *For what?* they wanted to know. Acuff never gave up campaigning for capital punishment.

But there were also those whose indignation, though strong, was second to their sense of loss. Archie Campbell spoke for many when he said, "String was the greatest guy in the world. I never heard him say one mean thing about another human being. He was really fine."

Despite the drunks and drugs and plane crashes and car wrecks that had taken so many lives in Nashville, this was the event that brought the city into the violent modern day, the Manson era. Musicians could be self-destructive, and accidents happened, but this was a big city, psycho-cult style murder. Music City could never again be the same sampler-sweet town it had always been.

Nashville had lost its virginity.

Johnny Cash

FOR all the dead and wrecked of country music, there have also been survivors, singers who have been around a long time and overcame serious personal setbacks. For these people, just to survive is quite an accomplishment. But to survive with one's dignity, class, and popularity intact is rare.

Johnny Cash is a rare man. Hank Williams and Roy Acuff were the guiding lights of modern country, but Johnny is its soul. You can hear it in his voice; you can see it in his face. He has the kind of charisma that defies description. Kris Kristofferson once said, "He comes in a room, you don't have to see or hear him to know he's there. Hell, people who don't know country from corn flakes know Johnny Cash."

J.R. Cash was born on February 26, 1932, in Kingsland, Arkansas and raised in a community called Dyess, which the government had established to give poor families land and a new start. Cash picked cotton and sang "from can to can't" (from the time you can see until you can't). He relaxed at night by listening to the radio, particularly *The High Noon Roundup*, which set his feet on a path from which they would never turn: "From the time

I was a little boy," he says, "I never had any doubt that I was gonna be singing on the radio."

It wasn't until after he graduated from high school and joined the Air Force in 1950 that J.R. learned to play the guitar (and gave himself a name, John, since the military wouldn't accept his given initials as a legal moniker). Serving mostly in Germany, he entertained fellow soldiers with gospel and country songs. He was honorably discharged in 1954 without having suffered any serious wounds.

"I had a crooked nose from a fight with a paratrooper in a honky-tonk," he wrote in his autobiography *Man in Black*, "a scar on my cheek left by a drunken German doctor who couldn't find a cyst he was trying to remove, and a left ear with the hearing temporarily impaired because a German girl stuck a pencil in it." Other than that, he says, he "was in good shape."

Returning to Memphis, he met a girl named Vivian Liberto, married her a month later, and worked as a door-to-door salesman. Failing to make a living at that, he went to radio announcer's school on the G.I. Bill, planning to become a disc jockey. Meanwhile, he met local boys Luther Perkins and Marshall Grant, an electric guitarist and bass player, respectively, and started playing with them every night. In 1955, they managed to get themselves on *Louisiana Hayride*, appearing on the show with Elvis Presley.

Thanks in large part to the red-hot Presley, Sam Phillips's Sun Records was starting to get some attention. Cash decided to give him a call.

"Mr. Phillips," he said, "my name is John Cash. I write songs and play the guitar and I wonder if you would listen to me."

Phillips said no.

Nearly a month later, selling appliances for a living and not too happy (or successful) at it, Cash tried again, this time securing an audition for himself and his Tennessee Two (Luther Perkins and Marshall Grant).

Phillips was impressed, gave them a recording deal, called the singer Johnny Cash, and released their first single in the spring of 1955, "Hey, Porter." It was a surprise hit. A subsequent release, "I Walk the Line," not only topped the country charts in 1956, but was a crossover hit.

One of his next and biggest hits came to him by chance. With a few hours to kill before catching a plane, he went to the movies and happened to see *Inside the Walls of Folsom Prison*, which had been made in 1951. Shocked by the prison conditions he saw in the film, he wrote "Folsom Prison Blues" on the plane. It took him less than an hour to write; it was a number four hit in 1956. Recorded live at Folsom Prison twelve years later, the song went to number one and stayed there for four weeks.

The success of Johnny and his group was due to a combination of factors. Musically, there was the raw, honest baritone of the tall man who usually dressed in black (beginning in 1971, Cash vowed *always* to dress in black onstage to show compassion for the poor and weak) and the pounding rockabilly beat of the Tennessee Three, who had added drummer W.S. Holland to the group. And, needless to say, the songs were also important because, according to Cash, "There's realism in them. They have true human emotions as well as being real stories."

The quartet was invited to join the *Grand Ole Opry* in 1957; a year later, after fifteen Top Ten hits, they jumped to Columbia Records, where they charted "Don't Take Your Guns to Town," "Smilin' Bill McCall," "Forty Shades of Green," and "Big River," among many other songs.

In those early days, Cash's home life was as solid and

as gratifying as his career. He and Vivian were very much in love and had four daughters: Rosanne (who is now a country star herself), Kathy, Cindy, and Tara. Johnny *should* have been a happy man.

But the singer's quick professional ascent and personal happiness were soon destroyed. In characteristic understatement, he says he started "to do a lot of bad things." Cash was constantly on the road, doing an astounding three hundred concerts every year. Not surprisingly, he had trouble keeping up his energy for the shows and travel, then sleeping when he had to. He often went drinking with bandmates, fellow singers, and fans after shows, and that was enough to bring him down—at first. But then he'd have trouble getting up for the next show, so he started taking stimulants, primarily Dexedrine. That left him wired and made it necessary for him to drink and/or take depressants to come down again afterwards.

For the most part, he was able to get pills from doctors wherever he performed, giving them a song-and-dance of one kind or another. He also got drugs from people in the music business who, he says, "wanted me to go down with them.

"They had a whole bunch of nice little names for them to dress them up, and they came in all colors," Cash says, adding that inside the bottles "which cost only eight or ten dollars for a hundred, came at no extra cost a demon called Deception.

"With a couple of those pills in me, I had courage and confidence. My energy was multiplied. If I'd ever been shy before an audience, I wasn't anymore. I was personable, outgoing, energetic—I loved everybody."

At first, that is. By 1959 he was addicted to pills, and though he was able to perform, his offstage life was a fog. He was regularly stopped for speeding, wrecked several cars, once leaped from a truck right before it flew off a five hundred foot tall cliff, and was frequently arrested for public drunkenness. More than once, he trashed hotel rooms in which he was staying.

As the new decade dawned, Cash went three years without making much of an impact on the charts. No surprise, since he managed to miss many recording sessions that his producer arranged for him. He finally reversed his chart slide with the 1963 smash "Ring of Fire," written by Merle Kilgore and a young singer/songwriter named June Carter, and with "It Ain't Me, Babe," a duet with Bob Dylan. But Cash's life and performing career continued to plummet. He was so chronically ripped that he failed to show up for concerts, and finally committed the greatest sin of all: on a Saturday night in 1965, he made a spectacle of himself at the *Grand Ole Opry*.

Emaciated and stoned, he went on stage; he says, "The band kicked off a song, and I tried to take the microphone off the stand. In my nervous frenzy, I couldn't get it off." That, he says, "was enough to make me explode in a fit of anger. I took the mike stand, threw it down, then dragged it along the edge of the stage." He says, "There were fifty-two lights, and I wanted to break all fifty-two, which I did."

Broken glass flew everywhere, over musicians and audience alike, and as Cash stormed off the stage he was met by *Opry* manager Ott Devine, who told him softly and painfully, "We can't use you on the *Opry* any more, John."

"I know," Johnny replied. "See you later."

Cash stalked out the stage door, got in his car, and crashed into a tree. The singer says, "I woke up in the emergency room at the hospital with a broken nose and a broken jaw. The car was totaled."

Had enough? Learned his lesson? Not Johnny. He continued to wreck hotel rooms—once, with an axe—

dropped firecrackers into men's room toilets, and then did something no one in country or rock had ever done before. In 1964, he was driving a camper that had a bent front wheel which grew hotter and hotter as it turned. Oil began to drip on it, but Cash was unaware that it had begun to smoke. As he drove through a national forest in California, the oil caught on fire and ignited the grass; strong winds quickly carried the blaze up the side of a mountain, burning everything in its path.

Firefighters spent two days snuffing the blaze, and Cash says, "I'm the only person that the United States government ever sued as an individual for starting a forest fire and collected." The bill: $120,000.

And still, Johnny managed to top himself.

On October 1, 1965, while returning from Mexico, Cash was arrested at the El Paso International Airport when Federal Narcotics Agents found a total of 1,163 upper and downers stuffed in a sock that had been tucked inside of his guitar.

He was carted off to jail and freed on bond. After pleading guilty, Johnny was fined one thousand dollars and given a thirty-day suspended sentence. He was lucky to get off as light as he did, and he knew it. That didn't stop his drug abuse.

About the only honorable thing Johnny did during this period was stand up to the Ku Klux Klan when they distributed leaflets that said Vivian was actually a "Negress" and that his children were "mongrelized." Cash quieted them by threatening a $25 million lawsuit and declaring, "If there's a mongrel in the crowd it's me, because I'm Irish and one-quarter Cherokee Indian."

But by this time, Vivian had had enough of Johnny not being there, or being blasted when he was. It wasn't the Klan, but the taunts her children endured at school —"Trash Cash"—that finally compelled her to file for divorce in 1966. The divorce was finalized the following year, and she married an Air Force man (talk about an about-face!) a year after that.

"Success is having to worry about every damned thing in the world except money," Cash lamented. But instead of having learned his lesson and cleaning up his act, Johnny got even worse. It all came to a head for him one night when he was in Georgia. After gulping down fistfuls of pills, he went out—and the next thing he knew he woke up in prison.

Calling an officer over, he asked, "What am I doing here?"

The sergeant answered, "Someone found you stumbling around the street, picking flowers." Cash was informed that by the time the police had arrived, he was unconscious and not breathing. Another time in Toronto if he hadn't been given mouth-to-mouth resuscitation, he'd have died.

(Contrary to what his prison songs, reputation, and ongoing fight for prison reform imply, Cash has spent relatively little time in jail. In addition to the day in El Paso, he was jailed overnight once in Carson City, Nevada, where he'd gotten rowdy and where the guards, he says, "slammed me against the wall and beat me in the kidneys. One of them knocked me out." But those were the *only* times the singer ever went to prison for doing anything outside the law. In Georgia, and on four other occasions, he was locked up simply because police were afraid he might hurt himself. Rumors of Johnny having committed murder and of a long career on a chain gang simply aren't true. Of course, it's easy to see how the legend grew, what with Cash melodramatically telling interviewers things like, "You . . . watch a cockroach crawl out from under the filthy commode, and you don't kill it. You envy the roach as you watch it crawl out under the cell door.")

Sitting there in prison, Cash wept at what he'd become, and made a vow that somehow, he'd change.

Enter June Carter.

June was a latecomer to the singing Carter Family, a country and gospel trio which originally consisted of Alvin Pleasant ("Doc"), his wife Sara, and Sara's cousin Maybelle, who was married to Doc's brother Ezra. The act broke up in 1943 when Doc divorced Sara and retired. Maybelle and her daughters Anita, Helen, and June continued to perform as Mother Maybelle and the Carter Sisters. They joined the *Grand Ole Opry* in 1950 (with the legendary Chet Atkins as their guitarist) and starred there until 1967 when Maybelle retired.

Maybelle and Ezra were early fans and boosters of Cash. When his drug dependency got the best of him, they did what they could to help him with love, support, prayer, and anything else he needed. June was always looking over their shoulders and had a much, much deeper interest in the singer.

June had married singer Carl Smith in 1952, bore a daughter, Carlene (who later became a top country singer in her own right), and was divorced by 1957. She fell instantly in love when she first met Cash—"Ol' Golden Throat," as she called him. Later, she described him as "probably the strongest, nicest, neatest man I've ever known in my life. The only thing that has ever been rough for him has been the fact that he's a chemically dependent person."

With Johnny finally wanting to help himself, June resolved to stand by her friend. She was determined to help rid him of his addictions, partly through any underhanded means she could think of: "I became a thief," she says. "I stole pills. I stole his car keys. I did everything I could." She added, "It hurts you so bad. I mean, you either want to be a little hero and help them out, or you manipulate things to make excuses for them so they can continue to do what they're doing. There comes a time when you have to learn to deal with it."

She also helped him to find religion in a big way. Cash said at the time, "I've always been a deeply religious person, but now the light's shining a little brighter than it did a few years ago. I've had a lot of straightening out to do in the past and I wasn't always honest about it but that's over now thanks to June and the good friends who've always stood by me."

Fortunately, he says, he didn't have as far to come back as other addicts because "I never, repeat never, used heroin or sniffed cocaine."

The bond between Johnny and June grew especially strong after his divorce, and in February of 1968, during a duet onstage in London, Ontario, Cash asked June to marry him. She accepted, and they solemnized it the following month. Two years later, son John Carter Cash was born.

Cash said later with an edge of bitterness that while the folks in Nashville "acted like they were proud of me when I straightened up," they were more than a little disappointed because, "I didn't go ahead and die so they'd have a legend to sing about and put me in hillbilly heaven."

He was kidding, of course. Maybe.

June was also there for Johnny when he suffered one of the most debilitating losses of his life: in August of 1968, Luther Perkins was seriously burned in a fire and died. Through tears, Cash said, "We may find someone to stand in for Luther but he will never be replaced." When he started wearing all-black, he said a part of that was for Luther.

Getting his offstage act together helped Cash reignite his professional career. After "Folsom Prison Blues" went back on the charts, he connected with a song that stayed in the number one position for six weeks early in

1969: "Daddy Sang Bass," written by rockabilly king Carl Perkins (no relation to Luther). He followed that with "A Boy Named Sue," which was recorded live at San Quentin and became the biggest of Cash's forty-eight crossover hits, reaching number one on the country charts and number two on the pop charts. (And in case you ever wondered, it wasn't your local radio station or Columbia Records that bleeped the "son of a bitch" off the end of the song. It was Cash himself, who later said, "It was taking a little while for a cleaner language to catch up with my new nature.")

Cash's duet with his wife, "If I Were a Carpenter," went to number two on the country charts in 1970.

Though Cash didn't rejoin the *Grand Ole Opry*, he repaid them in grand style for the embarrassment he'd caused. In 1969, when he signed with ABC to do a weekly TV variety show, *The Johnny Cash Show*—a summer replacement for *Hollywood Palace*—he taped it at the *Opry*'s famed Ryman Auditorium, giving the Ryman unprecedented national exposure. Indeed, he made a point of going back to many of the places he'd stiffed when he was drugged-out and performed for them free-of-charge. Naturally, now that he was a star of enormous stature, the venues benefitted mightily from his largesse.

Cash also made himself the darling of the anti-Smothers Brothers set by openly supporting the war in Vietnam. "I support our government's foreign policy," he told one interviewer, though he also stated, "The only good thing that ever came from a war is a song, and that's a hell of a way to have to get your songs."

For a while in the 1970s, it looked as though country music was going to lose Cash—not to drugs but first, to the movies (until his 1971 film, *A Gunfight*, starring Kirk Douglas, proved to be a major flop) and then to the fundamentalist faith that had helped to bring him back from the precipice. He took Bible courses, joined forces with evangelist Billy Graham, and said, "I don't have a career anymore. What I have is a ministry." But the staggering commercial failure of his 1973 Holy-Land-in-song documentary, *Gospel Road*, tempered those ambitions somewhat.

Then, for a while, it looked like the writing world might get ahold of him. Inspired by the success of his 1975 autobiography, Cash started writing a religious novel called *Man in White*, about St. Paul. But the opus took him nearly a decade to complete, and when it was finally published in 1986, the heartfelt but clunky novel did not do well enough to inspire a Man in Anything Else—or any more writing projects.

Johnny returned to having just a musical career, invigorated by one tidbit he'd discovered while writing the novel: "Paul sang in prison." And if it was good enough for Paul, Johnny reasoned, it was good enough for him.

During this entire period, his drug problem reared its head a few times.

The first time was in 1978. Cash was walking in a field stocked with wild game when he was attacked by an ostrich. The bird, Cash says, "had lost his mate in the winter freeze and had become hostile." It jumped at him, its feet striking his chest and knocking him down. "He broke three ribs when he hit me, and only my belt kept his big, dirty claws from ripping me open."

Cash had broken another two ribs when he landed on a rock, but he managed to crawl out from under the bird and make his way home.

Cash's doctor gave him painkillers, and the singer says, they "led to sleeping pills. Sleeping pills led to 'uppers' again, and soon I was back on that mood-altered, not-so-merry-go-round." This time, however, he was aware of what was happening and managed to kick the habit before it got back to what it had been.

In 1983, drugs struck again—for the last time. Cash

had fallen and broken his kneecap, and while he recovered, he "sang the same tune, different key." He took painkillers, "and of course sleeping pills in case the pain kept me from sleeping, and of course 'uppers' to kill the hangover from sleeping pills."

This time, though, the story took a different turn. "The pills, so many of them day and night, had burned holes in my stomach," Johnny says. He began bleeding internally and was rushed to the hospital. It took fourteen units of blood to replace what he'd lost. Then he underwent seven hours of surgery that "took out half my insides."

For a while, it was touch-and-go as to whether he'd even pull through: his heart stopped once, and he recalls, "I was as close to death as you can come."

June stayed with him; friends called or wrote, they weren't permitted by his side in intensive care; Waylon Jennings left an encouraging note for him every day, and Cash recovered. But because he'd been given morphine and other drugs, doctors suggested that Johnny spend some time at the Betty Ford Center to get clean. He knew they were right and felt that if nothing else, "the education I would get on my problem of chemical dependency would help me in the future to guard against any use of mood-altering drugs."

(Meanwhile, Johnny's daughter Rosanne, who was raised by her mother in Ventura, California, had started taking drugs in 1969 when she was fourteen. She did them "off and on for several years recreationally." She met singer/songwriter Rodney Crowell at a party at Waylon Jennings's house in 1975, and he convinced her to go to a rehab center. She says that if she hadn't, "I think I'd be dead now." She also married Crowell.)

Cash stayed clean and spent a great deal of time helping others—notably Jennings (see page 92) to lead drug-free lives as well.

Musically, Johnny continued to please and surprise. In 1985, he joined with Jennings, Willie Nelson, and Kris Kristofferson to record *Highwayman*—an album as well as a single—which went to number one. The next year, despicably, Columbia dropped Cash. An outraged Dwight Yoakam put it best: "The man's been there thirty fucking years making them money. He paid for the son of a bitch's office (*Columbia's Nashville boss Rick Blackburn*) . . . He built the building, man." Not renewing Cash's contract didn't stop Columbia from milking the cow one more time though. In March of 1992, they issued a seventy-five song retrospective that went all the way back to Sun's "Hey, Porter."

Wounded more than he realized at the time (he collapsed on stage a few months after being dropped, and underwent bypass surgery in 1988), Johnny was picked up by PolyGram and continued to record, five new albums to date, though he openly loathes the job (or nonjob) the label has done promoting them.

"If I hear 'demographics' one more time," he told *Rolling Stone* in 1992, "I'm gonna puke right in their faces." And with justification. Youth doesn't guarantee sales, or older age preclude them; just ask Elton John, Neil Diamond, and Ozzy Osbourne, all of whom had albums in the top one hundred of the pop charts the week the interview came out. Even Alvin and the Chipmunks were at fifty with a bullet.

Cash also continues to tour at home and abroad (where his fans are very loyal), singing up a storm despite severe vocal problems that began with an impacted wisdom tooth and ended, in 1992, with a metal plate being implanted to keep his jaw together.

"I sing songs and do the job I'm cut out to do," he says today. More than that, he just doesn't want or need.

And we, his devoted fans, couldn't be happier.

Roger Miller

ROGER Miller was a country singer who broke country rules and, for a short time, became a cross-over powerhouse. As he said in the middle 1960s, at the height of his fame, "I prefer to go in my own direction and let someone follow me."

It was a philosophy that served him well. He snared a record eleven Grammy Awards in 1964–5, had one of the most popular and oft-recorded songs of the decade, "King of the Road," and even got himself an eponymous TV show on NBC in 1966.

But while Miller was King of those roads, he was a slave to others—none of which did him any good.

Born on January 2, 1936, in Fort Worth, Texas, Miller was one year old when his father died and his dead-broke mother sent him to live with an aunt and uncle in Erick, Oklahoma. There, Roger milked the cows in the morning, walked three miles to his one-room school-house, and worked the cotton fields when he got home. Weekends were for cleaning the chicken coop.

He fell in love with music at the age of five when he got the chance to sing one of his own compositions in front of the three dozen kids who attended his school. Encouraged by the warm reception, he taught himself how to play guitar (which he bought with the eight dollars he earned from picking four hundred pounds of cotton), as well as fiddle, banjo, piano, and drums. He hoped that music would get him out of poverty as it had one of his heroes, the new country sensation Hank Williams.

At the age of fifteen, Roger was good enough to begin playing clubs in Texas and Oklahoma—not expecting to be discovered, but hoping he'd get enough experience to launch a career in country music—and he admitted, "Enjoying the time away from the manure."

After a three-year tour of duty in Korea, in which he drove a jeep and performed in a Special Services country band, Roger followed his heart to Nashville where he worked in a variety of musical positions while trying to get a toe-hold in the music business. He worked as a drummer for Faron Young, fiddled for Minnie Pearl, and played guitar for other stars. He also wrote songs and said he spent a lot of time "walking the streets of Nashville, trying to get anybody and everybody to record my songs."

Finally, he succeeded. In 1958, his "Invitation to the Blues" was recorded by Ray Price; the song went top-twenty. Miller's works were subsequently recorded by Jim Reeves, George James, and others. He also recorded his own songs, scoring top-thirty country hits like "You Don't Want My Love" and "Lock Stock and Teardrops."

But in 1964, after writing 150 songs, most of them "soft and uninspired," Miller found that he wasn't as happy as he'd hoped he'd be. He once said, "All I wanted to be was Hank Williams, and suddenly I was Andy."

He had a puckish sense of humor, and very much admired singer/songwriter Ray Stevens's mainstream hits "Jeremiah Peabody's Polyunsaturated Quick Dissolving

Fast Acting Pleasant Tasting Green & Purple Pills"
(1961) and the smash "Ahab the Arab" (1962) from an
album that made no secret of its nature, *1,837 Seconds of
Humor*.

Humor was not perceived as something the country-
buying audience wanted, by and large, but Roger wanted
to give it a try. Moving from RCA to the spunkier Smash
label, he recorded "Dang Me," with its playful "bup-
bup-bup-badoopadoo-doo-doo" refrain. To the surprise
of everyone but Miller, the record became a million-
seller in 1964. "Dang Me" won him five of the eleven
Grammys he took home during his two-year sweep.

Throughout the years, Miller would write and record
other humorous and irreverent songs, such as "You
Can't Roller Skate in a Buffalo Herd," the droll "My
Uncle Used to Love Me But She Died," "Do-Wacka-
Do," and "(The Day I Jumped) From Uncle Harvey's
Plane." However, his biggest success was the hobo-as-
minstrel song "King of the Road" in 1965, which sold
2.5 million copies, has been recorded by over three hundred singers, and snagged him his next six Grammys.

What was amazing about the country and pop success
of his two big hits is that, like his contemporary Jim
Reeves, he achieved them at the height of the British
Invasion, when the Beatles were way in and everyone
else was *supposed* to be fighting for the scraps they left
behind.

It helped that Miller was a multimedia star. His ready
wit and interaction with the audience put him in great
demand on the tour circuit, and he made many TV appearances. He also had an eye for up-and-coming talent,
and he did his best to encourage it. He was the first one
to record a song by Kris Kristofferson, the soon-to-be-
immortal "Me and Bobby McGee."

Miller's steady climb to the top was a dramatic contrast to his swift plunge from the peaks of popularity,

and it wrought havoc with him. He had a lavish lifestyle —he owned a Lear jet, luxury cars, and suits that cost over a thousand dollars each—and from 1966 on, his recordings just didn't pay the bills like they used to.

He began drinking heavily, which contributed to the failure of his first two marriages. In 1970 he crawled into what he later described as the "snake pit": he started popping amphetamines, often as many as eight dozen a *day*, which dragged his finances and his spirits even further down.

As so often happens, friends who saw what was happening tried to convince Roger to seek help, but to no avail. He had to come to the realization himself, which he did after two years. "I just got tired of falling down," he said. "You either mature or you die."

His much-anticipated comeback effort proved to be a bust. He wrote and performed songs for Walt Disney's dismal animated feature *Robin Hood* (1973), but though he admits the bottle beckoned, he refused to backslide. He had help thanks to his "Rock of Gibraltar," his new companion, Mary. Once a singer with the rock group the First Edition, she was introduced to Miller in 1974 by the band's front man, Kenny Rogers. They married in 1977, moved to Sante Fe, New Mexico, and had two children, Margaret and Adam.

Away from Nashville and the painful memories that haunted him there, he started touring and recording again, and a new generation of fans discovered his delightful songs. In 1982, producer Rocco Landesman felt that Roger was the perfect person to write the music for a new Broadway-bound musical production based on Mark Twain's *Adventures of Huckleberry Finn*.

Big River opened in 1985, and thanks to its timeless tale and the irresistible blend of Twain/Miller wit, it was a smash that ran for two and one-half years. The musical gave Miller's career—and confidence—a big boost. He got a particularly big kick from playing the role of Pap in the musical both in New York and on the road.

"I feel like a real writer at last," said forty-nine year-old Miller. Unfortunately, his joy was short-lived.

In October of 1990, Roger noticed that he felt hoarse whenever he sang. He went to see specialists at Vanderbilt University Medical Center. The news wasn't good: Miller was told that he had throat cancer, with the tumor growing right beneath his vocal cords.

He was given radiation treatment, and despite a severe drop in his weight, hair loss, and lesions that formed in his throat, Roger's spirits were high as the treatments appeared to be working. He said he fully intended to be around to see his kids grow up, and by January it looked like he'd beaten the disease. Though he was frail and weary, he said he was determined to work his way back to a full schedule.

Sadly, when he went for a checkup in February, doctors found that the cancer had resurfaced in his lungs and was also spreading to his brain.

Treatments resumed, Roger was outwardly determined to win again but inwardly holding out little hope that he'd beat the odds. He kept up a limited schedule of performing, and though weak, he went onstage at the *Grand Ole Opry* with other country superstars to pay tribute to Minnie Pearl, joining in a singalong prophetically titled "All My Trials, Lord, Will Soon Be Over."

As the cancer weakened him, Miller stayed home more and more. Friends came to visit in New Mexico, the last of whom was Waylon Jennings, who spent several days with his old friend early in October.

"Hang in there buddy," he remembers telling Roger. "There's still a lot of livin' to do."

The two sang a song together, and it was the last song Miller would sing. A few days later his breathing became labored, and he was flown to Century City Hospital in

Los Angeles where he died on October 25, 1992—a day before the Minnie Pearl show was aired.

Tributes were predictably plentiful and generous—Kris Kristofferson called him "a songwriter's songwriter and singer's singer"—but, of course, only when he was gone did the music industry, and Nashville in particular, acknowledge that a one-of-a-kind giant had left us.

But what he once described as his "depressive jazz" was a beacon for many stars who came of age in the 1960s and 1970s, particularly Waylon and the other "Outlaws." Without the irreverent Miller, the face of country music would have been much, much different.

Willie Nelson

HE'S been called the poet laureate of the heart of the Heartland, an American troubadour.

He's been called friend by a President and by the farmers of America.

He's been called an outlaw. A bum. A tax dodger. And —this one, he says, hurts most of all—a lousy singer.

Which of them is accurate? Where Willie Nelson is concerned, there's truth every which way you turn.

Born in Abbott, Texas on April 30, 1933, Willie went to live with his grandparents when his parents divorced. His grandmother was an amateur songwriter, and young Willie showed an interest in her music, so much so that he started writing songs when he was five. When he was six, his grandfather bought him a guitar and showed him how to play it.

As a boy, Willie's other musical influences were the *Grand Ole Opry* broadcasts and the blues and spirituals he heard blacks singing in the cotton fields, where he worked alongside them for $1.50 a day. Not that he was always working when he was out in the fields. He says, "I didn't like picking cotton one bit," and so he often ended up daydreaming. "I used to stand in the fields and watch the cars go by and think, 'I want to go with *them*.' "

It would be a while before he got to do that, though music *did* finally manage to get him out of the cotton fields. When he was in the sixth grade, he was paid from eight to ten dollars a night to play polka with the John Raycheck Band, entertaining the area's Polish and Czechoslovakian population.

Apart from the money, these gigs were important in another way: "Playing (*guitar*) with no amplification," Willie says, "with all those tubas and trombones and drums, there was no way anyone could really hear me, so I could make my mistakes young without being noticed."

Meanwhile, Willie's sister Bobbie had married bass player and sometimes fiddler Bud Fletcher, who formed a band called, of course, Bud Fletcher and the Texans, which included Bobbie on the piano and high school student Willie on the guitar. They achieved a considerable degree of local fame, even performing on the radio from time to time. Willie remembers with a laugh, "When I found myself singing over the radio, I didn't think life got much better than that."

After a short stint in the Air Force—he was discharged because of back problems dating back to his hay-baling days—the eighteen-year-old Willie married waitress Martha Jewel Mathews, who was two years his junior. Willie earned his living doing odd jobs during the day, from selling Bibles door-to-door to deejaying and playing at night in any local joint that would have him.

He admits that, "Me being an entertainer, a singer in a beer joint, and Martha being a waitress, sometimes in the same beer joint," they often ended up, "drinking too much." Back home and inebriated, they would be at one another's throats because she winked at this guy or he smiled at this gal.

Things always looked better for the couple in the morning though, and in 1953, daughter Lana was born, followed by Susie in 1957, and Billy a year later. Willie says money was so tight during those years that "we'd live in one place for a month, then pick up and move when the rent would come due."

Despite the financial bind, he knew he couldn't keep working day and night jobs. He was wearing himself out, and worse, "the nightlife was calling me," and he was only too willing to answer. He had to commit to a nine-to-five life or to music. He says, "It was no choice."

Willie had diligently kept up the songwriting he'd begun when he was a boy, and says that "we didn't have any money, but I did have some new songs I thought I could sell to somebody."

He was right.

Thanks to his club work, he'd managed to make some connections in the music business. In 1959, he sold a pair of songs for fifty and one hundred and fifty dollars, respectively: "Family Bible" and "Night Life." Claude Gray took "Family Bible" to the top ten on the country charts. Ray Price's recording of "Night Life" made the top thirty and became what Willie calls "one of the most-recorded songs in history." Yet, while over seventy artists have covered the song, Willie never saw a dime above the one-fifty for which he'd sold all rights.

"But so what?" he said much later. "The fact that both songs became hits encouraged me to think I could write a lot more songs that were just as good."

It also encouraged him to move to Nashville, and in 1960, just shy of his twenty-seventh birthday, Willie put his family in their 1950 Buick and headed for Tennessee. His recent track record opened a few important doors for him, and he was able to put three more songs in the top ten: "Crazy" sung by Patsy Cline, "Hello Walls" sung by Faron Young, and "Funny How the Time Slips

Away" from both Billy Walker and Joe Hinton (whose version also made it to the top fifteen on the pop charts).

But his fondness for "nightlife" and for the bottle was stronger than ever now that he had some money. While his family was back at their comfy trailer, he'd be out drinking and cheating on his wife. He, in turn, had reason to believe she had cheated on him, and Willie says that he was "mad enough to shoot somebody" had any of the men he suspected admitted sleeping with his wife.

"The guys I was after had a little more sense than I had," he says, "or else they didn't want to get shot over a piece of ass."

He and Martha continued to fight, sometimes violently. Martha vigorously denies the story Willie has told often, that she was so angry at her soused husband one night that she waited until he was asleep, sewed him up inside a bedsheet, and beat him silly with a broom handle. However, in a recent interview she was willing to discuss stories that she once picked up a knife and chased her naked husband around the yard and, on another occasion, bit his finger through to the bone ("Slowed up my guitar playing," Willie notes).

He was frequently despondent over the state of their relationship and his inability to fix it. Once, in 1962, he went so far as to try and commit suicide by getting drunk at Tootsie's Orchid Lounge, which was where he frequently partied, then lying on the dark street in front of the Hitching Post, which was where Martha worked, to wait for a car to run him over. Happily, Martha found our hero before a motorist did, and she hauled him to the sidewalk, where she left him to sleep it off. Shortly thereafter, she put the kids in the car and drove off. The next time Willie heard from her, it was for a divorce.

The divorce, he says, just "lasted and lasted . . . and cost and cost." For months, he said, "the money I was

making off my songwriting either went for booze or lawyers."

Helping to see Willie through these dark days was
singer Shirley Collie, whom he'd met in 1962. They
married the following year and bought a farm outside of
Nashville. Determined, now, to sing his own material
and make big recording artist money, Willie cut two LPs
in 1963–1964: *Here's Willie Nelson* and *And Then I Wrote*,
the latter of which did manage to spawn the top-ten hit
"Touch Me." Willie even got to sing on the *Grand Ole
Opry*, though he wasn't particularly well-received. No
matter, he told himself. They were the ones who told
Elvis to go back to driving a truck.

Unfortunately, Nashville's tastes were running to a
smooth, easy style, and the nasal Nelson baritone just
didn't fit in. Subsequent records didn't sell, and his "just
in case" sideline, hog farming, was also a bust. By 1968,
Willie says he was drinking heavily and his wife "was
boozing as bad as I was." Worse "we were all swallowing
enough pills to choke Johnny Cash when he was at his
worst."

Deja vu: the couple fought. To escape his dismal home
life Willie toured, taking newcomer Charlie Pride with
him and, in the process, breaking taboos against black
singers at various venues in the South. He once kissed
Charlie full on the lips so the unruly crowd would be too
stunned to boo. By the time they recovered, Charlie's
smooth, strong voice had won them over.

On the road, Willie resumed his philandering ways,
but was particularly dazzled by one lady he saw, bushy-
tailed young factory worker Connie Koepke, who was in
his audience one night. Willie was suddenly Mr. Gentleman; he introduced himself and, within five minutes,
was in love. Connie toured with him and, in October of
1969, bore him a daughter, Paula, in Houston. Shirley

didn't find out about it until she opened the bill, which had been sent to the house.

She called him every name she could think of ("and Shirley was an eloquent lady with plenty of insults in her repertoire," Willie says) and then split. Connie moved in and, though Willie wasn't divorced, they went ahead and married in April of 1971. The divorce from Shirley followed in September.

In the meantime, just days after Connie and Paula moved to Nashville, Willie's luck turned bad again when his house burned down. Willie was out at the time, but when he got the news he rushed over. After determining that his wife and daughter were all right, he ran into the still burning house to retrieve not a prized guitar, not an important manuscript, but the tin can that contained his stash of pot. He didn't want the firefighters to find it, pointing out, "In 1969, you could get life in prison for being caught . . . with one joint."

Fed up with Nashville and with records that weren't selling—he'd cut eighteen by now—Willie moved his family to Austin, Texas in 1971. There the singer grew himself beard and braids, donned his trademark bandanna, and started to tour, courting the still-rebellious and disenfranchised youth of the era, kids who liked folk and country and honky tonk and blues and rock and didn't care what it was called or how it was fused. At the same time, Atlantic Records, new on the country scene and looking to make a mark with something untraditional, signed the renegade in 1973.

Though his albums sold extremely well, Atlantic decided to ditch their Nashville efforts. Nothing personal: it was just too far afield from the soul to which they were accustomed. They bolted one album too soon. Willie went to Columbia in 1974, where his next record, *Red Headed Stranger*, was released the following May and was a smash; to date, it has sold over 2.5 million copies, though it happened over Columbia's near-dead body.

Willie says, "They thought it was underproduced, too sparse, all those things. Even though they didn't like it, they had already paid me a bunch of money for it, so they had to release it under my contract. And since they had money in it, they had to promote it."

The label also didn't want to release Willie's choice for a single, "Blue Eyes Crying in the Rain." So what happened? It went to number one on the country charts, number twenty-one on the pop charts, and won a Grammy.

Backed by this success, Willie—along with Waylon Jennings—spearheaded the so-called Outlaw Movement, which drew inspiration from the country-rock fusion triumphs of Bob Dylan and Gram Parsons, and consisted of artists who did country their way, ignoring what was fashionable, in, or acceptable to Nashville.

But even Nashville has trouble ignoring sustained record sales and, eventually, Music City acknowledged his innovation and talent as a singer. In 1983, he won the Country Music Association award for album of the year, for his duet album with semi-Outlaw Merle Haggard, *Poncho and Lefty*. The following year, he won a Grammy for his duet with non-Outlaw (indeed, non-country) Julio Iglesias, "To All the Girls I've Loved Before." He had gone from being a musical pariah to being a giant.

Meanwhile, in its ongoing effort to appeal to youth, Hollywood beckoned, and Nelson acted in films like *The Electric Horseman, Honeysuckle Rose, Barbarossa,* and *The Songwriter.* A favorite of President Jimmy Carter, Willie sang the national anthem at the Democratic National Convention in 1980 (accidentally leaving out the section that begins, "And the rocket's red glare . . ."). After participating in the famous "Live Aid" benefit, he got the idea in 1985 of doing "Farm Aid" and its sequels, which not only raised money for farmers but called attention to the dire financial condition of the people who grow our corn and raise our beef.

He continued to smoke pot ("I think most sensible human beings know it's not something you send people to the penitentiary for") and enjoy his whiskey. He'd, however, cut way back on his former passion, tequila, saying that it was something he'd drink "down to the worm. Down *through* the worm." On the other side of the worm, of course, was his old nemesis the street. He also didn't allow cocaine or pills on his tour, his motto being, "If you're wired, you're fired."

At last, he was on top of the world. His marriage was solid. He had a new daughter, Amy. Unfortunately, what goes up——

In 1984, the Internal Revenue Service decided that there was something fishy about Willie's returns going back a half-dozen years. They concluded that due to some questionable tax shelters, he'd underpaid to the tune of over six million dollars. Ten million dollars more in penalties and interest were added, bringing the total debt to $16.7 million.

Willie felt like he'd had the wind knocked out of him, but agreed to pay, provided the IRS wait until the conclusion of his $6.5 million lawsuit against Price Waterhouse, the accounting firm that he said had screwed things up for him by getting him into the tax shelters.

The IRS said no. No grace period.

(Price Waterhouse attorney Allen Young called Willie's charges absurd, declaring, "We only did his accounting and taxes. We are not his investment advisers." A formal statement from the firm said, "Mr. Nelson and his advisers made all of the decisions regarding tax shelters . . . those decisions and the economic consequences that resulted from those decisions were Mr. Nelson's responsibility.")

With interest payments increasing by some five to six thousand dollars daily, Uncle Sam seized most of Willie's holdings for auction: twenty-plus properties, including a twenty-two acre fishing camp in Texas, a 688 acre movie set, a golf course, a Lear jet, and more. Also seized were many of his personal belongings, though the IRS permitted memorabilia such as gold records and instruments to be sold for seven thousand dollars to the Willie Nelson and Friends Showcase, an organization that held the items for Willie. Musicians organized fundraisers, farmers pitched in money, and at least Willie's home, a forty-four acre ranch in Austin, was spared the auctioneer's gavel.

The singer was very reluctant to accept all of this so-called "Willie Aid," but the sad truth was that the property auction didn't make much of a dent in his debt, raising only $2 million because of the depressed real estate market.

But he refused to become dispirited about his debt. He told *The New York Times*, "I've been broke before and will be again. Heart-broke? That's serious. Lose a few bucks? That's not." He joked with *Rolling Stone*, "I've been callin' around lookin' for one of those suicide machines. I'll go on national TV, hook myself up to that machine and tell everyone I have 'til seven o'clock to get $16 million. If I don't get it, I'm pulling the plug."

He wouldn't have to. American sponsors would fork over a bundle to get a spot on an "event" show like that.

In June of 1991, Willie put out a new album called *Who'll Buy My Memories? (The IRS Tapes)*, a collection of early acoustic Willie, sans accompaniment. He intended to use the profits from the $19.95 recording to pay off the remainder of his debt, though the fact that he got out at all was a major coup. After months of haggling, the usually intransigent IRS bent long enough to give him access to tapes they'd seized.

Artistically, the collection of twenty-five short songs is a breathtaking listen. Financially, though, it was a major disappointment. Willie needed to sell four million copies to earn enough to fill the bill (literally): he sold in the area of a quarter-million copies. That brought the debt down by just $750,000, which is a lot of money under ordinary circumstances but less than Willie needed.

The only option left to him was to push hard on the road and whittle away the debt, collecting roughly fifty thousand dollars a show and playing two hundred of them a year (not *all* of that money goes to Willie; he travels with a crew of some twenty-five roadies and musicians, all of whom are paid very generously).

As if this publicity weren't bad enough, in the early days of 1991 a woman sued Willie for $50 million, charging breach of promise when he refused to marry her. She said that in January of 1985, they'd made love for nine hours straight. A liaison, she says, that Willie finished with a backward somersault—while they were still coupled. "Shirley said she'd be glad to testify on my behalf," Willie told a reporter.

Connie didn't offer to come to Willie's defense though. In 1987, she filed for divorce at roughly the time fickle Willie met and fell in love with Ann Marie D'Angelo. He made her his fourth wife in 1991, and they had two children, Lukas Autry and Jacob Micah.

However, the cruelest blow of Willie's fifty-eight years came on Christmas morning in 1991, when his thirty-three-year-old son Billy was found dead in his log cabin in Davidson County, Tennessee.

Life had not been kind to Billy. An aspiring gospel singer and songwriter who was largely underwritten by his dad, Billie had a serious drinking problem. His mother Martha had died in December of 1989, and his wife Janet had left him soon thereafter, taking their daughter Rae Lynn with her. These two blows, plus four arrests for drunk driving, convinced Billy to seek help. He entered a rehab center in 1990, very much wanting to get better. And though he came out clean, he couldn't stay that way.

On December 24, 1991, Billie was in a good mood. He bought some clothes, got a haircut, and hung out with a friend, Buddy Frank. Frank left at two in the morning, and apparently rationalizing it as a holiday celebration, Billy started doing some serious drinking.

And, it seems, he became depressed about being alone, and about having to rely on his father for money.

Sometime thereafter, he slipped a noose around his neck and hanged himself. An autopsy showed that he was well beyond the legal limits for intoxication.

When he was told of his son's death, Willie broke down and blamed himself to a degree for having been away so much, "busy trying to pay the rent." Billy was buried in the family plot in Vaughn, Texas. The tearful Willie said at the time, "I've never experienced anything so devastating in my life." Then he added, "Alcohol didn't kill my son. My son was an addict. Alcohol just happened to be his addiction."

Willie confronted his sorrow head-on. Less than three months later he threw himself into Farm Aid V and continued to work hard on his touring and new recordings, still chewing away at the tax debt. He also busied himself with a pet project called the Outlaw Music Channel (a.k.a. the Cowboy Television Network).

Though the outcome of his battle with Price Waterhouse remains in limbo, Willie has moved on from the pain and turmoil of the past. He exudes an air of resignation about so many things such as bureaucracy and the fact that so many people are no longer as good as their word, but he still is, in his own way, the bad boy he was when he first went to Nashville, the kid who wants to shake things up.

"It's the only way I know how to do things," he says. "My philosophy has always been to shoot straight, make sure you're the one still standing, then take your loved one's hand and move it on. More than that, no one can ask for. And more than that, no one really needs."

Waylon Jennings

WILLIE Nelson may be an Outlaw to the bone, but he's also an Outlaw with a sense of humor, a sense of fun.

Not so the other leading figure in musical gunslinging, Waylon Jennings. He's always tended to take life more seriously, perhaps there's a good reason for that: namely, the fact that he barely missed dying in one of the most famous disasters in music history, a disaster that claimed a man who was his mentor and closest friend.

Would things have been different *had* he gone? Of course not. But the doubt is always there, along with the guilt.

The son of a truck driver, Waylon was born in Littlefield, Texas, on June 15, 1937. He learned to play guitar when he was a youngster and was deejaying on a Littlefield radio station at the age of twelve. A country fan, he was also drawn to the fledgling rock and roll movement. At the age of twenty-one, he began toying with ways of merging the two.

He received encouragement from Lubbock, Texas, disc jockey Hipockets Duncan, the man who had discovered local boy Buddy Holly four years before. Duncan not only hired Jennings as a DJ for country station KLLL but also helped to arrange concerts for the singer.

Whenever Holly was in town, he'd stop by the station to give an interview or visit his old friends. Hipockets introduced him to Waylon. Holly heard him perform and was so impressed by the young man's talent that he offered to produce Waylon on vinyl. Jennings didn't need to be asked twice.

"He was the first man who ever had any faith in me as a singer," Waylon says. "He was a friend all the way."

Holly's involvement with Waylon's career didn't stop there. Holly and his wife Maria were living in Manhattan at the time, and she recalls, "He actually wanted Waylon to come and move in with us—because Buddy felt like that way he could really come to know Waylon and his feelings, and write songs that matched them."

When Holly split with his old band the Crickets—in large part due to conflicts with their former producer, Norman Petty—he formed a new band for a tour he was planning early in 1959. He hired Tommy Allsup to play guitar, Carl Bunch on drums, and offered Waylon the chance to join them on bass. Waylon took an immediate leave of absence from KLLL, and although he'd never played an electric bass before, he learned—fast. He smiles as he remembers what Holly told him when he agreed to do the tour: "Here's the bass—you learn it. Now, here are my albums—you learn 'em. You've got a week and a half to do it."

The band rehearsed in Texas and, in mid-January, joined Holly in New York for a week of rehearsals, then they set out for Milwaukee, Wisconsin, for their first gig. Also on the bill were J.P. Richardson, a.k.a. the Big Bopper ("Chantilly Lace"), Ritchie Valens ("La Bamba"), and Dion and the Belmonts ("A Teenager in Love").

After the January 23 opener, the so-called Winter Dance Party played a different city every night: Kenosha, Wisconsin on the 24th; Mankato, Minnesota on the 25th; Eau Claire, Wisconsin on the 26th; Montevideo, Minnesota on the 27th; St. Paul, Minnesota on the 28th; Davenport, Iowa on the 29th; Fort Dodge, Iowa, on the 30th; Duluth, Minnesota on the 31st; and Green Bay, Wisconsin, on February 1st.

The 2nd was to have been a free day, but the promoters were able to book the entertainers into Clear Lake, Iowa. Since it was in the same general westerly direction as their date on the 3rd, in Moorhead, Minnesota, the stop made sense. Buddy agreed to the gig, though he wasn't happy. It was the dead of winter, and he was sick of the buses that he described as "dirty and cold" in a phone call to his wife, Moreover, because of the grueling schedule, none of the performers had been able to get their stage attire cleaned and pressed.

"When they called 'em rock and roll pioneers," Waylon said later, "they were talkin' about the music. But that pretty much described the living conditions too."

Prior to the Clear Lake show, Buddy told Waylon and Tommy that he'd decided to charter a plane so he could go ahead to the next stop, take care of last-minute arrangements for the show, and get their wardrobe cleaned. The two bandmembers agreed to go with him. However, when the Bopper got wind of the plan, he literally pounced on Waylon and asked him to give up his seat. The Bopper had caught a cold and felt that the only chance he had of getting over it was if he didn't have to ride the damn cold bus all through a night that was expected to get down to fifteen degrees.

At the time, wide-eyed Waylon felt like a kid out of school. He enjoyed hanging with the other musicians, even when conditions were less than ideal, and he was happy to give the Bopper his seat on the plane.

Meanwhile, Ritchie Valens was feeling left out. He

wanted to fly ahead too, and throughout the night he bugged Allsup about switching places with him. Unlike Waylon, Allsup wasn't keen to go by bus, but finally, just before departure, he agreed to Ritchie's suggestion that they flip a coin for the seat. Valens won.

The plane took off just before one A.M. with twenty-one-year-old pilot Roger Peterson at the controls. Peterson had been flying for four years, but he was not certified for instrument flying. When darkness and snowfall forced him to rely on them, he apparently misread the gyroscope while executing a turn, mistaking down for up and descending rather than climbing. The right wing of the Beechcraft Bonanza hit the snow-covered ground of Albert Juhl's farm and was torn off; the fuselage hit an instant later, compacting like an accordion, bouncing some fifteen yards, then tumbling through five hundred feet of snow and rock before hitting a wire fence.

All of the occupants, save Peterson, were thrown from the wreckage; all had died on impact.

It wasn't until noon that the buses carrying Waylon, Allsup, and the rest of the entourage reached Moorhead. Allsup was the first to enter the hotel lobby, where the clerk informed him what had happened. Fighting back tears, he walked back to the bus and, his voice choked, he said, "Boys—they didn't make it."

Incredibly, arrangements were quickly made to continue the tour with replacement bands. Waylon and Allsup were asked to continue—and they did, as a tribute to Holly, though Waylon admits they were emotionally numb for each of the nightly gigs. Only when the Winter Dance Party ended on February 15 and the young men returned home did the depth of their loss hit them.

In many ways, Waylon never recovered. "Everything seemed just a waste after Buddy died." In 1960, he named his third child Buddy, and even today he says,

"There's never much time that goes by that I don't think of him."

Emotionally, he wasn't prepared to play again and went back to disc jockeying. It wasn't until 1963, when Waylon met Herb Alpert of A & M Records, that he went back into the studio. However, Alpert didn't invite him to sleep at his house and get to know his music. A & M wanted Waylon as a pop singer; he bristled at that and walked out on the deal after just one album.

Settling in Phoenix, Arizona, Waylon returned to live performing and working local clubs, backed by his band the Waylors. Waylon earned some local celebrity, and in 1965, RCA Records signed him to sing country. He moved to Nashville the next year and, produced by Chet Atkins, he began a slow climb to the country chart top ten, winning a Grammy in 1970 for his country version of "MacArthur Park."

But the label's fingerprints were still on the arrangements; they picked the musicians and often the songwriters. While good things were happening for Waylon professionally, he was bugged by the fact that no one since Holly had let him do his kind of music his way. In 1973, at a DJ convention in Nashville, he and good friend Willie Nelson performed together and officially inaugurated what quickly became known as the "Outlaw Movement," country that dealt with alienation and misery instead of marriage and hooch, often using wild west metaphors and thicker, more complex instrumentation. The men recorded together and scored one of country's first platinum albums in 1976, *Wanted! The Outlaws*.

But Waylon was a renegade in every sense of the word. When he'd first moved to Nashville he'd roomed with Johnny Cash and joined him in his boozing and pill-popping ways. Waylon says, "Neither one of us could handle it . . . It got to the point where it nearly killed both of us. . . ."

Beginning in 1972, after going through a phase of using amphetamines, cocaine became the drug of choice for the singer, and over the next twelve years, it became more and more of a habit. Early in 1977, the Nashville Metropolitan Police Department named Waylon an honorary police chief; on August 24 of that year, he managed to bump the late Elvis Presley off the lips of the folks in Nashville by getting himself busted in a major way.

It started in New York, where a nosy courier had looked into a package addressed to Waylon, discovered cocaine, and alerted Federal Drug Enforcement agents. The agents let the package go and, in Nashville, followed a secretary and the parcel from the airport to a recording studio where Jennings was producing an album for aspiring Outlaw, Hank Williams, Jr.

Jennings was arrested and faced fifteen years in jail and a twenty-five thousand dollar fine. Released on bond, he was off the hook by October, the charges dropped because—among other things—no one had had any right to go peeking in the package in the first place and, when agents arrived at the recording studio, they hadn't actually found the drugs on Waylon's person.

Waylon learned nothing from the close call. He just wiped the sweat off his brow and went back to pushing powder up his nose. By 1981 he was spending $1500 a day on the drug and living in a perpetual stupor; at one point the owner of a recording studio sued him not just for overdue rent but for allegedly leaving the place a wreck.

"I think my own mother might sue me next," a bitter Waylon said at the time.

He'd probably have deserved it. He burned his way through the $3 million he'd been advanced by RCA on a new contract in 1984, and he indulged in both free-wheeling sex and, on at least one well-known occasion, the trashing of hotel rooms.

None of this was helping Waylon's marriage to singer Jessi Colter, his fourth wife. Married in 1969, he was not only untrue to her but generally uninvolved with their son Shooter, who was born in 1979. Still, she was devoted to Waylon and refused to give up on him. Jessi even found a way to use her pain: one night in 1975, when Waylon called out a name in the middle of the night, she was moved to write her hit song "I'm Not Lisa."

Drugs weren't doing much for his career, either. On the road, it was often touch-and-go as to whether he could perform at each gig.

"I'd be out on the bus, they (*the band*) would be putting hot and cold towels on me to keep me from hyperventilating, then when I'd get on stage I'd cool right down."

Usually, he was able to get through his dates—but not always. At a concert in Portland, Oregon, he could barely stand as he mumbled his way through a few tunes before being booed off the stage by an angry crowd. He remembers giving a magazine interview while stoned: "I don't know how (the reporter) got any sense out of me at all."

In the recording studio, he says his attention span was "short and I would get bored immediately, and I'd keep people around the studio for a week at a time, day and night. It'd take me that long to cut one side, because I would go to sleep some, and wake up and see where I was really messed up and didn't do something right. I wasn't in control of things, and I knew it. I was smart enough to know when not to drive," but, he concludes, "it was a mess."

By 1981, he had virtually lost all interest in eating. Jessi took to tricking/cajoling/forcing him into drinking milk shakes filled with honey, fruit, vitamins, and other things to keep him going. He couldn't sleep, and although he'd lay awake at four in the morning, staring into space, thinking "about what (cocaine) was doing to me, to my people and to my family, . . ." he couldn't bring himself to kick the habit. Not that he didn't try. In 1982, he rented a house in Malibu intending to go cold turkey. Unfortunately, he found that "California isn't a real good place to get off drugs."

Finally, in Nashville, cleaned-up Johnny Cash went to visit Waylon one day and had a long, long talk with him. Cash himself had recently kicked his own addiction to painkillers and told his friend, "I want to show you my big bright eyes." What Waylon saw in them was a happy man, one who looked "saved" to him, and he decided, once and for all, that he wanted to be saved too.

But while other musicians had gone to the Betty Ford Center in Rancho Mirage, California, to get clean, that wasn't for Waylon. He had always been a do-it-yourselfer. He rented a house again, this time in isolated Paradise Valley, near Scottsdale, Arizona.

Alone except for his wife and son, Waylon breathed the clean air, walked in the fields and hills, sat outside and asked himself what he wanted from life.

"It took me a couple of mornings sitting out by myself in the wilderness to be able to say I was quitting," he says, but after four weeks of being clean he felt good and ready to throw himself back into arms of temptation.

Cash says, "I appreciate everybody's giving me the credit for Waylon's recovery, but . . . nobody but Waylon did that."

It's a debatable point. In any case, upon his arrival in Nashville, Waylon called together everyone who worked with him on tour or in the studio and said that he wasn't going to tell them how to live their lives, but if they wanted to be around *him* there were to be no drugs.

His bandmates were only too happy to oblige. He made the successful *Turn the Page* album and, in 1985, teamed up with Willie, Johnny, and Kris Kristofferson for their hugely successful *Highwayman* project. Waylon didn't disappoint fans who wondered if sobriety or age would temper the ornery singer. As recently as the fall of 1992 he was still kicking up dust with the release of his album *Too Dumb for New York City, Too Ugly for L.A.* He sniped at Billy Ray Cyrus and the current trend toward hunkiness by saying, "The video thing has put much too much emphasis on appearance." Then he said, laughing, "I'll tell you, if me and Willie were starting out now, we'd be in a lot of trouble."

But he said that at least he'd be equipped to deal with it. The experience of being clean was, says Waylon, "a new high for me." He got close to his family and, together with the Cashes, they'd have regular "sobriety parties." He says today, "I spent twenty-one years of my life on drugs, and I have no excuse for that. I would have been a lot more successful sooner if I had never touched them."

True enough. But at least he was alive, which was more than could be said for an artist who out-Outlawed —and outdrugged—them all.

Gram Parsons

NO one was more important to the nascent late 1960s fusion of country and rock than Gram Parsons. And with the possible exception of the Doors' Jim Morrison, no one in music was as egregiously self-destructive as Gram Parsons.

Without his recklessness, perhaps his music wouldn't have been as adventurous and rich as it was. It's a debatable point. Rocker Eddie Van Halen put it well in 1985 when he said, "Creation is like trying to get through a wall. You can blow it down and get to the other side quickly, or you can take your time and build a door. I guess stuff [drugs] will get you there faster, but which one do you think will leave you with a roof still over your head?"

Gram was born Cecil Ingram Connor on November 5, 1946, in Winter Haven, Florida. Passionate about popular music from the time he was a young boy, he was especially fond of Elvis Presley, whose songs he taught himself to play on the guitar and piano. As a teenager, Gram became deeply interested in the folk sounds of the Kingston Trio, and Peter, Paul and Mary.

When Gram was thirteen, his father, Cecil "Coon Dog" Connors, a factory manager and frustrated singer/

songwriter, grew despondent over work and over his un-happy marriage (he apparently suspected his wife Avis of having an affair). He ended his life with a bullet to the head. The alcoholic Avis wed wealthy New Orleans businessman Robert Parsons. Robert adopted the boy and changed his name to Gram Parsons.

Gram wasn't happy with his new family—he hadn't been thrilled with the old one, either—and buried himself in music. In 1960 he formed a group called the Pac-ers, which performed rockabilly hits, and in 1962 he founded the Village Vanguards, which became a popular group around town. The next year he joined yet another group, the Shilos.

Avis died of liver failure in June of 1965, the same day Gram graduated from school. In September, Gram en-rolled in Harvard University as a theology major. But he got into LSD at Timothy Leary's old stomping grounds and was usually too stoned to go to class; he later joked, "I was there about four hours and fifteen minutes."

He was actually there through February of the follow-ing year. Then he headed to New York, hoping to build a career singing and playing the guitar and piano. He also continued experimenting with hallucinogenic drugs.

Settling in the Bronx, he and a friend from Boston, Barry Tashien—formerly of the marginally successful group the Remains—formed the International Subma-rine Band. They began playing clubs and making demo tapes, then landed a relatively high-profile job, recording a song for the film *The Russians Are Coming, The Russians Are Coming*. They did some recordings for Columbia that went nowhere. But none of it was the country, folk, and rockabilly sounds that Gram had grown up loving, and he abandoned ship.

The young musician headed to Los Angeles where so much music was "happening" then—the Doors, Jeffer-son Airplane, the Beach Boys, and others. He formed a new International Submarine Band and cut the album *Safe At Home*, which was country flavored with rock. It bombed.

Marginally more successful was his relationship with young Nancy Martha Ross. They became inseparable and in 1967 she bore him a daughter, Polly. Unfortunately, though he loved Nancy and asked her to marry him, he quickly rescinded his offer, realizing that he wasn't ready to settle down in any way, shape, or form.

After the failure of *Safe At Home*, Gram didn't sit idle. When rocker David Crosby left the successful rock group the Byrds, Gram was invited to join. Though his stint there lasted about as long as his studies at Harvard, he managed to move the band towards country, resulting in their classic *Sweetheart of the Rodeo* "folk-rock" album and enabling them to do an historic gig at the *Grand Ole Opry* in March of 1968, singing Gram's "Hickory Wind."

However, Gram adamantly refused to do a tour of racist South Africa with the band and quit in July. He was also at odds with some of the members over instrumentation and their reluctance to record more of his country songs. (The Byrds restaffed and lasted till 1973, though sales after *Sweetheart of the Rodeo* were increasingly flat.)

Although the other bandmembers were bitter about Gram's departure, founding member Chris Hillman liked him and, perhaps more importantly, liked the southern influence he brought to their music. Hillman left the band and, with high hopes for creating a new musical genre, formed the legendary Flying Burrito Brothers with Gram.

Their first two albums remain classics of country-rock: *The Gilded Palace of Sin* in 1969, and *Burrito Deluxe* a year later. Unfortunately, the buying public didn't get it and the records flopped. (Gram wasn't alone in finding country-rock a hard sell. Mike Nesmith of the then hot Monkees was also a big country-rock advocate, yet the group's 1969 single "Listen to the Band"—one of their best—was only a modest success.)

Gram and the Burritos parted company. He was annoyed that the band wanted to sell out, and move away from country, while they were sick of his drinking and the company he was keeping.

Drinking was something Gram had *always* done, since his earliest days in high school, but it was exacerbated by a motorcycle crackup in the spring of 1970 that put him in the hospital for several weeks. He was determined to have an agony-free recovery, and between the painkillers he was taking and the liquor he was imbibing, he succeeded.

As for his friends, Gram had taken to hanging around with the Rolling Stones while they were in Los Angeles recording their album *Let It Bleed.* Gram grooved with Mick Jagger and Keith Richards. Roadie Jim Seiter told *Rolling Stone* reporter Ben Fong-Torres, Gram got into the Jagger trip, "Painted nails, all that effeminate shit. He'd come out of the house, holding hands with Keith, skipping along . . . in these faggy outfits and the other guys would say, 'We can't go on stage with this fucker.' "

All of that aside, Gram did help the Stones create some great music, his uncredited influence obvious in a number of country-tinged songs from this period.

The Stones returned to Europe, and Gram pursued a solo career—though he went to France to work with them, uncredited, in 1971. That year was important for another reason: he got married, though not to the mother of his daughter. In 1969 he had met a stunning, blonde model, sixteen-year-old Gretchen Burrell, and he married her two years later. Matrimony did nothing to domesticize Gram, just the opposite, in fact. Friends and co-workers say he seemed to resent it when Gretchen was around.

As much as Gram had given to music over the previous five years, the Village, then L.A., and finally Europe gave something to him: an increasingly insatiable appetite for drugs, particularly acid. LSD and alcohol frequently left him wrecked, fighting with Gretchen (once, police came to their hotel room, maced Gram, and took him to jail), destroying hotel rooms, having affairs, or screwing up songs onstage.

Despite his various addictions, he could still write music with the best of them. Warner's Reprise label signed him, assigning top talent to work with him, including his and Hillman's protégé, Emmylou Harris, a twenty-three-year-old Joni Mitchell wannabe who had previously cut an unsuccessful album. Though Gram was so drunk on tequila during the early sessions that he literally couldn't stand, let alone sing, he managed to pull himself together to do the album. The result, *GP*, was yet another commercial disappointment when it was released in 1973, as was *Grievous Angel* which came out in January of the following year.

Gram didn't second-guess himself or the material, which he knew was good. But after *GP* flopped, he wondered if the public would ever catch on. Reprise felt that touring would help and he agreed.

In the meantime, his personal life was in a complete shambles. His house in Laurel Canyon (L.A.) burned down in July of 1973—apparently from his having been smoking in bed—and he was hospitalized due to smoke inhalation. His relationship with long-suffering Gretchen finally hit bottom, reportedly because of Gram's open affection for Emmylou. Divorce proceedings were initiated shortly thereafter.

In 1973, Gram was in surprisingly good spirits as the tour began, putting much of his disappointment behind

him as he began to work with Emmylou and the Fallen
Angels Band prior to touring in support of the second
album. He was emotionally together and in good voice,
and he was clicking with his audiences when they hit the
road. Both Emmylou and his bandmates felt that if the
twenty-six-year-old could just get some help for his various chemical dependencies, he'd really be able to turn
his life around.

But it wasn't to be.

On September 17, 1973, he headed to Joshua Tree,
California, to get away from music and the crowds in
L.A. He checked into the Joshua Tree Inn with three
friends: his aide and chum Michael Martin, Martin's
girlfriend Dale McElroy, and Gram's lover Margaret
Fisher. Ironically, Dale and Michael rode out to Joshua
Tree in her car—a hearse.

On September 19 Martin went back to L.A. to get
more pot. Gram spent the next day drinking Jack Dan
iels and tequila like they were pop, bought heroin from a
dealer and shot up, then returned to his room at the Inn.
Margaret went out a while. Apparently, while she was
gone, Gram also injected morphine and may have done
cocaine as well.

Not surprisingly, he passed out a short time later.
When Margaret returned around a quarter to midnight,
she found him cold and blue and without a heartbeat.
She tried to bring him around, but after her unschooled
attempts at artificial resuscitation and pounding on his
chest had failed, she phoned for an ambulance.

The comatose singer reached the Hi-Desert Memorial Hospital at a quarter past twelve; he was not breathing and had no pulse, and after fifteen minutes doctors
gave up trying to revive him. The coroner's report said
that he'd died of drug toxicity. No kidding.

Yet that wasn't quite the end of Gram Parsons's odyssey. He'd never wanted a simple dirt nap. He wanted to go out in the blazing glory he'd never known in life.

To that end, Gram and his manager Phil Kaufman had once made a deal, whoever outlasted the other would take his dead friend to the desert and torch him. Now that Gram was gone, Kaufman intended to make good. Just one problem: stepdad Robert Parsons had quickly arranged for his son's body to be shipped to New Orleans.

But that didn't stop the devoted Kaufman and his accomplice, Michael Martin. They went to Los Angeles International Airport in the beat-up old hearse, found out where Gram was, flashed fake papers and some double-talk at the hearse driver, and absconded with the casket.

It was early evening as the two men plus Gram reached the Joshua Tree Monument. There, the duo opened the coffin, poured gasoline on the body, and ignited it. Rangers didn't find the smouldering remains until the next day. What was left of the singer was belatedly shipped to New Orleans for burial. The body thieves were fined $300 each, though not for having stolen the corpse. Amazingly, there was nothing on the books that made it illegal, though one police officer did joke that they should be charged with Gram Theft Parsons. No, they were fined for having taken the coffin. They also had to fork over an additional $750 to replace the charred coffin.

Naturally, fans and co-workers lamented the loss of the country pioneer, though Emmylou took it hardest of all. She was in shock for months, and she said, "I felt like I'd been amputated, like my life had been whacked off. It's amazing how much he changed me."

In order to keep her mind off her sorrow, she developed a solo act. Backed by her new Angel Band, she began building a career. Parsons's fans already knew her distinctive voice and comprised her core audience. As her following built, she kept his songs and style alive and became a country superstar in her own right. But she has always harbored bitterness about the way in which Gram is remembered, complaining to one reporter, "People talk a lot about Gram Parsons, and they write a lot about Gram Parsons, but you never hear Gram Parsons on the radio."

It's sad, in a way, that her debut album, *Pieces of the Sky*, sold 130,000 copies, over three times more than Gram's top-selling album.

Parsons was one of the true originals, and it's fair to say that countless bands and even the Outlaw stylings of Waylón Jennings and Willie Nelson wouldn't have been what they were without Parsons's trailblazing. Indeed, in his 1988 autobiography *Willie*, Nelson credits Gram with having spearheaded the movement in which "country music is mixed up in everything," a blend that led to the Eagles, the Band, the Allman Brothers, Leon Russell, "and God knows who else."

Never knowing what else Gram might have done remains one of the great tragedies of contemporary music. When one listens to *Gram Parsons & the Fallen Angels Live 1973* (released in 1982), it's clear how bold and exciting the material was. However, it's also clear that he was too innovative to have become a commercial giant, too rooted in country at a time when the mainstream wasn't that interested. Had he lived, he'd have gone along selling just enough records to keep some label happy.

And what delights the rest of us would have had when we caught up to him!

Hank Williams, Jr. and Jett Williams

UNDER the best conditions, it's tough for the children of successful entertainers to make their marks in the same industry. The musical junkyard is littered with failed offspring, from Frank Sinatra, Jr. to Dino Martin to the down-but-not-out Julian Lennon. And Hank wasn't just a celebrity: he *was* country music.

But Hank Jr. managed to pull it off, not without a struggle, but better than just about any son-of since Carl Philipp Emanuel Bach.

Randall Hank Williams was three years old when his father died. Hank, Sr. adored the boy, whom he'd lovingly nicknamed Bocephus, after a wooden dummy used by *Grand Ole Opry* star Rod Brasfield. Unfortunately, the two didn't spend much quality time together, as Hank, Sr. was either touring, under the influence of drugs, drink, or both, or on the outs with his ex-wife Audrey and not permitted to visit.

When Hank Sr. died, the youngster's ambitious mother—her own performing career thwarted by a lack of talent—taught her young son how to walk, talk, and sing like his father and pushed him into the spotlight. Bocephus didn't seem to mind it either, enjoying the attention he received when, at the age of eight, and billed as Hank Williams, Jr., he made his debut in Swainsboro, Georgia.

"I walked out on that stage with my hands stuffed into the pockets of my little black suit," he says, "and I sang 'Lovesick Blues' in my little eight-year-old voice. The audience loved it. They went crazy shouting about 'Hank's little boy.'"

When Hank wasn't in school—where he was a superb athlete and extremely conscientious about what he ate and drank—he toured with his mother, singing his father's old songs and enjoying being Hank's little boy. In 1964, when he was just fourteen, he fulfilled the man-sized task of recording his father's songs for the sound-track of the MGM film *Your Cheatin' Heart*, which were lip-synched onscreen by star George Hamilton.

With Hank, Sr.'s songs and reputation as a launching pad, Hank, Jr.'s recording career took off. His version of "Long Gone Lonesome Blues" made the country charts, and when he was sixteen he scored a second hit with the appropriately titled "Standin' in the Shadows."

In 1969, Hank, Jr.'s name joined the Walkway of Stars at the Country Music Hall of Fame, and he toured and recorded like mad. He was twenty-one when he had his first number one hit in 1970 with "All For the Love of Sunshine," which he recorded with the Mike Curb Congregation. In between that and his next number one country hit, "Eleven Roses," which went to number one in 1972, he hit the top ten one dozen times.

However, he was increasingly unhappy at being a Hank Sr. clone, recording his father's songs or soundalike songs or songs his father left behind but never recorded; hearing from folks who knew his father how much he reminded them of him.

Wesley Rose—whose father was songwriter/publisher Fred Rose—says that he couldn't help being "haunted every time I see that boy walk in the door."

Hank was also becoming more and more uneasy with the big photos of his father projected on a screen behind him while he sang his Sr. medley. He recalls, "I used to cry all the time. There's no doubt I was haunted by Daddy. I'd sit in front of a record player, play Daddy's records, get the biggest bottle of Jim Beam I could find, and try to communicate with him.

"Hell," he told *Billboard* magazine, "that had to end."

Something else that had to end was his increasingly self-destructive lifestyle.

The pressures of the road and of his borrowed stardom drove him to give up his life of fitness and abstinence. He began to escape into alcohol and recreational drugs, despite knowing full well what they did to his father. In 1973, he ended up in the hospital after gulping down a few too many barbiturates. But pain succeeded where common sense had not: "Takin' a bottle of Darvon and tryin' to kill yourself and gettin' pumped out is not fun," he said afterward.

Sobered by his near-brush with death, Hank knew he had to clean himself up. He also knew he had to be true to himself, musically.

His own tastes were varied. When he was growing up, musicians of all kinds used to stop and visit, from Perry Como to Fats Domino to Jerry Lee Lewis to Al Hirt. He listened to everything, and what he found he enjoyed was a rougher style of country, one that incorporated elements of rock and blues and of Cajun style music from Louisiana, styles that the powers-that-be in Nashville just didn't like.

Well, screw Nashville, he told himself. In 1974, he left Music City and moved to Cullman, Alabama, leaving behind his mother (who objected to what he was doing) and the Nashville establishment. In Alabama, with the help of pals and colleagues like Charlie Daniels, Chuck Leavell (former keyboardist for Gregg Allman), and Toy

Caldwell of the Marshall Tucker Band, he cut *Hank Williams Jr. And Friends*, which featured the kind of music *he* wanted to perform.

It took a year for the record to reach the stores. The label wasn't convinced that it would sell and dragged their feet to the contractual limit; it was finally scheduled to be released when Hank suffered an accident that nearly ended his life.

Vacationing in Montana, he went out hunting with some friends on Mount Ajax on August 8, 1975. At an elevation of some nine thousand feet, he slipped from a ledge and fell five hundred feet. That he survived the fall is a miracle, though it didn't look as though the miracle would last very long. He landed face-first on a big rock and sustained staggering head and facial injuries: one eye was pushed outside its shattered socket; his nose was ripped away; his forehead was opened to the brain, which was punctured by rock and bone; his jaw and gums were destroyed along with most of his teeth; and his cheekbones were smashed.

To put it mildly, the prognosis for his recovery was lousy.

"Doctors said, 'He's not going to make it,' " Hank says today.

Complicating his recovery further was the fact that his mother died less than three months later, on November 4, distraught over her son and over her own precarious financial situation.

Hank spent nearly a year in bed, during which time his face was almost entirely reconstructed in nine operations. Even at that, things didn't go perfectly: to this day he wears sunglasses constantly. "I'm not being Mr. Cool," he says. "I wear these glasses because (of) the surgery . . . on my right eye."

After the operations, he spent another year and a half recuperating. He received a lot of love and support from his soon-to-be-wife Becky, who says that when she first saw him after the accident, "He thought I was just gonna be grossed out, but it really didn't bother me at all." Hank Jr. used this enforced downtime to figure out exactly where he wanted to go, musically. Money wasn't a problem: he was earning an average of a half million dollars a year from royalties on his father's compositions. Creative satisfaction was the issue, and what he decided was to push even more towards different country hybrids than on his previous album.

The result was 1977's *The New South*, which was produced by fellow rebel Waylon Jennings. (It was on this album that they were working when the infamous Jennings drug bust took place.) When it was finished, Hank went out on the road and many of his traditionalist fans deserted him, often walking out of his concerts when he refused to play Sr.'s songs. After all, they reasoned, he was willing to use his dad's name to get them in the door and then he refused to give them any of his songs. Had that fall on his head knocked all the good sense out of him?

But Hank stuck to his guns. He made some missteps along the way, such as his silly recording of the Bee Gees old smash "To Love Somebody" (borderline country singer Gary Puckett had already covered it to much, much better effect), but he stayed with his new sound.

Finally, in 1978, his song "I Fought the Law" made it to the top twenty, and a year after that he struck gold. Literally. The title cut from his *Family Tradition* album got him back into the top five on the country chart, and he followed it with four more hits, after which a song he wrote, "Texas Women," went to number one. That was March of 1981, and it was Hank's first number one hit in nine years.

He had his next number one hit in November, the autobiographical "All My Rowdy Friends (Have Settled

Down)," which he wrote as a tribute to all the former wild men who were important to him: Jennings, Cash, Kristofferson, and George Jones. It was so popular it inspired a sequel three years later, "All My Rowdy Friends Are Coming Over Tonight."

The truth was, at that time, most of them had "settled down" more than Hank. He'd gotten off drugs back in 1973, but, bored and depressed, had discovered cocaine while recovering from his fall. Though he'd managed by-and-large to kick it by 1979, he got himself into trouble several times over the next few years before going entirely clean. For example, in 1981 he was allegedly drunk during a show in Sherman, Texas, put on a lousy show, was sued by the promoter, and ended up having to pay $160,000. The next year, he missed a gig, reportedly because of drugs, and had to pay nearly $100,000 in reparations. Even with a seven figure income, that kind of overhead will kill you.

Hank told *Music City News* that he decided to take a leaf from friend Waylon Jennings's playbook and, so far, he's managed to live by it. "I smoke a few Salems and drink a little whiskey," he said. "But when it comes to me and my show, we don't put up with any drugs— zero."

As an example of how confident Hank had become in his own right, he recorded a number of his father's songs, including "Move It On Over" and "Honky Tonkin'," the latter of which went to number one in August of 1982. Manager Merle Kilgore said at the time, "When he proved that he could do it his way, he went back and did Hank, Sr. stuff." (Actually, the record had been planned as a duet with Tanya Tucker, but Hank wasn't satisfied with her vocals and decided to release it as a solo song.)

That year was a great one for Hank in another way. On October 30, he had a total of nine albums on the country charts. The only other artist in history who ever charted that many records at once was Elvis, and he achieved it in 1978, a year after his death.

These days, Hank is still a hit on the charts, still in great demand on the road, and happier than he's ever been. He married his fourth wife, Mary Jane Thomas, in 1990. They divide their time between a home on the Tennessee River, not far from his office in Paris, Tennessee, and another home in the wilds of Montana, on three hundred acres near the Idaho border. He's back to his athletic, outdoorsy ways, enjoying his four children, and still surprising his fans. In 1989, he did a duet using his father's long-lost recording of "There's A Tear in My Beer," and won a Grammy. As if that and his numerous Country Music Association awards weren't enough for his mantel, he's even won a pair of Emmy awards honoring his theme music for TV's *Monday Night Football*, which he began singing in 1989.

In fact, there's only one place where Hank hasn't been able to get what he wants. He won't talk about it, but his rebuilt teeth gnash whenever anyone else does. The matter of the long, long court battle with his half-sister.

Cathy Stone, a.k.a. Jett Williams, says that Hank, Jr. used to deny vigorously "that he knew anything about me, and recently we (Jett and her husband Keith) have heard rumors that he says my name will never cross his lips." (They're not rumors, Cath.) She says with a touch of irony, "Certainly he knows about me now."

Hank Williams, Sr. met Bobbie Webb Jett in Nashville in 1951, at a time when his relationship with wife Audrey was at a nadir. The two became lovers, and Bobbie became pregnant in April of the following year, three months after Hank and Audrey split up and a month before their divorce became final. In August of that year, Bobbie moved into the boarding house run by Hank's mother Lillian Stone in Montgomery.

In October, when it became clear that Hank was going from Audrey to another woman, Billie Jean Jones Eshliman, he signed an agreement with Bobbie Webb Jett providing money for her and her child, but also stipulating that the baby had to be turned over to his mother. Hank told Bobbie to take it personally: he very much wanted the child, but he realized he wasn't in love with its mother.

As it turned out, the baby girl was born five days after Hank's death. Bobbie named her Antha Belle, after her maternal grandmother, and though Hank was gone she did as she'd promised: she gave the baby to Lillian and left town. Bobbie died in 1974 at the age of fifty-one, never having seen her daughter again.

Lillian officially adopted the girl and renamed her Cathy. Sadly, Cathy's stay was brief: a year later, Lillian was divorced from William Stone, and a year after that she died. Since neither William nor his daughter Irene wanted the little girl, Cathy was sent to a boarding home. She lived there until February 1956, when she was adopted by Wayne and Louise Deupree of Mobile, Alabama. It wasn't until Cathy was twenty-one that her adoptive mother tells her that she was the daughter of Hank Williams.

"I thought my mother was kidding," Cathy says—and who could blame her? But as startling as the information was, it helped to explain to Cathy why, when she was "sad or lonesome," she would turn to writing songs for consolation.

For the next ten years, though Cathy was certainly curious if she were entitled to a share of Hank, Sr.'s royalties, her primary interest was in learning more about her natural mother and father, and about the circumstances surrounding her birth. In the interim, she graduated from college, married, and settled in Montgomery.

By September of 1984, Cathy was in a somewhat different frame of mind. Her marriage was failing, and writing songs just wasn't doing the trick anymore. What she wanted to know was if she'd "been screwed" out of a piece of her father's estate.

Introduced to Keith Adkinson, a hard-nosed Washington-based attorney who'd worked for the Senate Rackets Committee, Cathy told him her tale, and he agreed to pursue the matter for her. He also encouraged her to sing and, after making a demo tape, she went to see Owen Bradley, the legendary producer/artistic director who had worked with Patsy Cline, Loretta Lynn, and many others.

Bradley liked what he heard, thought the attractive blonde had charisma, and agreed to work with her. But he told Cathy that she had to get even better, be the best she could be before she recorded or went out on the road. Cathy says, "He made it clear that being the child of Hank Williams was as much a curse as it was a blessing. Because of who I was, people would expect more of me." Just ask Hank, Jr., Bradley said.

She tried. Hank didn't want to know from her.

While Bradley coached Cathy in music, Keith pursued her legal case and became husband number two in September of 1986.

The path to getting a piece of the Williams royalty pie has turned out to be rockier than Cathy had expected, and as of this writing, her pursuit of what she views as her fair share of the Williams estate is still tangled up in the courts. She says things would be easier if she and Hank, Jr. could sit down one-on-one and "set things right, personally," though she admits the chances are slim. Putting broken families together is tough enough without millions of disputed dollars to complicate matters.

Professionally, though, she's well on her way thanks to

a masterstroke: in August of 1989, she reunited her father's old team and two months later debuted using the stage name of Jett Williams and the Drifting Cowboys Band. Though she has yet to achieve the success of her half-brother, she says, "Despite the 'rain' that has fallen on my life, I can't help but feel I've been blessed."

Sounds like terrific lyrics for a song. Let's hope it has a happy ending.

Mel Street

IT'S been said that George Jones and Mel Street are the finest singers country music has known. Certainly they've got to be on anyone's top-ten list.

Two other things are certainly true. First, Street earned his reputation in spite of the fact that his records didn't sell nearly the numbers they deserved to. And second, there's no telling how far Street might have gone had he lived past his forty-fifth birthday.

Born on October 21, 1933, in Grundy, West Virginia, King Malachi Street always loved to sing. He began doing it professionally as a teenager, appearing on local radio shows. When he married wife Betty, he put his dreams on hold to put food on the table, becoming a construction worker and settling in Niagra Falls, New York.

But even there, not exactly the heart of the country market, he found himself drawn to local clubs and earned himself a sizable following. Realizing that he would only be happy if he were singing, he saved up enough money to return to West Virginia. Once there, he opened a car paint and body shop to pay the bills, then put together a four member band and did the local club scene.

In time, the honky tonk singer with the dark good looks landed on a local TV show *Country Showcase*, where in 1969, he came to the attention of Tandem Records. The following year they released his first single, "House of Pride." But it was the B-side of the record, a song Mel wrote called "Borrowed Angel," that drew the most attention. It took two years, but "Borrowed Angel" eventually became a top-ten hit.

Street did an inordinate amount of label-hopping over the next few years, unhappy with either sales, management, or both. He moved from Tandem to Royal American Records to Metromedia to GRT to Polydor to Mercury, cutting records like "Lovin' On Back Streets," "Smokey Mountain Memories," and "Close Enough for Lonesome," which earned him critical acclaim and cracked the top twenty, but never reached the top of the charts or made him a major draw. Even though he was well-received wherever he went, most of his dates were still in clubs and small theaters.

Street wasn't an egomaniac, hungry for fame and money. He had a nice house in Hendersonville, Tennessee, and he was making money. What he wanted was to be heard, to investigate new areas of country, to encourage new talent—he was the first to record an Eddie Rabbitt song.

Failing that, he tried to console himself with drink. That made his home life a shambles, and drove him to drink even more, the same story as so many others. The difference with Mel was that he would usually stay sober enough to record or perform, then hit the bottle after the last note had been sung.

After five years of failing to set the world on fire (possibly because he was so damp), Mel moved out of his home in the early weeks of 1978 in an effort to find himself spiritually and give up booze. He succeeded, moved back home, but was still so chronically depressed that the only solution was to start drinking again.

His wife later said that during this period, he'd been so depressed that she tiptoed around him, afraid he'd blow up. She wanted him to get professional help but didn't dare suggest it. Mel was the kind of guy who had to come to conclusions on his own. All she felt she could do was nurse him through his suffering.

In the middle of October, 1978, Mrs. Street says her husband suffered "a complete and total breakdown of his mind." He was deeply depressed, had a hairtrigger temper, drank heavily, and wasn't even having fun anymore when he was making music.

On October 20, 1978, Mel was so depressed he cancelled a show at George Jones' Possum Holler, a Nashville club. The folks there were understanding; Street didn't do a lot of that, and if he wasn't up to it they didn't want him giving a half-hearted performance.

The next day, his forty-fifth birthday, Mel's mood seemed surprisingly upbeat as he sat with his wife and his brother Cleve at the kitchen table, having breakfast, talking about growing up with Cleve, and taking good-natured taunts about his age.

Shortly after ten A.M., he yawned, excused himself, dragged himself upstairs, and took a .38 from one of his drawers. He opened his mouth and put the barrel inside, and without a word to his family or a note saying why he felt he had to do this, he squeezed the trigger.

In the days that followed, no one could point to a specific "thing" that had finally driven Mel to take his life. It seems to have been a combination of disappointment about where he was and dread of where he was headed.

Nowhere. At forty-five, Mel felt he was never going to make his mark, except in blood. Perhaps he'd said all he needed to say in his last single, which was released just

days before he took his life: the title was "Just Hangin'
On."

His hero, George Jones, sang at his funeral, and there
was no question, now, who had the best voice in Nashville, though this wasn't the way Jones wanted it.

Johnny Paycheck

THERE are country music Outlaws, musical rebels like Jennings and Nelson, and then there are real country music outlaws, live desperadoes who would just as soon pick a fight as a guitar.

For years, the king of those outlaws was Johnny Paycheck, a full-fledged rebel who went from rockabilly to rockin' Nashville, at one point in the 1970s calling himself John Austin Paycheck after Music City's rival, just to stick it to the establishment.

Of course, that he even lived to see the middle 1970s was pretty astonishing in itself. Paycheck may have one of the strongest, surest, note-perfect voices in country history, with thirty-three hit singles, six gold albums, a platinum album and a double platinum album to prove it. But he also had devils in him, and over the years he did just about anything they told him to.

Where'd they come from? At five-foot-five, perhaps he suffered a touch of the short man complex. Or maybe he was out and about in the world when he was still too young. Or maybe he was just ornery. Or all of the above.

When asked, Paycheck describes the root of his problems this way: "I've never kissed an ass or licked a boot and I won't ever compromise what I believe in . . ." he says proudly. Then admits, "I've been like a window blind. I come up, then I have my problems, then I come back down."

Born Donald Eugene Lytle in Greenfield, Ohio, on May 31, 1938, the future hellraiser got his first guitar when he was six. Within three years he was performing in local talent shows, and at thirteen he got his first professional gig at a local club. Two years later he left home and roamed the Southeast, playing anywhere that would have him and knocking down any drunk who told him he was too young or too wet-behind-the-ears to be out without his mama.

Wanting to see more of the world, Lytle joined the Navy, but quickly ran afoul of authority. He went AWOL, was caught, and as if he weren't in enough trouble, he punched out a superior officer. His actions earned him a court-martial in 1956 and two years behind bars, though he did make a valiant effort to escape incarceration by sawing through the ceiling of the shower room.

After his release, Lytle took the name Don Young and, once again slinging a guitar, drifted down to Nashville. There he hooked up with Porter Wagoner in 1958 and sang with his backup group, the Wagonmasters. The next year, he shifted over to Faron Young's Country Deputies, and the year after that went to Ray Price's Cherokee Cowboys. He ended his grand slam by moving to George Jones's Jones Boys in 1962, managing to hold on there for four years.

Meanwhile, Lytle also did some rockabilly recording on his own for Mercury, without any chart success. In 1964, frustrated by a half-dozen single flops, he defiantly assumed the name Johnny Paycheck—after a Golden Gloves fighter who'd been felled by Joe Louis in the first round—switched to the Hilltop label, and in 1965 scored a hit with "A-11." The following year, he connected with "Heartbreak, Tennessee" and also co-founded Little Darlin' Records, which offered a hard-driving alternative to Nashville's increasingly soft and fluffy sound. There, he had his first top-ten hit, "The Lovin' Machine" and also wrote Tammy Wynette's debut hit, "Apartment #9." After several false starts, Johnny Paycheck seemed well on his way to becoming a bonafide superstar.

The operative word is "seemed."

As his brief stint in the military suggested, and as his nearly-as-brief stays with various bands underscored, Paycheck needed to do things *his* way. And his way was "drinkin' up a storm" and playing music the way he wanted. He had always been unpredictable, but he grew more so as the decade dragged on and his record sales slowed. Paycheck began spending more and more time on the West Coast, he was arrested for breaking into a house in Nashville and fined fifty dollars, and when Little Darlin' finally closed down, the singer moved to San Diego.

What he did there, and with whom, he has never said, and there's a good chance he really doesn't remember much of it. The bottom line was that drink and drugs caused what was left of his life to go to pieces. "Everything fell apart there," he told *The Journal of Country Music*, "and I wound up in L.A. And I was living just bumming off the streets and working clubs for beer, you know, and just, oh, just about give up."

However, CBS producer Billy Sherrill hadn't given up on the singer, whom he'd tried unsuccessfully to sign years before. Locating Paycheck in 1970, he and the singer's longtime friend Nick Hunter were shocked at the condition of the long-haired, bearded, scraggly, dead-broke, wafer-thin singer. But they were determined to get him back into fighting trim.

Paycheck crashed at Nick's home in Denver, sang at a

local club to rebuild his confidence, and met and married his wife Sharon. With a little meat on his bones (though still scraggly) he returned to Nashville in 1971 to record for Sherrill.

Johnny made his comeback with love songs, scoring with "Don't Take Her, She's All I Got," the infusion of money coming just in time for him to make good on a bad check he'd passed at a hotel, a crime that earned him an eleven month suspended sentence and made him the brunt of countless Johnny Badcheck jokes. He followed "She's All I Got" with hits like "Someone To Give My Love To," "Something About You I Love," and others, but the tunes (or he, or both) grew tired after several years.

The money ran out again and Johnny filed for bankruptcy in 1976. But the scrapper and his patron Sherrill weren't quite ready to give up; they cut "Take This Job and Shove It" in the fall of 1977. The song rocketed up the charts. Suddenly, the thirty nine-year-old former near-derelict was hotter than ever, a millionaire who was no longer a balladeer but a musical spokesperson for blue collar workers everywhere.

Paycheck was amazed and delighted. He says that people walked up to him and wanted to shake his hand. Once, he recalls, a man came up to him and said, "I just want to thank you. That song of yours gave me the courage to walk in and quit my job. Now I'm president of my own company."

But of his sudden, enormous fame, Paycheck also admits, "I didn't handle it too good. I got into drugs and drinking real bad."

That's an understatement.

Like the last time, he was anything but apologetic about his chemical recreation. "I'll try anything once to see if I like it," he said. "And if I like it, I'll stick with it, no matter what anybody says." The only caveat, he said, was that what he did to himself must not hurt anyone else. Which, of course, wasn't how it turned out.

On April 8, 1981, on a flight about to leave from Denver to Casper, Wyoming, where he was to perform, Johnny refused flight attendant Helen Espinoza's request that he fasten his seatbelt. When the pilot announced that the plane wouldn't leave until he did, Paycheck shouted, "Tell that bitch I have my seatbelt on."

Not content to leave bad enough alone, bandmember James Murphy reportedly grabbed Helen's arm and made a lewd suggestion; Espinoza sued Paycheck, who ended up paying her $175,000.

The same night as the tiff on the plane, he went home with a woman who was in his audience and, in December, was socked with charges that while he was at the woman's house he seduced her twelve-year-old daughter. The charge was later reduced from statutory rape to misdemeanor sexual assault, and Paycheck escaped with a thousand dollar fine and a year's probation.

Obviously, April was not Paycheck's lucky month: one year after those two encounters, the Internal Revenue Service came after him for over one hundred thousand dollars in back taxes. The state of Tennessee also claimed back taxes. And there was one more hit for Johnny, though not the kind he wanted. He was arrested in Raleigh, North Carolina, for having failed to pay $26,000 in reparations for a cancelled concert.

In October, he filed for bankruptcy a second time, but fully intended to make good his debts.

In 1983, he and CBS ended their relationship. CBS says they dropped him, but he says they've got it backwards that he just got sick of the "back-stabbing stench" and walked away from them. Regardless, he was unsigned. Paycheck wandered from one small label to another, had some minor hits, and then hit rock bottom, lower than even his lowest days in Southern California.

He drank heavily. He did massive amounts of cocaine. In 1984 he said, ". . . cocaine isn't a killer drug and neither is alcohol . . ." Of course not. Shortly after that, he sunk even lower.

In December of 1985, after bumming around far more than he was performing, Paycheck headed north to Ohio to visit his mother for Christmas. On the nineteenth, he stopped at the North High Lounge Barroom in Hillsboro. While he stood drinking at the bar, he was recognized by thirty-seven-year-old Larry Wise and his friend Lloyd Bowers. The men came over and engaged the singer in conversation.

Paycheck wasn't sure whether the guys were seriously enjoying their talk or making fun of him because of his poor background. At half past eleven he got his answer, when one of the men asked Paycheck if he wanted to go out and have a bite with them— a little bit of deer meat and turtle soup.

"What do you think I am," he shouted at them, rising, "a hick that came into town yesterday?"

The other men also rose. The words grew more heated.

Finally, Paycheck snarled, "I don't like you! I'm going to mess you up!"

One of the two men made a preemptory strike, throwing a blow at the singer. Paycheck ducked and returned the blow, connecting, according to Paycheck. Wise then picked up a beer bottle and came at him. Wise denies it.

Barroom owner Ernest Turner rushed around the bar in an effort to separate the men, but before he could reach them, Paycheck had drawn a .22 caliber pistol and fired. Paycheck would later claim that it was an accident, that he was aiming at the ceiling.

Turner froze. Wise stumbled back, his hands on his

temple, then turned and staggered from the bar. According to Wise, Paycheck ran after him yelling "I'm sorry, I didn't mean to do it." None of the other patrons moved. Wise's partner ran to help his friend.

Taking a quick, cautioning look around, Paycheck pushed the gun in his pocket, left the Barroom, and climbed into his car. Driving to a friend's house and tossing away the gun en route, he had a glass of milk and crashed on the friend's sofa.

Wise, meanwhile, had been rushed to the hospital. Although there was blood everywhere, the bullet had only grazed him. Remarkably, a big bandage and a few aspirin later, he was back at the Barroom.

The police found Paycheck the next morning. He was arrested, tried, and found guilty of aggravated assault and tampering with evidence (because he'd thrown the gun away). It didn't help that the singer had once cut an album called *Armed and Dangerous*, which the prosecution used as evidence of the guy's volatile nature. Paycheck's checkered career finally looked as if it had come to an end as he was sentenced to nine and one-half years in prison.

Paycheck remained at liberty while he appealed, but he used the time to send wildly conflicting messages to the public. On the one hand, as part of the "Just Say No" movement, he spoke out against the drugs that had helped corrupt him. He also recorded an album of gospel songs.

On the other hand, when some Hell's Angels friends of his went on trial in Louisville in July of 1988, he showed up to support them. His appearance made the papers, causing many to question his choice of friends and whether he was serious about being a law-abiding citizen.

His concerts were erratic affairs, more of them bad than good, and he drank and was rowdy in public. Finally, in February of 1989, he went before a judge on appeal and asked for mercy, saying his wife would suffer (as though she hadn't already) if he were put behind bars and couldn't earn a living.

He got the slammer, sent to the Chillicothe Correctional Institute to serve out his sentence.

Whether it was the prospect of growing old in a cell or the prophet in the wilderness syndrome or both, prison made a new man of Paycheck. For one thing, he says that the overcrowding at Chillicothe was horrendous, and tensions among the prisoners ran very high. If you didn't learn to get along with these people, you had a world of trouble on your hands. Paycheck may have been a scrapper on the outside, but without drugs or drink he found he didn't have quite as much spine as he *thought* he had.

Secondly, he says that prison helped him get his "priorities straight. You never really know what your priorities are until they take it all away from you, and then you look and see what is valuable to you and what isn't: freedom, family, friends."

Once he got over the shock of where he was and mucked through the weeks of depression that followed, Paycheck learned that he still had friends. Fans didn't forget him, writing to him in prison, and he says, "That was very important to me and is one of the main things that got me through" those early days. He also made friends behind bars, "good old boys in there that really respected me and been fans of mine for years."

He realized that he wasn't alone *or* doomed, that prison could be a beginning instead of an end. He studied and got his General Educational Development high school equivalency degree. He also called in friend and former convict Merle Haggard, and together, they gave a riproaring concert for the inmates.

For nearly two years, Paycheck was a model prisoner.

And he got his reward in January of 1991, when Governor Richard Celeste commuted his sentence. The singer's only obligations were to stay out of trouble and perform two hundred hours of community service.

Paycheck was free from prison, but was he truly free of the past?

After a year on the outside—a quiet, productive year in which he gave up drinking and even cigarette smoking—he knew he was free.

"There's certain people that say, 'Ah, he ain't never gonna change,'" he said, "but those people are just—they're just assholes, that's all. Anybody can change."

Though Johnny had pulled himself up by his bootstraps before and fallen back down, this time he really does seem to have made it back.

"I'm singing better than I have in twenty years," he told reporter Daniel Cooper shortly before appearing at Fan Fair in Nashville in 1992. "I'm stronger." And he says that he intends to continue performing community service even when his debt to society is paid. He enjoys going out and talking to children about the dangers of "drugs and alcohol. I tell them it'll kill them, more than likely, and it'll ruin them for sure."

Though most of these kids weren't even alive when "Take This Job and Shove It" was released, one look at the craggy face, no longer hidden behind a Manson-like beard, and they know that Paycheck speaks the truth, that this is a man who's been there.

By the time of Fan Fair in the spring of 1992, he had changed his name once again to Johnny PayCheck. But he was was still preaching his new gospel, singing with a strong voice, touring, and playing a gig every other day. And, most importantly, he was still clean and sober.

Badcheck? No more. At long last, it looks like Payday for the star.

Stevie Ray Vaughan

THE five-years-younger brother of Jimmie Vaughan, star guitarist of the Texas-based Fabulous Thunderbirds, Stevie Ray was born in Dallas, Texas in 1956. He grew up listening to his brother's collection of blues albums, his favorites being B.B. King and Lonnie Mack. He was already a prodigious guitarist and singer by the age of eight.

The boys tended to practice late into the night, but their parents—asbestos worker Jimmie Lee and secretary Martha—didn't stop them, loud as the musicians were. Stevie later said, "I can't tell you what my parents mean to me, what they've done for me, my brother. We have a lot to pay back for."

While he was still a young teenager, Stevie played with the acid-rock band Blackbird. After failing music theory in his senior year, the seventeen-year-old dropped out of high school to become a musician, performing with the Nightcrawlers and a succession of groups including Texas Storm, the Cobras, and Triple Threat. The names accurately reflected the kind of hard, fiery country and blues mix that Vaughan burned from his '59 Stratocaster Rosewood.

Vaughan was eventually spotted by singer Jackson

Browne, who took him under his wing and let him do some recording in his private studio; however, it was Vaughan's electrifying performance at the Montreaux (Switzerland) Jazz Festival in 1982 that brought him to the attention of CBS records. A close friend of Stevie's, singer Angela Strehli, was surprised that the CBS executives hadn't heard him all the way back in New York, saying that Vaughan plays "louder than God."

The following year was a great one for the artist: he released his first album, the rockin' country/blues record *Texas Flood*, and also played lead guitar for David Bowie on the singer's *Let's Dance* album and tour. He brought down a sold-out house during his Carnegie Hall debut in 1984.

That same year, secure that he had a future in music, Vaughan bought a home on nearly nine acres in Valente, Texas, for himself, his wife Lenny, whom he married in 1979 in a club dressing room before a gig, and their two children.

Eclectic influences ranging from Jimi Hendrix to jazz could be found in Stevie's subsequent albums, but his skills at synthesizing various forms was such that rather than alienating the fans who were first attracted to his country blues, he slowly built on this following.

"What I'm trying to do," he said in 1985, "is take everything that's ever excited me and put it together." He added that nothing was more important to him than the integrity of the music: "I'll go back to bars before I ever go commercial, because it's important to keep this music alive."

By 1986, his family and friends also convinced Vaughan that it was important to keep himself alive. He had acquired a fondness for drugs and alcohol when he was young and impressionable while hanging around bars after performing. Although music was too important to him to screw around before performing, he did pot (among other things) during his downtime.

Vaughan enjoyed recording, and his records typically went gold. His autobiographical *In Step* won a Grammy. But his heart was in performing live. Audience feedback energized the cool dude in his trademark riverboat gambler's hat, and he gave listeners performances that they didn't forget.

On August 26, 1990, at the Alpine Valley Music Theater outside of East Troy, Wisconsin, Vaughan was in rare form, even for him. This was understandable considering that onstage with him were guitar legend Eric Clapton; Louisiana blues singer/guitarist Buddy Guy; up-and-coming Georgia blues star Robert Cray; and Stevie's brother Jimmie, whose presence was a surprise for Stevie and the audience.

After a climactic twenty-minute verion of "Sweet Home Chicago," Guy was so blown away by Stevie's performance that he told a friend, "I had goose bumps."

The performers wrapped up the show shortly after midnight, after which the bulk of the musicians and their entourage boarded the four Bell 206B Jet Ranger helicopters for the trip back to their hotels in Chicago. Vaughan linked up with Jimmie and Jimmie's wife Connie to wait for the helicopters to return, which would have been some ninety minutes later.

However, before they left, Peter Jackson, Eric Clapton's tour manager, came over and told the Vaughans that there were three empty seats on the fourth chopper. Stevie said they'd take the seats, and Peter went off to make the arrangements. However, when Peter returned a few minutes later, he told Stevie that he was wrong.

"I'm really sorry," he said, "but there's only one seat."

The exhausted Stevie turned boyishly to his brother and sister-in-law.

"Listen," he said, "would you guys mind if I took that seat? I'd really like to get back."

They encouraged him to do so and, after hugging them both, Vaughan climbed aboard with pilot Jeff Brown, Clapton's assistant tour manager Colin Smythe, Clapton's agent Bobby Brooks, and Clapton's bodyguard Nigel Browne. At 12:40, with crowds still filing from the noisy outdoor theater, the chopper lifted off.

A thousand-foot-tall ski slope towered into the darkness three-quarters of a mile southeast of the theater. The helicopter was headed in the direction of the slope as it took off in what the National Transportation Safety Board later described as conditions of "darkness, fog, haze, and rising terrain."

The pilot was unaware of the slope and, seconds after he and his four passengers were airborne, he banked the craft and slammed into the far side of the slope, just one hundred feet from the summit. It was what the NTSB called "a high-energy, high-velocity impact at a shallow angle," and it scattered wreckage over a two hundred foot area.

No one survived. And no one in the theater heard the crash.

Upon landing back in Chicago, the other chopper passengers dispersed quickly without waiting for the fourth to arrive. Only when a satellite heard the Bell's emergency locator bleating four hours later was a search mounted, and it wasn't until 6:15 A.M. that the twisted wreckage was located, along with the broken bodies of the five men. Reached in their rooms, Jimmie and Clapton were rushed to a morgue to identify the remains.

Vaughan had died exactly four years after his beloved father, near whom he was interred.

After an investigation that lasted two years, the NTSB placed the blame for the crash on pilot error. Their findings did little to assuage the grief of Vaughan's friends or millions of hardcore fans, for whom Buddy Guy spoke tearfully when he said, "Stevie is the best friend I've ever had . . . and the best person anyone will ever want to know.

"He will be missed a lot."

Tammy Wynette and George Jones

THE odds against making it in the music business are staggering enough for anyone. But considering the impoverished backgrounds of so many entertainers, their sagas are all the more inspiring.

Elvis Presley may be the outstanding example of a star who rose from poverty, but even he had it relatively easy compared to others, such as Tammy Wynette. Before Tammy made it big, women singers were used mostly as backup or opening acts. Kitty Wells and Patsy Cline were exceptions, though Kitty sang a *lot* of duets with established male stars and Patsy may or may not have been singing with them in private. Nashville was still Boy's Town, U.S.A.

Tammy helped to change that by headlining her own shows at a time when that just wasn't done. To this day, she remains the top-selling solo female artist of all time —Barbra Streisand notwithstanding—having sold over one hundred million recordings.

Not that the trailblazing didn't cost the woman a great deal.

Born Virginia Wynette Pugh on May 5, 1942, in Elvis's old stomping grounds of Itawamba County, Mississippi, Virginia was just nine months old when her fa-

ther died of a brain tumor. The girl's mother Mildred
left to go to Memphis to work in an aircraft factory,
sending Virginia to Red Bay, Alabama, where she lived
on a farm with Mildred's parents. Two years later, the
girl's mother returned and remarried.

Like many other entertainers, Virginia was exposed to
music in church, and it was there, as a little girl, that she
first entertained thoughts of one day becoming a performer. She recalls, "I might not have been the best
singer in church, but boy I was the loudest. And the
quartets were just so distinguished looking. The women
wore frilly chiffon dresses, stuff that I'd never seen before, never had. And I wanted to be part of that so bad."

Popular singers fueled her desire. When she was in
the fields picking cotton to help pay the bills, she'd listen
to a small radio. She recalls, "I'd hear George Jones and
Melba Montgomery and I'd think, 'I could sing as well
as she can, I know I can.' I can't," she laughs, "but in my
mind I could."

Perhaps her ambition was genetic. In 1939 and 1940,
Virginia's father had cut some records. He also left behind an attic full of instruments. His dying wish to Mildred was that if their daughter liked music, she would
encourage her to sing and play. Mildred and her parents
did that, and Virginia learned to play piano, guitar, organ, accordion, and flute. She even wrote a few songs in
what little free time she had.

Unfortunately, she managed to get herself side-
tracked. While she was a senior in high school, Virginia
met and fell in love with frequently unemployed construction worker Euple Byrd, who was seven years her
senior. Over her mother's strenuous objections, the seventeen-year-old dropped out of high school to get married.

Virginia Byrd had two daughters, Gwendolyn and Jac-
quelyn, before things began to unravel for her. The cou-

ple was living in a ramshackle log cabin with cardboard insulation, and they did their cooking in the fireplace. In 1964, Virginia was felled by a kidney infection, and severely depressed by her illness and the state of her life, she followed it with a nervous breakdown. The young woman was hospitalized and given a dozen electroshock treatments, which she says, "were horrible, but they helped me."

While she was in the hospital, Virginia learned she was pregnant again. When she was released and her strength returned, she took stock of her life. *This* wasn't what she wanted for herself or her daughters, and she refused to raise a baby where they were living. Filing for divorce, she moved to Birmingham, where she had a sympathetic aunt and uncle, and got a job as a beautician.

It's difficult to understand just what a big step that was for a young woman of that time and place. Today, she says, "A man's word was God in our home and everywhere down there. In the Deep South where I was born that's exactly how we lived. They still do." She adds, further, that no one had ever been divorced in her family, and that her mother thought she was "the worst thing in the world for doing that." Her mother tried to *make* her work things out with Euple, but Virginia couldn't—and wouldn't even try.

Working long hours in the beauty parlor, gutsy Virginia was just starting to get up on her own two feet when daughter Tina arrived prematurely. The baby weighed only one and one-half pounds and, worse, quickly came down with spinal meningitis. Virginia spent every free moment at the baby's side and, miraculously, Tina gained weight and overcame her illness.

But the medical bills were enormous, and Virginia wasn't making enough to cover them. She entertained

thoughts of earning extra money by singing, but wasn't
sure how to go about it. Fortunately, fate intervened.

Virginia often tuned in to WBRC-TV's *Country Boy
Eddie Show*, a local show which was broadcast from six to
seven A.M. each weekday morning and where, as it happened, her uncle worked as an engineer.

One day she happened to ask him, "Why does he not
have a girl singer on that show? He's got five or six guys
that're singing, and there's not even one girl. I don't
think that's fair."

Her uncle agreed and mentioned it to Eddie Burns,
the Country Boy himself. A few days later, Eddie Burns
asked Virginia to come and audition.

"I was scared to death," she says, her woes compounded by the fact that she couldn't find anyone to
watch her kids and had to bring them with her.

She needn't have worried. Eddie liked what he heard
and offered her a job that paid $35 a week. Billed as
Wynette, Virginia won the hearts of both viewers and
Eddie. After a few months, Eddie took her aside and told
her that she was too good for the show. He urged her to
go to Nashville and try her luck with the record companies.

In 1966, Virginia drove to Music City and began making the rounds, often leaving the three girls in the car
while she walked into offices, trying to get an audition.
Things got a little better for the girls when Virginia wed
her second husband, Don Chapel, who was not only a
songwriter but was a clerk at the Anchor Motel in which
she lived. At least they could stay home and watch TV
while mom was away.

Disappointment followed disappointment, and when
she finally got in to see producer Billy Sherrill it was a
fluke. His secretary wasn't at her desk, so Virginia was
able to stroll right into his office.

Guitar in hand, Wynette sang for Sherrill; he saw a lot

of potential in her, recalling, "I thought she had a real unique style—like a little teardrop every now and then appears."

He told Wynette that he'd let her know when he had a song that might be right for her. She thanked him for his time, not really believing he'd ever call her. But, true to his word, Sherrill phoned just a few days later: he had a song called "Apartment #9," co-written by a newcomer named Johnny Paycheck, that he wanted her to record. Sherrill also said he had a stage name that he felt would be more commercial: Tammy Wynette, inspired by the fresh, young movie character played by Debbie Reynolds.

Tammy was on her way. "Apartment #9" was a hit, entering the charts in December 1966 and making it to the top twenty. Her next recording, "Your Good Girl's Gonna Go Bad," made it to number three. She finally reached number one in March 1968 with "Take Me to Your World." However, it was her next two songs that really put her over the top.

The first was "D-I-V-O-R-C-E," about which Tammy was getting more first-hand knowledge than she wanted. Her marriage to Chapel was on the rocks after just two years: she felt that he was trying to use her newfound music connections for his own benefit (which he denies).

Tammy, also, insists he took some photos of her as she stepped from the shower or got dressed. She describes the subsequent selling of the photos as a "sickening, low-down thing to do," and calls her ex-husband "a loser, and that's all you can say about him."

Back to the musical "D-I-V-O-R-C-E."

Tammy says, "I remember thinking when I first heard the song, 'How ridiculous that I didn't write this song, because how many times have I spelled out words in front of my kids?'" She adds that she cut the song dur-

ing her struggles with Chapel: "I was doing it at the time
—it went right along with my life." It also went to number
one on the country charts in June of 1968 and stayed
there for an impressive three weeks.

Her next smash was an about-face, one that she co-
wrote with Sherrill. The idea for the song was Sherrill's,
who said he played with it for over a year and got nowhere. In August of 1968, at a recording session, the
musicians took a twenty minute break and Sherrill took
Tammy aside. He told her he had a song title but no
song. As soon as he said, "Stand By Your Man," she
jumped on it, recalling, "We just sat down, and it was
one of the fastest songs to ever come to me. It was almost as if it was meant to be."

The song was written in just twenty minutes, and
Tammy says that after she sang it she went to Sherrill
and "begged him not to release it. Every line I wrote, I
thought, 'Oh gosh, this sounds so stupid.' I didn't have
confidence in myself."

She should have. The song came out at a time when
the fledgling women's liberation movement was picking
up steam, and "Stand By Your Man" became an anthem
for those who wanted no part of it. It was a big crossover
hit that also became Tammy's theme song.

Feminists trashed the song. Tammy admits being
"confused by the reaction I got. There's nothing in that
song that says to take any kind of abuse. Nowhere in that
song does it say, 'Be a doormat.' It simply says, 'If you
love him, you'll forgive him.'" She said that that was
what she believed, and she saw nothing wrong with it.

Ironically, Tammy herself couldn't have been a more
modern woman if she'd tried. She says, "I put my career
before my children when I first came to Nashville. If I
had put my children first, we would have starved to
death. I did what I had to do, what I was forced to do."
She adds that when she got her first tour bus, she

couldn't afford a driver and drove it herself. She says, "I did a lot of things women wouldn't attempt to do."

Meanwhile, Tammy's personal life was coming out of its tailspin thanks to the country superstar whom she met when they toured together, the man who was to become husband number three.

Born in September of 1931, in Saratoga, Texas, George Jones earned money as a child by singing on street corners. Dropping out of school in the seventh grade, he began his career in earnest in 1947, playing guitar for the duo Eddie & Pearl. After a stint in the marines, he worked clubs throughout Texas before signing with the Starday label in 1952. Thanks to constant touring and more than 250 albums, he became one of the most popular (and surely one of the five best) country singers of all time. From 1955 to 1971 Jones placed thirty-one songs in the top ten.

Jones married Tammy on February 16, 1969 and the couple set up housekeeping at Jones's home in Lakeland, Florida where he owned a theme park, Old Plantation Country Music Park (and which he sold soon thereafter so they could return to Nashville). They continued touring together and also began recording some of the most successful country duets in history. Sadly, the life they shared offstage, a life in which Tammy had put so much hope, was anything but harmonious.

When they first got married, Jones was already a heavy drinker on his way to becoming an alcoholic. Tammy told interviewer Alanna Nash that on several occasions, he backed out of gigs because he was "so strung out he thinks the FBI's chasin' him, and he has to hide out." Once, when he found himself out of liquor, a desperate Tammy hid his car keys. Undaunted, an equally desperate Jones climbed aboard his lawnmower and rode it ten miles for a drink.

In July of 1973, Jones disappeared for several days on

a drinking binge. Fed up, Tammy filed for divorce.
When he came back, he persuaded her to give him another chance, Tammy recalling, "He knew I was very
upset with him, and he got out the guitar, and all he
would do was strum it and sing, 'We're gonna hold on,
we're gonna hold on . . .' " Tammy says that she really
wanted to be mad at him, but he just kept playing and,
eventually, she softened.

The song that grew from Jones's plaintive chorus,
"We're Gonna Hold On," became a smash for the duo,
and in large part because of their baby daughter, Georgette, born on October 5, 1970, Tammy gave him another chance.

But the second chance failed to stabilize the singer.
He continued to drink, becoming so drunk on one occasion when he thought Tammy was going to leave him
that he went on a rampage that nearly destroyed everything in the house. Sometimes, Tammy herself would be
on the recieving end of his verbal outbursts.

In December of 1974, the tension was at its peak when
they went into the recording studio to cut what turned
out to be the number one hit "Near You." Billy Sherrill
was producing the record and remembers, "They really
weren't speaking, then. It was bad. Toward the end,
Jones wouldn't sing anything the same way twice for
Tammy, and it was hard for her to phrase with him and
all that. They just carried on. It made it miserable to try
to do, and I thought, 'God, this needs to stop.' "

The couple got home around midnight after that session, George apparently feeling guilty again and saying
he'd make things better. Tammy wanted to believe him
—and the next morning, before leaving for a dental ap-
pointment, she agreed to give the relationship one more
try.

While she was gone, George packed up his things and
moved out. *He* wanted to be the one to leave, not her.

Tammy filed for divorce in January and it became final in March.

But if the couple had been unhappy together, things didn't exactly work out for them apart, either. At least, not initially.

Professionally, Tammy was a wreck. She suffered from the Wynonna Judd syndrome. She remembers that the first show she did alone, she had "never been so scared in my life. Wouldn't you know, somebody yelled, 'Where's George?' I shook for about five seconds and pretended I didn't hear. Then I got to where later on I'd joke about it. I'd say, 'I don't know where he is, and he doesn't know, either.'" It took a while, she says, before she was comfortable performing before big crowds on her own.

Things weren't much better personally, Tammy feeling "utterly lost and lonely." A mysterious, still-unsolved bombing at her house left an "entire wing . . . burned to the ground," and the conflagration became a metaphor for her social life.

She briefly took up with one of her bandmembers, Rudy Gatlin (who also played with the Gatlin Brothers), then fell in love with Burt Reynolds. When she couldn't get Burt to commit to her, she met and impulsively married real estate mogul Michael Tomlin, but she ended the marriage after just forty-four days.

Jones, meanwhile, had continued success on the charts, including his Tammy-written song "These Days (I Barely Get By)," but by 1978 he'd added cocaine to his list of addictions. Squandering his fortune, he was forced to file for bankruptcy. Perpetually stoned, he stopped eating and dropped to under one hundred pounds. He stopped coming to concerts, earning himself the nickname "No-Show Jones". When he did show up, he would sing for a few minutes, invite the musicians to play and sing, head over to the bar, and stay there for the rest of the show. On one occasion he got into a fight with his longtime friend, songwriter Earl "Peanut" Montgomery, who was trying to convince him to straighten out. In one oft-told tale, George got a gun and tried to cut his concerned friend down. Though charges were pressed, Peanut later dropped them.

With his world caving in around him, Jones—no dummy when he's sober—finally realized he needed help. He checked into a rehab center in Alabama in 1979, saying "I had no other direction. Every which way I turned I got more paranoid, made the wrong decisions."

Though he came out clean, and even reteamed with the forgiving Tammy for some successful recordings and concert engagements, he quickly slipped back into old habits, getting back on the bottle and cocaine.

Fortunately, love saved the day for both stars.

For George, it was meeting divorcée Nancy Sepulvado in 1980. The two were introduced by a mutual friend and, because she lived in Louisiana with her children, they got to know each other over the phone. She says, "We hit it off—I saw a good man on the inside who needed help."

Jones says, "Before Nancy came into my life, I didn't think anybody cared. I was filled with self-pity, I thought my world was over (that) there was no way back."

It took two years before Nancy was able to completely win Jones's confidence and convince him to come to Louisiana, where she promised to help him beat his reliance on both alcohol and cocaine.

"Anybody who ever saw her (*Nancy*) mad wouldn't wonder what made me straighten up," he laughs. But it would be simpleminded to believe it was her temper alone that did it. What had happened was that she'd forced him to look hard at his life, at his health, forced him to tell himself, "I've had enough of this. When you're young, you take most things for granted—the money, the attention, the fans. But I can appreciate it all now. I'm older and I know what it is to have it all slip away." He smiled as he said, "My old body couldn't take it anymore, either."

He managed to get clean again and, as of this writing, has remained so. When he was inducted into the Country Music Hall of Fame in 1992, the sixty-one-year-old singer publicly thanked Nancy for having "saved my life."

As for Tammy, after Burt she began seeing an old friend, Jones's accompanist and songwriter George Richey, and the couple married on July 6, 1978. For the first time in her life, she felt as though things had stabilized—but not for long. In September, they returned home to find eight big X's painted on the door of their home. A day later, someone who was apparently trying to abduct young Georgette was scared away.

Then, a week after that, another still-unsolved near-disaster befell Tammy—the mother of all ills. As she was getting behind the wheel of her car in a parking lot in Nashville, a lone figure approached wearing a stocking over his head. Pressing a gun to Tammy's side, he forced her to get onto the interstate and drive. After they'd gone eighty miles, he had her pull over and drive into the woods, where he beat and strangled her and left her for dead. But Tammy was still alive and, crawling to a nearby house, phoned for an ambulance and the police.

On fifteen other occasions, her home was broken into and the word "slut" was painted on TVs, mirrors, and elsewhere. To top it off, while she and several musicians were sleeping in her tour bus, someone set it on fire. Fortunately, everyone managed to escape unhurt.

Tammy was unable to make sense of it all. Who was behind it all? Radical feminists? People angry with her (justifiably, mind you) for having supported Governor George Wallace in his aborted 1972 Presidential bid?

Fans of George Jones?

Regardless of who was behind the assaults, she and her husband quickly worked a three-man security team into their budget.

Meanwhile, the supposedly traditional Tammy caught flak from fans and the press in 1983 when seventeen-year-old daughter Tina ran away from home and ended up in a halfway house before landing in a foster home. Through it all, the singer refused to go after her.

Was it okay to stand by your man, but not by your daughter? Tammy said that she loved Tina but going to get her would accomplish nothing. "Every time she gets upset when I'm on the road, she's going to do this same thing."

Tammy had no intention of giving up her career to wet-nurse a grown young woman, and it was years before mother and daughter were reconciled Tina, ironically, signing on as a backup singer for her mother.

Tammy continued to tour and record. She wrote her autobiography *Stand By Your Man* in 1979 (it was made into a TV movie two years later, starring Annette O'Toole). She also tried acting—something Burt Reynolds had once encouraged her to do—with a continuing role on the afternoon soap opera *Capitol* in 1986. She got so-so reviews for a role that was not exactly a reach, playing Darlene Stankowsky, a singer who supported herself by working as a waitress in Washington D.C.

But controversy and setbacks weren't quite finished with Tammy.

Stress and bad health had always plagued Tammy, and in the eighties, it almost seemed like she'd joined the Plague of the Month Club. Over the years, she underwent nineteen different kinds of surgery, including a hysterectomy, the removal of her gall bladder, an appendectomy, and an operation for gangrene-infected intestines caused by unsanitary conditions in a *previous* surgery. She'd even had the broken end of her pinky fused.

Because she couldn't afford to cut back on her performing schedule during this time, she took scads of painkillers since the earliest of the operations. "When you're bent over double and have to perform in front of thousands of people," she said, "you have to take something to relieve it." Predictably, she became addicted to them and, in 1986, entered the Betty Ford Center to try and kick the habit.

While she was there, making progress, Tammy fell ill and was taken to the hospital, where doctors cut out two feet of her intestine. Lying in bed, hurting constantly for four months, she got back on painkillers, from which her doctors had to wean her slowly.

Recovering from all that, hoping she could finally see some daylight, Tammy and her husband were forced to declare bankruptcy in 1988 when a mall developer defaulted on a loan Tammy had co-signed. She worked hard to earn money over the next three years, concertizing and taxing her not-unlimited stores of strength.

The 1990s. New decade . . . new crisis. Tammy found herself stressed-out to the max in January of 1992 after crossing swords with Hillary Clinton who, when asked by *60 Minutes* about the alleged infidelities of her husband, then-Presidential candidate Bill Clinton, snapped, "I'm not sitting here, some little woman standing by her man like Tammy Wynette. I'm sitting here because I love and respect him and I honor what we've been through together."

Well, Ms. Pugh returned fire, criticizing Hillary's "obvious insensitivity to all 'little women' in the country who stand by their men," and seething for days, in private, over the remark. Later, Hillary publicly apologized, and Tammy buried the hatchet and hugged Hillary when the two met later at a Democratic fundraiser.

Tammy continued to push herself that year, undertaking an ill-advised tour of Australia, collapsing twice onstage and still refusing to slow down. Finally, on May 2, 1992, right before a performance in Brantford, Ontario, she suffered terrible chest and abdominal pains and was rushed to a hospital. Doctors determined that she was suffering from intestinal inflammation and was rushed seven hundred miles to a specialist at Barnes Hospital in St. Louis.

Happy fiftieth birthday!

After a week of tests, doctors decided that surgery (and the removal of half of her stomach) was necessary to relieve a blocked bile duct. Due to the complexity of the procedure, and because of the scar tissue from her other operations, the surgery took fourteen hours. Over the next few days, everyone from George Jones to Burt Reynolds kept in close contact with Richey, who rarely left his wife's side during her long recuperation.

Tammy was back on her feet that fall, slowing down a tad to spend time with her grandchildren and also to safeguard her health.

"The old saying, 'The show must go on' does not apply to me anymore," she said. "I've tried that. The show must go on as long as I'm able."

Still, she doesn't regret any of the decisions she's made. "I think I'm a better person for having gone through what I did," she says, adding that a life of quiet and comfort has its drawbacks. "The sad part about happy endings is there's nothing to write about."

But she's only at the half-century mark. Knowing Tammy, it's not *quite* time to close the book on this remarkable woman.

Dolly Parton

HERE'S how Dolly Parton sees it.

"I'm not offended at all by the dumb blonde jokes because I know I'm not dumb. And," she says, "I also know that I'm not blonde."

You could pack a book with the wit and wisdom of Dolly Parton. One of the most engaging and forthright figures in contemporary music, she had the honesty and courage to tell the late Cliff Jahr of *The Ladies Home Journal* just where she got the inspiration for her "look": "I always liked the look of our hookers back home. Their big hairdos and makeup made them look *more*. When people say less is more, I say more is more. Less is less. I go for more."

For a while, Dolly was the truest, purest country songstress around, then she became a crossover hit and, like Elvis, managed to turn herself into something of a self-parody. Things that had once been attributes and characteristics became trademarks and caricatures.

Dolly herself admits, "It takes a lot of money to make me look this cheap," and "I look like the girl next door . . . if you happen to live next door to an amusement park." For the record, she swears her breasts are not the result of implants. "I do have big tits," she says in her inimitable way. "Always had 'em." As for the wigs, the beauty with the naturally light-brown hair says that she started wearing them because she was too busy writing and singing to go to the beauty parlor.

In a way, of course, you can't fault her for going where the spotlight was brightest. Since her impoverished childhood, the driving force in her life has always been to *be* somebody. And the bigger and more successful that somebody became, the happier she was.

Always, though, there were the controversies and heartbreak to remind us that, beneath what friend Merle Haggard calls "that bunch of fluffy hair, fluttery eyelashes, and super boobs," she was still a very human being.

Born on a farm in Locust Ridge, Tennessee on January 19, 1946, the fourth of twelve children, Dolly Rebecca Parton knew from a very early age that she wanted to be an entertainer. A rich one.

She began singing in the church choir, taught herself to play an old mandolin when she was six, began writing songs when she was seven, and at ten she was singing them on Cas Walker's radio and TV shows in Knoxville. At twelve, she made her debut on the *Grand Ole Opry*— though just barely. She says that right before she went on, the managers "told me I couldn't go on because I didn't belong to a union." Through tears, she says she happened to see Johnny Cash "and just walked up to him and told him I had to sing." She says that Cash walked her out onstage, introduced her to the crowd, and sing she did.

Upon graduating from high school in 1964, the ambitious and optimistic Dolly packed up and moved to Nashville, where her compositions became hits for Bill Phillips ("Put It Off Till Tomorrow" in 1966) and Hank Williams, Jr. ("I'm In No Condition" the following year). She also did some recording of her own for Mon-

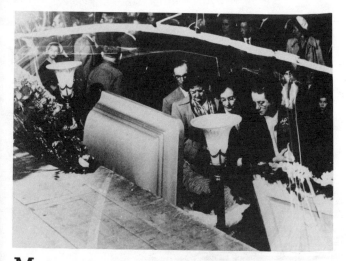

Mourners file past the open coffin of Hank Williams in Montgomery's Municipal Auditorium. (AP/Wide World)

Roy Rogers weeps at the funeral of son Sandy. (AP/Wide World)

Johnny Horton, who died at age 35. (*AP/Wide World*)

Early publicity shot (1958) of Jim Reeves. (*AP/Wide World*)

A bondsman and U.S. Marshal accompany Johnny Cash to the Federal Courthouse in El Paso after his drug bust. *(AP/Wide World)*

Waylon Jennings enters a Nashville court to defend himself after the August, 1977 cocaine bust. The charges were later dropped. *(AP/Wide World)*

Johnny Paycheck is led from Highland County Common Pleas Court after being found guilty on two charges stemming from the barroom shooting.
(AP/Wide World)

Federal investigators examine what's left of the death helicopter of Stevie Ray Vaughan. *(AP/Wide World)*

Tammy Wynette's eight-year-old daughter Georgette comforts her after her abduction and beating. *(AP/Wide World)*

The Mandrell car crash. That's her Jaguar on the left. *(AP/Wide World)*

Barbara Mandrell being wheeled into surgery at Baptist Hospital. *(AP/Wide World)*

Tanya Tucker horses around with Glen Campbell at the Roxy Roller Disco in New York in September 1980, while *Soap* star Jimmy Bayos looks on. The original caption described Glen as her "husband-to-be." *(AP/Wide World)*

Lorrie Morgan at the Country Music Association Awards in 1989. *(AP/Wide World)*

Billy Ray Cyrus greets a young fan backstage, showing off the sleeveless, neckless shirt he wore during his concert. *(Author's Collection)*

From day one, Dean avoided the spotlight like it was the sun and he was Count Dracula (hmmm . . . same initials). Until fairly recently, in fact, he *never* toured with his wife. He finally went with her to Lake Tahoe for a four day gig in September of 1992 and, reportedly, was so bored he left early. Turns out he doesn't even *like* country music.

Dean spends most of his time running his contracting business, or living comfortably on the couple's sixty-five acre Nashville estate with its antebellum mansion or at their retreat in Hawaii.

"He's sort of shy and quiet," Dolly says, in one of her characteristic understatements.

From the beginning of Dolly's relationship with Wagoner, her constant separation from Carl was the subject of talk that theirs was an open marriage. Folks around town said that Wagoner and Dolly did more than sing and write together, though she categorically denies that there was anything sexual going on.

"We were lovers of music, and I suppose we had one of the world's most unique relationships. We were not lovers as you know lovers."

People didn't believe her. Especially after the split, when published reports quoted Wagoner as saying that the two of them did, in fact, have an affair. Did he think Dolly would have others?

Wagoner says, "Regardless of what it was or who it was—I mean her family, her own blood—she would turn her back . . . to help herself."

After Wagoner, there was talk about Dolly and Merle Haggard, who toured with her, he riding in her bus or she in his. Haggard admits that he was madly in love with Dolly, but says it was unrequited.

"Dolly wouldn't even come close to discussing any kind of future with me," he wrote in his 1981 autobiography *Sing Me Back Home*. "It was as though it was all an impossible dream—of mine." Haggard says that every time he broached the subject of a relationship, she'd tell him, " 'Don't you understand that I *love* Carl? I really *do*.' "

Dolly said at the time that she was sure her marriage would "last forever. It's just too right, and too natural, and too comfortable, and too secure."

But that was in the middle 1970s. By the next decade, she had a different attitude toward marriage, or at least a broader definition. She told *Playboy* that if she wanted to make love with someone other than her husband, "I would. (And) if I should do it, it would affect nobody but me and the person involved." Sex, she said, "is an overwhelming emotion. Natural as breathing . . . if I feel the need to express any emotion, I'm gonna do it. . . . I really like it, and I'm not ashamed to say it."

But it was a two-way street, she told *Redbook*, and what Carl did when she was gone was his business, "as long as he don't love somebody more than me. I like the fact that he's got his friends. He takes his girlfriends to dinner and to lunch. Now, whether he goes to bed with them or not, I don't care . . . if he wanted to, that's fine. Same with me."

With straight talk like that, it's not surprising that gossip about affairs continued, centering around Dolly's music director, who left his job in 1982 to study medicine. Was it he about whom Dolly was speaking when she told a reporter that she'd suffered "an affair of the heart that left me shattered"? Word from the set of her film *Rhinestone* in 1984 was that she and co-star Sylvester Stallone were doing more than rehearsing their lines when the two of them made that miserable film, having late night dinners after long days of filming.

(Conversely, there were zero reports of romance from the set of the 1982 film *Best Little Whorehouse in Texas*, as co-star Burt Reynolds was getting over his busted liaison with Sally Field. He was in a constant set of pique, reportedly throwing tantrums on a regular basis. Burt says, "Yeah, I was pissed. I loved Dolly, but I was still pissed.")

The list of reported lovers is long, and Dolly—to be private or provocative, it's difficult to say which—will say nothing about any of the men in particular. She did tell interviewer Cliff Jahr—off the record—that if she did have an affair, she wouldn't take out an ad announcing it.

"Let 'em all wonder," she said. "It don't bother me."

Carl, of course, can teach the sphinx a thing or two when it comes to keeping quiet. You won't find out much about his or Dolly's private life from him.

While all of this was being discussed in whispers, Dolly was catching some pretty vocal hell from country fans for a career move she made in 1977. Determined to have more impact on the pop charts, she ditched her Nashville managers and homespun Travelin' Family Band for a Los Angeles team. Long-time supporters accused her of selling-out, charges which greatly upset her.

"I'm not leaving country," she said at the time. "I am just taking it with me."

It's a debatable point. Dolly wasn't exactly attempting a Gram Parsons-like fusion of country and some other musical style. However, true to her word, it was a country song she (and a steel guitar) took to the top of both the country and pop charts: "Here You Come Again," which also won a Grammy and earned her the Academy of Country Music's Entertainer of the Year award. The following year, Nashville's Country Music Association hopped on the bandwagon, tapping her as Entertainer of the Year.

Die hard Nashvillians were still bitter, but Dolly kept on truckin' her way up both charts. To soften the blow of her biggest "defection," her movie debut in 1981 in the smash hit *9 to 5*, she saw to it that the film premiered in Nashville.

(And she was pretty much forgiven by the remaining hardcore holdouts in 1982 when she opened her four hundred acre Dollywood theme park in Pigeon Forge, thirty miles from Knoxville. Folks will overlook a *lot* when it's good for the local economy.)

As if all of this weren't enough to keep Dolly busy, other problems began to dog her. One surfaced in 1974, and the five-foot-tall Dolly has had to fight it constantly: the battle to keep her weight closer to its normal 105 than to its (so far) uppermost limit of 165.

"When I was about thirty," she says, she first started "getting to be a little porker." The culprit: "those fried clams at Howard Johnson's," which she always inhaled when she was on the road. Dolly says that to combat the problem, she went on one "crazy diet" after another, from "yucky liquid protein" to fasting. None of it worked to her satisfaction.

Health problems compounded her weight problem. Dolly's menstrual cycle had always been unpredictable, and for years she suffered from debilitating cramps and headaches. In February of 1982, she underwent minor gynecological surgery in an effort to correct the problem. After a short rest, she undertook a grueling tour. Late in the summer, while performing at the State Fairgrounds in Indianapolis in a driving rain, she began hemorrhaging and collapsed. She was forced to call off the rest of the tour and undergo a partial hysterectomy.

After the operation, depression set in big-time. She ate herself silly and went up to 165 pounds, and she says, "For about six months I woke up every morning feeling dead." At her worst, she says she kept looking at the gun she keeps on her nightstand and telling herself, " 'You're either going to blow your brains out or get off your fat ass and lose weight and get into a better place in your mind.' "

Obviously, Dolly chose the latter (or this would be quite a different entry!). Though her weight is still a potential problem, she has been diligent about keeping it from getting out of hand.

Elsewhere, the years have been unkind to her multimedia career. Her hugely-hyped ABC series bombed, and though she got fine notices for her ensemble work in the 1989 film *Steel Magnolias*, her starring vehicle *Straight Talk* died at the box office in 1992. The defector is no longer in great demand in Hollywood, though Nashville and her country fans still love her. Her recordings continue to sell and her concerts still sell out. On the curious matter of her husband, whatever may have gone on in the past (or continues to go on on the road), she now leaves big slabs of time to be home alone with him.

"When Patsy Cline had her car accident," Dolly says, "she came to the *Opry* on crutches and sang, even though she was clearly in pain. Someone said it was great she did that for the fans, and Patsy said, 'I didn't do it just for the fans. It was also for me. You don't get anywhere wallerin' in misery.' "

"I don't waller. Never have. I believe in gettin' on with things and movin' ahead. Cripes," she told Jahr, "I want to be an eighty-year-old lady whose sex life they're still wonderin' about."

Loretta Lynn

*T*HIS has been a life.

Ups and downs? Loretta's had them, major league. In her bestselling autobiography *Coal Miner's Daughter*, she wrote, "My life has run from misery to happiness"—and more than once, often without the kindness or generosity this hard-working, loving woman deserves.

But as she herself says, "We don't deal the cards, we play the hand. That's just the way it is."

The hand Loretta was dealt was one of awesome poverty. Born on April 14, 1935 in Butcher Hollow, in eastern Kentucky's coal-mining hills, and named after movie star Loretta Young, Loretta was married when she was thirteen to a boy she met at a school dance, six-years-older World War II veteran Oliver Lynn (a.k.a. "Mooney," from his moonshining days, and "Doolittle" because he was so little as a child). She dropped out of school in the eighth grade, and within four months was pregnant—even though, she admits, she didn't know quite how she got that way. She really *did* believe she'd been found under a cabbage leaf, and didn't understand quite how sex worked.

She discovered fast, though, that it was something she

felt possessive about. When she learned that her husband was cheating on her, she wrote to one woman to get lost, then spied on the woman to watch her angry reaction when she went to the post office. She threatened another woman with "a mouthful of knuckles."

Loretta doesn't say things without first thinking about them, and if she's thought about them, she means it. Reportedly, Doo stopped.

Loretta had four children by the time she was eighteen. Betty Sue was first, followed by Jack Benny (named for her favorite comedian), Ernest Ray (who was delivered by Caesarian section, though Loretta was a minor and couldn't sign her own consent form), and Clara Marie. Twins Peggy and Patsy (after Patsy Cline) came later, when Loretta was twenty-nine. That was also the year she became a grandmother for the first time, thanks to Betty Sue.

She lost several other children due to miscarriages, one of which resulted in blood poisoning that almost cost her her life.

Doo held a variety of jobs over the years, coal mining, farming, and logging. None of them paid much, which made it difficult to feed all of those mouths. Then Doo had an idea.

Loretta's family, the Webbs, had always been musical, but no one ever thought of turning music into a vocation. Not until Doolittle bought Loretta a guitar for her eighteenth birthday, and she started singing and writing songs. Six years later, when they were living in Custer, Washington, not far from the local Grange Hall—the ambitious young man finally got together some local musicians and arranged for Loretta to perform there.

Never mind infidelity, Loretta says today: "He got me into this business. That's enough to kill him for."

Before long, Loretta's Trail Blazers had steady gigs throughout the area, and appeared on Buck Owens's TV show, which broadcast from Tacoma. She was seen by an aspiring producer, who signed her to his start-up label Zero Records and released her first record, "I'm a Honky Tonk Girl," in 1960.

Thanks to Loretta's vigorous station-to-station promotion, the record went to number fourteen on the charts, though Loretta admits that when she and her Blazers were informed about their accomplishment, "We were so stupid we didn't know what the charts meant."

She made her debut on the *Grand Ole Opry* on October 15, 1960, and became a member two years later. She also signed with Decca that year, went to the top ten with "Success," and finally hit number one in 1966 with "Don't Come Home A'Drinkin' (With Lovin' On Your Mind)." Her second number one hit was "Fist City," an autobiographical tune she wrote that carried a warning: mess with my husband and you'll lose some teeth.

Life was good. Loretta became country music's first female millionaire. In 1976, her autobiography became a huge bestseller and spawned a hit film in 1980, which made a star of (and won an Oscar for) Sissy Spacek. Even Loretta's sister, Crystal Gayle, was a hit. Born Brenda Gail Webb (she got her nickname from the Krystal hamburger chain), she started as a singer with her sister in 1970, when she was nineteen. Then Gayle struck out on her own, hitting it big in 1977 with the crossover smash "Don't It Make My Brown Eyes Blue." Crystal says that she and her sister have had a friendly rivalry ever since, and that they "would never let our careers get in the way of the deep love we have for one another."

In 1971, at the age of fourteen, cousin Patty Loveless —nee Lovelace—also got into the act, specializing in songs of heartbreak.

But while music has spared Loretta from the pain of poverty, there have been downsides as well, foremost being the assaults on her health due to her hectic touring schedule. She has passed out God-knows-how-many times in hotels, in transit, and onstage ("If you really want to try something unusual, try passing out in front of five thousand people," she says).

She has also suffered from bleeding ulcers and, since she was seventeen, from migraines so severe that they cause her to throw up uncontrollably. The headaches are so bad, in fact, that she once contemplated taking her life with the pearl-handled gun her romantic husband purchased for her as a Valentine's Day present. She went so far as to put the gun to her head before thinking better of it. Instead, she became addicted to painkillers, an overdose of which once landed her in Nashville's Park View Hospital. Afraid to give them up, she ended up on a psychiatrist's couch in a successful effort to get clean, though she wasn't able to root out any psychological causes for the headaches.

Perhaps, she speculates, it's tension caused by the subconscious fear of never knowing how and when trouble will strike. For example——

In 1982, the way-unprejudiced Loretta found herself the subject of unwanted publicity when she was sued by a black security guard for having turned to him during a concert and said, "Black is beautiful, ain't it brother?" It was an innocent, offhanded remark that according to the guard—led to his drinking and impotence. The man filed a lawsuit that dragged on for four years before being dropped.

In 1986, Loretta and Doo were involved in a car accident that landed her in the hospital with a concussion.

And then there are family problems, such as Ernest's wife giving birth to stillborn twins, Ernest having a kidney removed, and Patsy, at fifteen, eloping with a nineteen-year-old truck driver. Loretta brushed off comparisons with her own childhood, saying, "I knew my only future was to be married and have children, but these kids could have had everything." (PS: the marriage didn't last.) There was also Doo's loooong relationship with the bottle, which finally drove him to hop on the wagon.

"He quit," says his wife, "when he realized he didn't remember an awful lot in the morning."

Not to put too fine a point on these and other domestic problems, Loretta said after seeing the film version of *Coal Miner's Daughter*, "If the movie had told everything, there'd have been fifty hours of fighting."

But nothing in her very full life prepared Loretta for the tragedy she suffered in 1984, one from which she still hasn't quite recovered—and says she never will.

In *Coal Miner's Daughter*, Loretta wrote of son Jack, "Of all my kids, he's the one I feel most sentimental about." Quiet, handsome, the father of a daughter, Lora, and a son, Jeffrey—"Who," Loretta admits, "is the apple of my eye"—Jack always made her happy. When Jack and his wife Pat broke up, Loretta says she couldn't stop "bawling" for weeks. He subsequently remarried, he and his wife Barbara having a young daughter, Jenny.

Jack spent most of his time on the family's five thousand acre ranch outside of Waverly, Tennessee. A year before, excessive drinking had resulted in liver problems and also contributed to his being thrown from a horse, which landed him in the hospital with a neck injury. During the hospital stay, says sister Patsy, "he straightened up" and became a teetotaler.

On the afternoon of July 22, Loretta was returning to Nashville from Kansas City on her quarter-million-dollar tour bus. Taking it easy on the ranch, the thirty-four-year-old Jack got on the back of his quarter horse Black Jack and told a hand, "I'm goin' ridin'," and headed off. Several hours later—it isn't known exactly when, but darkness was already falling—they entered the Duck River which cuts across the ranch.

The horse was steady as they made their way across, but the river runs deep in several sections and the current can be unpredictable. Apparently, the water rushed over Black Jack at some point and knocked Jack off.

When he didn't show up the following day, people at the ranch started getting antsy. It wasn't like Jack to camp out without telling anyone, and besides, he hadn't packed to do so.

A search party was dispatched late in the day. They found Jack two days later when a motor boat spotted Black Jack standing under a bluff, his master's body floating in the water beside him.

In an eerie coincidence, that same day, an assistant had gone to Loretta's cabin in the bus to see if she wanted any coffee. Loretta was unconscious and ghostly-white. She was rushed to the Good Samaritan Hospital in Mount Vernon, Illinois; when she came to, she said she was afraid of something she couldn't put her finger on.

She wasn't told of the tragedy until Wednesday, July 25, when Doo walked quietly into the private room, sat on the side of the bed, took her hand in his, and told her the terrible news.

Doo did the best he could to console his wife, containing his own grief for her sake, then took her back to Nashville on a chartered plane. Hysterical all the while and wailing that she didn't want to live, Loretta was put in the hospital for observation.

On Friday, July 27, the day of the funeral, she was oblivious to the three hundred mourners, which included the elite of Nashville, and had to be supported constantly by her husband and friends. Widow Barbara was in somewhat better shape, for the most part retaining her composure and telling four-year-old Jenny that daddy was "riding horses with Jesus."

Loretta remained in seclusion throughout August, then threw herself back into work to keep from losing her sanity altogether. Much later, she was finally able to deal with Jack's death by clinging to a strongly held belief she'd outlined in her autobiography: "people take different forms, and death doesn't end things."

People in Nashville doubt that anything could ever end Loretta herself. She's slowing down somewhat as she nears her sixtieth birthday, but she hasn't come close to stopping.

"I don't think anyone ever does, really," she says. A believer in reincarnation who maintains she was a Native American and an Irish girl in past lives, Loretta says, "I think we keep on goin' till we get it right."

Most of her fans would agree that Loretta's gotten pretty close to it this go-around.

Barbara Mandrell

FOR the longest time, Barbara Mandrell seemed to live a charmed life, a fairytale existence in which she rode talent and beauty and a distinctive R&B style to the top and became one of the handful of female country superstars.

Then she took a different kind of ride, nearly losing everything in a mixmaster of a crash.

Born in Houston, Texas, on Christmas Day, 1948, Barbara was raised in a musical family. By the time she was eleven, she could already play bass, banjo, steel guitar, and saxophone. She became one of the Mandrells; the group was comprised of her parents and two boys from outside the family, Brian Lonbeck and Kenneth Dudney, and Barbara. They appeared on TV shows in the late 1950s like *Hometown Jamboree*. When she was twelve, Barbara soloed in Las Vegas as the Sweetheart of the Steel Guitar.

Her first solo recordings, made when she was seventeen for the small Mosrite label, were undistinguished and unsuccessful pop-style ditties. She toured Korea and Vietnam with Johnny Cash in 1966–7. On May 28, 1967, Barbara wed seven-years-older Ken, who was no longer a Mandrell but a navy pilot. When Ken was sent overseas later that year, she went to to stay with the rest of her family, which had moved to Nashville. Intoxicated by the singers she saw and heard at the *Grand Ole Opry*, Barbara was bit bad by the country bug, and with her father as her manager, she signed with Columbia in March of 1969, hitting the charts at once with soulful recordings like "I've Been Loving You Too Long" (an Otis Redding tune), "Do Right Man—Do Right Woman," and "Treat Him Right." Barbara joined the *Grand Ole Opry* in July of 1972, moved to ABC/Dot in 1975, made the top five that year with "Standing Room Only," and had her first number one record in 1978, "Sleeping Single in a Double Bed," a song that virtually every other artist in town had turned down.

Barbara stayed on top of the charts and was the Country Music Association's Female Vocalist of the Year in 1979, and their Entertainer of the Year in 1980 and 1981 —an unprecedented feat for a female artist. Her 1980–1 NBC series *Barbara Mandrell & The Mandrell Sisters* brought her an even larger audience; the popular show would have run for years if Barbara hadn't "felt it would be physically impossible for me to continue at that pace every week."

Meanwhile, she and Ken had two children, Matthew and Jaime. The family lived in a mansion with its own helicopter landing pad. Life wasn't just good, it was perfect.

Until September 11, 1984.

Barbara and the children were in her silver 1982 Jaguar, heading home to Hendersonville, Tennessee after clothes shopping for Matthew, then fourteen, and Jaime, eight. Matthew was sitting next to his mother, Jaime behind her. They didn't always wear their seatbelts, though this time they did as Barbara headed east on Route 31.

Heading west in his 1981 red Subaru was nineteen-year-old Mark White, a University of Tennessee mathematics major who had just bought archery equipment at a sporting goods store. Mark hadn't bothered to put his seatbelt on.

Route 31 is a five lane road—the middle lane is for turning—and both Barbara and Mark were in their respective inside lanes. For reasons that will never be known, just before 6:30 P.M., Mark's car drifted into the turning lane. But he didn't stop there; he continued to move diagonally, toward Barbara's lane.

The car in front of Barbara's swerved to the right to avoid the on-rushing car. Barbara saw it at the last instant and gasped. Almost directly in front of the Victory Baptist Church, Mark's car slammed head-first into Barbara's, crushing the left front of her vehicle. The front of Mark's car was completely caved in.

Cars swerved left and right to avoid the collision, motorists pulling over quickly to see if they could help. One ran to a pay phone to call for the police.

Barbara and her family were in a bad way. Though Barbara later said, "Without those seat belts, we would have been tossed and broken like cheap toys," things weren't so great as it was.

The children were hurt, though not as severely as Barbara, since her side of the car had taken the brunt of the impact. Matthew's face was severely cut, and doctors later determined that the seat belt had caused some minor internal injuries. But he was alert and, after the collision, turned to ask his sister if she were all right. She told him she was, and then he looked at his mother and saw her, lying unconscious and bent over the steering wheel.

Barbara had suffered broken ribs, a smashed thighbone, a fractured ankle, broken toes, and various lacerations. Her mouth was bloody inside and out, and her face badly bruised from having been thrown against the steering wheel. She had a severe concussion, glass was embedded in her right leg, and leather and plastic from the steering wheel were buried in her left arm.

Jaime undid her belt, pushed open the door, and stood on wobbly legs on the grass beside the road, looking back at the wreckage.

People were running toward her, asking if she were all right. She didn't say anything, she couldn't. "I was still feeling the hit," she recalls.

She started back toward the car to help her mother and brother, and then she went down, conscious but unable to stand. She became terribly anxious then, suddenly discovering that she couldn't move her head; she felt better when someone pointed out that that was because she was sitting on her long ponytail.

When the ambulance arrived, paramedics gently took Matthew from the car and lay him on the grass beside his sister. A man came over and gave him money he'd found on Barbara; he told him to keep it safe.

A motorist came over and washed the blood from the children's faces. Then someone recognized the driver of the Jaguar, and rumors spread through Nashville that Barbara Mandrell was near death or already dead.

The two children heard people saying that their mother was dead. A friend of the family, who happened to be driving by and stopped, assured the youngsters that it wasn't so, even though he didn't know that for a fact.

Workers pried open the door, and Barbara was placed on a stretcher. She was awake now and muttering incoherently, unable to respond to questions or statements, registering no emotion when told that the children were all right.

By the time the jaws of life could be used to get Mark from the wreckage of his car, he was dead, crushed and bleeding from the ears, nose, chin, neck, chest, and arms. Ironically, on the seat beside him was a pamphlet entitled *About Facing Death As a Christian.*

An autopsy revealed no drugs or alcohol in his system. The setting sun hadn't been a problem, nor was he driving excessively fast. There had been no attempt to brake in the short distance (142 feet) he'd strayed.

What had happened? All anyone could think of was that Mark had been working too hard and had simply dozed off. Not that it matters.

The Mandrells were rushed to Baptist Hospital in Nashville. Barbara's father recalls that as dazed as the singer was, "every time the doctor would move her leg . . . she whammed him one in the face."

Barbara underwent three hours of surgery to have the glass removed from her leg so the thigh could be set, and then she was placed in traction. She was in constant physical pain and in deep grief over the death of Mark White, mourning for what his family had to be feeling. She was also having a great deal of difficulty coming to grips with the fact that one's life could end so suddenly, and through something utterly beyond your control.

After nineteen days, doctors decided that Barbara might heal better in her own surroundings. She went home and just lay in bed for nearly two months, staring into space, eating little, and talking even less.

"I had never been so depressed," she wrote in her 1990 autobiography *Get to the Heart*. For a time, no one was even sure she'd be the same Barbara she'd once been: she'd suffered a brain trauma. It took months for her memory, emotional stability, and even her voice to return to what they were, though even now, she says, she still has trouble driving in traffic.

It wasn't until June 10, 1985 that Barbara returned to the stage and, as though celebrating her own rebirth, she had her third child, Nathan, in September of 1985—almost a year to the day after the crash.

"A third child was not exactly on our list of priorities," she laughs. But since doctors had *originally* suspected that she had cancer, "Given a choice between a baby and a tumor," she says, "we knew which one we would prefer."

Barbara is still a top recording artist and a big draw on the concert trail, and she's also a poster girl for the National Safety Council's wear-your-seatbelt campaign. But she also spends more time than ever with her family, and admits that the accident has changed her.

"The old Barbara used to be more impulsive, more spontaneous, more optimistic," she says. Today, she says she treasures every day as though it were her last.

That may seem like a ghoulish way to live, but as one of those rare country birds who has managed to *survive* an accident, Barbara doesn't care. For her, being live and pessimistic is better than being dead and on Memorex.

Tanya Tucker

TEN years before anyone ever heard of Madonna, country music had a *blonde terrible* of its own, a pre-Madonna, as it were, a singer who was fond of dressing in tight bodysuits or miniskirts, and whose license used to read MS BAD ASS.

It was appropriate. In 1972, Tanya Tucker's gutsy, sexy recording of "Delta Dawn" bowled listeners over, especially when they discovered that the artist was only thirteen.

Born October 19, 1958 in Seminole, Texas, and raised in Wilcox, Arizona, Tanya was determined to be a singer from the age of nine, when she walked up to artist Mel Tillis at a fair, told him she wanted to be a singer, and gave him a sample of her now-famous pipes. He was so enraptured that he invited her onstage to sing during his set. Tanya's parents encouraged her dream. In fact, her father Beau—a jack-of-all-trades—paid for his daughter's demo, which made the rounds of the labels in and out of Nashville. When it came to the attention of Tammy Wynette's mentor, producer Billy Sherrill, he was sufficiently impressed to offer her a recording contract.

But the headstrong youngster, who would soon be

nicknamed "The Texas Tornado" by the press, boldly rejected the seasoned Sherrill's choice of a first song, "Happiest Girl in the Whole U.S.A." (which became a hit for Donna Fargo) and, instead, recorded "Delta Dawn" after hearing Bette Midler sing it on *The Tonight Show*.

It was her butt on the line, she reasoned, and the gamble paid off. The record was a hit, and she followed it with the top-five country song "Love's the Answer." Her third single, "What's Your Mama's Name," hit the number one spot. In May of 1973 and her next number one song, "Blood Red and Goin' Down," was inspired by a sunset, though more disc jockeys than not took it to mean something else altogether, and many were offended. The double-entendre title had industryites wondering what Tanya would do next: would she smooth some ruffled coats and do something sweet, or would she push the outside of the envelope even further?

Hint: the title of her next recording was "Would You Lay With Me (In a Field of Stone)." Written by David Allan Coe—an ex-con—the song went to number one in March of 1974. The deejays and Nashville executives may have had a rough time digesting Tanya, but the music buying public had no such problems.

Hot as a smoking gun, ninth-grader Tanya dropped out of high school to pursue her career. She jumped from Columbia to MCA, and after several more number one singles made the career-stalling move of covering rock-and-roll songs that Elvis Presley, Buddy Holly, and others had originally recorded. Though her *Greatest Hits* album went gold (her first album to do so), she lost her grip on the country charts and didn't make a dent on the pop charts, which was one of the reasons she'd tried a new sound in the first place.

"I think it was just a searching period," she says. "I wasn't leaving country music, because that's my roots, but I was searching and trying to cut bigger and better records."

Tanya wouldn't return to the top of the country charts for years. Until then, like Madonna, the press she got was not for music but for her romances with a slew of celebrities, including country star Merle Haggard, rocker Andy Gibb, actor Don Johnson, and, when she was twenty-two, a sizzling, highly publicized relationship with the twice-older Glen Campbell.

Campbell was a crossover artist of enormous stature when they met. He had recorded over thirty-five albums, one third of them gold, and had enjoyed country and pop chart triumphs with songs like "By the Time I Get to Phoenix," "Wichita Lineman," "Galveston," and "Rhinestone Cowboy." His TV series, *The Glen Campbell Goodtime Hour*, had a healthy run from 1968 to 1972.

But while his career was earning him millions of dollars a year, his personal life was a bust. He'd been married at the age of seventeen to Diane Kirk; the relationship went bust in 1958, after three years. His second marriage, to Billie Jean Nunley, lasted from 1959 to 1976. His third marriage, to Mac Davis's ex-wife Sarah, hung on by its fingertips from 1976 to 1979. That relationship had had *its* share of publicity as well. The press wrote that Campbell had stolen her from his friend, charges he vigorously denied.

"They were already apart," he told *People* Magazine at the time, "and anyway Mac and I were never friends. . . . People were very rude and stupid concerning that whole thing."

Tanya had first met Campbell in 1972, when she got his autograph at the *Grand Ole Opry*. For her, it was infatuation at first sight. She carried his photograph in her wallet, and seven years later, when she heard that he and Sarah had split, she was on the phone to him.

"I heard that you and Sarah are separated," she told

him. "I'm really concerned and I want to know if there's anything I can do for you."

It so happened that Campbell *could* think of something. "Yeah," he said. "Come over and let's sing some songs together."

She did, and Campbell swears they "just talked. No sex." Not then, anyway. The two fell hard for one another, Campbell lovingly describing her as "a raunchy young broad." They became a professional as well as a personal duo.

"Our voices blend so well together," Tanya said at the time, "that it's almost sinful not to work together."

They sang together in Las Vegas, in Monte Carlo, in Honolulu, taped a TV special together, cut hit duets like "Dream Lover," and even sang the National Anthem at the Republican National Convention in 1980. Campbell sang backup vocals on several of Tanya's hit songs, including "Pecos Promenade," which was used in the movie *Smokey and the Bandit II*, and "Can I see You Tonight," which went to number four in 1981.

They were inseparable, and just before giving her an engagement ring onstage in Hawaii—with a wedding scheduled for fourteen months later, on Valentine's Day, 1982—Campbell said reverently, "There's a bond there I'm not going to break."

Ah, the dreams of the everyday country star.

The truth was, the honeymoon had already began to cool early in 1980, when they would have what Tanya calls "disagreements" over silly things. Then she got tired of Campbell's reportedly voracious sexual appetite, calling him "the horniest man I ever met. . . . I mean, I thought I could handle a lot. . . ."

But Tanya reports that the biggest problem was Campbell's jealousy and his concern about their age difference. He was fearful that strapping young men would come on to her. Though she assured him "it takes two to do anything and I wasn't interested in anybody but him," he was beyond furious when the chauffeur reported that she'd gone out to dinner and didn't tell him —even though she was with a female friend.

Tanya remembers her inamorato saying, "If I could lie to him about that, I could lie about other things."

The relationship went *splat* as, the next day, Campbell dropped her from his European tour, pulled out the financing on a boutique she was planning to open in Beverly Hills, and stopped talking to her.

She was hurt, but not exactly out in the cold. Though her solo career had stalled during the relationship, she still had her Beverly Hills home and a three thousand acre ranch in McEwen, Tennessee, which her father ran for her. She also was young, and had time.

Tanya didn't return to recording immediately. She wanted to do country, but wasn't sure how fans would react after she'd been cut loose by one of the industry's kings. She also didn't want to come back until she had the goods to make it work.

After three years, Tanya found herself cash-poor (more on which in a moment) and was forced to make her move. She released "One Love At A Time," which hit number three early in 1986, then grabbed the number one spot with "Just Another Love" in October. After that, she placed record after record in the top ten and began touring to support her albums *Girls Like Me* and its appropriately titled 1987 followup *Love Me Like You Used To*. It was then that she faced her second major personal crisis.

She says that "boredom" and being alone again had driven her to substance abuse, and her return to performing only reinforced that need. "You get applause and admiration," she said, "and then you're back in the hotel room by yourself."

Not one to sit alone and read a book, she turned to

alcohol and cocaine, which temporarily boosted her spirits while at the same time draining her pocketbook.

For nearly a year, her worried parents had urged her to get help. Though she says, "I think they overreacted a lot," she finally came to the conclusion that "that stuff's not good for you." In February of 1988, Tanya entered the Betty Ford Clinic. She got clean and stayed clean, though there was a good reason. No sooner had the ink on those headlines dried than she made new ones in 1989 by giving birth to a daughter, Presley Tanita, out of wedlock. Two years later she had a son, Beau Grayson. Tanya has never revealed the names of the father or fathers, and says she has no intention of doing so.

Surprisingly, usually conservative Nashville was behind Tanya. She'd tried things the old-fashioned way, and men had treated her wrong. She had Music City's blessings to be a nineties woman.

But if Tanya's still picking the songs she'll sing, so to speak, she gave a little too. She's toned down her tight fitting stage costumes, chucked her wild ways to care for the kids, and returned to a more traditional Nashville sound.

Summing up the state of her life and career, she says today, "I don't want to be called a risqué mother of two. Being called a *little* risqué mother of two is better."

So is selling lots of albums and winning awards. In 1991 she was the Country Music Association's female vocalist of the year, honored as much for her amazing comeback as for individual achievements. In November of 1992, after more than twenty-five top-five records in twenty years in the business, *What Do I Do With Me* was her first album to go platinum, ironically, with sales roughly the same as those of Madonna's highly touted *Erotica* album. Sex still sells, but not as well as good music.

Yet Tanya feels that reaching these new plateaus is just the beginning.

"I'm definitely still moving up the mountain," she says. "I feel there's a lot more for me to do, and I'm going to take my best shot at doing it."

Reba McEntire

REBA McEntire empathizes with what Tanya and other women have had to go through in Nashville, thanks to the double standard of the industry—and the audience.

"If a man is sexy," she says, "that doesn't offend the men in the crowd. They know the women are just having fun. But if a gal is sexy and something of a come-on, the women in the audience take offense. They don't want their husbands or their boyfriends seeing that."

Further, she says that women have to *do* more than male singers in order to succeed. Men can sing about being gunslingers, convoy drivers, killers, or whatever, but when a woman sings to an audience, the listener has "to believe that she's singing from personal experience, and that there's a consistency of the message in her songs."

In other words, women aren't supposed to fake it.

Reba admits that singing autobiographical songs wasn't always true about her. From the time she was a child, all she really wanted to do—to paraphrase Gypsy Rose Lee—was to entertain us.

Reba was born in Chockie, Oklahoma on March 28, 1954, the daughter of a rodeo rider. A tomboy from the time she could walk, Reba loved her father's world and became a young roping and barrel racing star herself. To keep a balance, of sorts, Reba's mother taught her, her older brother Dale, and her younger sister Martha to sing, which the McEntires would do as they traveled from rodeo to rodeo. She also instilled in the children a love of country and folk music, particularly the music of Patsy Cline.

Reba made her public debut at the age of five in the lobby of the Cheyenne Hotel, impulsively singing "Jesus Loves Me" for a group of cowboys who were just hanging around. One of the men gave her a nickel, and the experience—singing, not being paid—was so exhilarating that Reba says, "After that, I was hooked."

Because the family was constantly on the road, it was a while before Reba got to do anything serious about music. It finally came together when she, Dale, and Martha were in their early teens. They'd stopped traveling so much so they could concentrate on their schooling. But there was still time for music, and they formed a group called the Singing McEntires, performing throughout their native Oklahoma on weekends and holidays.

After graduating from high school, Reba accompanied her father to the National Rodeo Finals in Oklahoma City. There, Red Steagall, a horse breeder and an up-and-coming country singer himself, gave her the opportunity to sing "The Star-Spangled Banner" before the competition. Steagall was dazzled by the singer's magnificent, clear contralto, so much so that he cut a demo with her. He sent the recording to Polygram/Mercury, and in November of 1975, Reba signed with the label. Her first single was released nearly to the day that she wed rodeo star Charlie Battles, who was thirty-one, divorced, and the father of two boys.

But Reba wasn't calling the shots. The label was telling her what songs to sing and how to sing them, and that hurt her. Her career sputtered along, and in 1978 she was actually booed off the stage in Fort Worth after an uninspired rendition of "Proud Mary." Rather than turn in her spurs, she decided to take charge of things.

To begin with, instead of playing with someone else's band, she organized one of her own. She also started to sing the way *she* wanted to instead of imitating Patsy Cline, Dolly Parton, or Loretta Lynn, or whoever else the record company felt she should be at different times.

Most importantly, she sang the kind of songs she wanted to. At the time, rock and roll was dominating the charts, and Nashville—following the lead of Dolly Parton and others—tried to synthesize the styles and create crossover hits. The results were disastrous, including many of the rockin' tunes on Reba's first two albums. As the decade ended, she resolved only to write and sing songs "my way—from the heart." But they were contemporary in a way that other country songs weren't; Reba's songs were about women confronting and triumphing over life's problems instead of succumbing to them or crying into their pillows.

The newly recountrified Reba reintroduced herself in 1979 with a popular version of Patsy Cline's "Sweet Dreams," then scored a top-ten country single of her own in 1980, "(You Lift Me) Up to Heaven." She followed that with several other hits before "Can't Even Get the Blues" came out in 1983 and went straight to number one.

Well aware that careers in music can fall as fast as they rise, she and Charlie bought a 215 acre ranch in Stringtown, Oklahoma, and when she wasn't on the road, she was helping him to raise cattle.

But hit followed hit for the neotraditionalist, who was one of the handful of singers who was devoted to resuscitating non-rock country music. But her devotion and long stays on the road was not without a price. In June of 1987, she filed for divorce from her husband.

"We had our differences, our ups and downs," she said later. "I guess things really started to go wrong when I made 'Entertainer of the Year' (the prestigious Country Music Association award she won in 1986). Charlie thought it was time for me to slow down, when I was thinking things were just beginning." She says that his suggestion was so hurtful that she was in love with him one day, "and the next day, I was out of love."

Reba moved to Nashville and, since that day, has not seen Charlie or his two sons.

Reba survived the divorce and the backlash from fans who felt that they'd been betrayed, who felt that Reba was no longer the ideal Christian woman, that her uplifting songs were a lie.

"One woman said my songs were the reason she stayed with her husband," Reba recalls. "Another said, 'How dare you? I've had you on a pedestal for years.'"

The anger was a surprise and a disappointment, and Reba answered every letter personally, not explaining what she'd done but asking for people's understanding and compassion.

Meanwhile, she plunged back into her work, her experiences (the listener has "to believe that she's singing from personal experience. . . .") giving a new dimension to her work. Unlike Dolly, she didn't abandon her country sound, but as *Billboard* put it, she "traded in her well-scrubbed cowgirl look for a classy, uptown image."

Result? The following year she won the Grammy for "Best Country Vocal Performance/Female," performed in New York City's bastion of classical music, Carnegie Hall, and had her first platinum record, *Reba McEntire's Greatest Hits*. She made movies, most notably *Tremors* (1990), playing a survivalist who takes on an army of giant worms in the desert, and in June of 1989, she mar-

ried her road manager and longtime friend Narvel
Blackstock. A son, Shelby, was born in February.

Reba had everything: a perfect home life, soaring record sales, and she was constantly in demand on the
road. It was this popularity, in fact, that led to the greatest tragedy in her life.

In March of 1991, Reba was on a concert tour of the
Midwest when she was asked to perform in San Diego,
California, on Friday, March 15. The night was free, but
she had a gig in Fort Wayne, Indiana, on Saturday night;
to make it, she and her entourage would have to fly instead of taking the tour bus. She accepted.

The concert was a smash, ending—as they usually did
—with Reba singing "Sweet Dreams." When it was
over, Narvel convinced his wife that they should stay in
San Diego for the night. She was still fighting a case of
bronchitis that had put her in the hospital in Nashville
just a month before, and he felt it was important for her
to get a good night's sleep. Instead of flying with the
musicians that night, they arranged to take a commercial
flight the next morning.

Both Reba and Narvel were asleep at 1:30 A.M. when
two planes took off from Brown Field, one with the
seven bandmembers and tour manager Jim Hammon,
the second with the stage crew and bandmembers Joe
McGlohon and Pete Finney—Pete having swapped
spots at the last minute with bandmate Michael Thomas.

The twin-engine Hawker Siddeley jet carrying the
band and Hammon was in what pilot Don Holms and
co-pilot Chris Hollinger believed was a flawless ascent to
the east, climbing at two hundred miles an hour. Holms
had just gotten off the radio with a flight service specialist at nearby Montgomery Field, who had assured him
that, yes, it was okay to remain below 3,000 feet. Unfortunately, the specialist—who has never been publicly
identified—assumed that Holms, like the pilot of the

other plane, knew about the Otay Mountains that lay dead ahead. The highest peak was 3,572 feet; what the specialist meant was that it was all right to fly 3,000 feet *above that*.

But Holms knew nothing about the mountains. He was talking about sea level, which would have put him at least 572 feet shy of clearing the mountain. The misunderstanding resulted in tragedy.

At 1:40 A.M., as the plane soared through the dark skies, one wing scraped a peak. The plane cartwheeled ahead, the nose slamming into the cliff, followed by the other wing, and then the rear of the fuselage. The nearly full fuel tanks exploded, and the plane literally disintegrated. From impact to fireball took less than five seconds; all of the passengers perished, never knowing what hit them.

The explosion was visible twenty-five miles away in San Diego, and before there was even any notification of who or what might have been involved, emergency medical teams and volunteers rushed to the sight.

When they reached the still-burning wreckage, Sgt. Michael O'Connor of the San Diego sheriff's office says they found "a grisly scene. Clothing and bits and pieces of broken musical instruments were everywhere."

In addition to the pilot, co-pilot, and Hammon, the dead were Chris Austin, a singer/songwriter; Kirk Capella, the bandleader and keyboardist; Joey Cigainero, a keyboardist; Paula Kaye Evans, a singer; Terry Jackson, the bass player; Tony Saputo, the drummer; and guitarist Michael Thomas. All were in their twenties and thirties.

At 2:30 A.M. in the morning, authorities phoned one of Reba's associates at the Sheraton Harbor Island Hotel. He was told what had happened, and called Reba's room. Narvel answered the phone and was told to come over—something had happened to one of the planes.

As Narvel pulled on his pants and shirt, his wife asked sleepily, "What is it?"

He said, "I don't know yet." Then, deciding that it wasn't fair to lie to his wife, he said, "I think there's been an accident with one of the planes."

"How bad?"

"I don't know," he said, then told Reba to go back to sleep while he looked into it.

Sure.

Instead, Reba went to the bathroom, washed her face, then knelt by the bed and prayed as she waited for her husband to return.

When he did, she says, "It was a nightmare."

Narvel told her that the plane had gone down, but they didn't know how and exactly where, and whether or not any of the passengers were still alive.

"We were hoping and praying that there might be some survivors," Reba says. "We radioed the second plane carrying the crew and Joe and Pete. They got off their plane for a refueling stop in Memphis and were told."

Weeping openly in the plane, the crew and surviving musicians returned to Nashville, where Narvel said that he and Reba would meet them. He told them they'd head out as soon as they'd heard from the rescue team.

But dawn's light confirmed everyone's worst fears: no one had survived the crash. Narvel immediately put in calls to the families of the victims, feeling they should hear the news from a friend, not from TV or newspaper reporters.

Reba remembers, "It was so hard for him to do that. How do you tell a daddy that his boy is dead . . . or a husband that his wife is gone?"

The couple returned to Nashville for the funerals at the Christ Church in Brentwood, Tennessee, stopping en route to see Jim Hammon's wife Debbie. Debbie urged Reba not to let this stop her from performing, which she could tell was on the singer's mind.

"Jim worked all this time to help you get where you are today," Debbie told her. "He'd kick your butt if you thought about quitting."

Waylon Jennings, who had given up his seat on board the Buddy Holly death plane, also phoned Reba with some important advice: "Don't let guilt set in," he said. "There's nothing you could have done."

At the star-studded funeral, Johnny Cash sang the song "Jim I Wore A Tie Today," mentioning each bandmember in the song. While radio stations nationwide honored the fallen entertainers, country stars like Merle Haggard, Charlie Daniels, and Lorrie Morgan pitched in to honor concert dates Reba was unable to fulfill. Benefits featuring the likes of Eddie Rabbitt and Kenny Rogers raised hundreds of thousands of dollars for the families of the dead. One San Diego fan made a particularly touching gesture: the attendee had (illegally) taped the show, then sent the recording to Reba so she would have a treasured memento of the band's final concert.

Reba knew that if she sat around mourning, grief "would have eaten me up. I knew I had to get out there, and I knew I wanted to." So she took Dolly Parton up on her generous offer to lend her friend bandleader Gary Smith, who helped Reba assemble a new band. Incredibly, on April 7, less than a month after the disaster, Reba was back on the road. However, it was several months before she was able to sing her signature song again, "Sweet Dreams," performing it out of deep appreciation for an audience in Wallingford, Connecticut, that sat in a driving rain to listen to her sing.

She also went right back into the recording studio, cutting her saddest and most poignant album, *For My Broken Heart*, which was released in October.

"For me, singing sad songs often has a way of healing a situation," Reba says. "It gets the hurt out in the open —into the light, out of the darkness." Obviously, the music-buying public was able to relate to her pain: *For My Broken Heart* became Reba's most successful album to date, going double-platinum in nine months. By the time she released her twentieth album in December of 1992, *It's Your Call*, Reba was the top-selling artist in the history of MCA/Nashville.

Though Reba freely admits, "I don't think I'll ever stop grieving," she adds, "Evidently, I was not meant to go on that plane. God must have things for me to do."

And she is busy doing them: recording, performing (she agreed to do a remarkable 125 concert dates in 1993), acting, and overseeing her ninety-employee Star-struck Entertainment company, which not only manages her career but handles other entertainers and is heavily into music publishing.

She is also into another business: air safety. After the crash, she founded what she intends to be the safest charter airline company on the planet, Starstruck Aviation Company. However, Reba learned something about the best laid plans of mice and country signers when she survived a close call herself on the night of November 6, 1992. She, Narvel, and three others were onboard Star-struck's Hawker 25 twin-engine jet. After takeoff from Gallatin, Tennessee, en route to a sold-out date in Madison, Wisconsin, the pilot determined that the nose gear wasn't working properly. He turned back, unsure whether the plane would take the stress of landing; everyone braced for a crash that, fortunately, didn't occur. Later, investigators found the cause of the problem: someone had left a flashlight in the gears during inspection.

Reba was understandably shaken by the incident, but she boarded another plane to Wisconsin. Her publicist,

Jennifer Bohler, points out, "She wasn't even late for the show."

But that's what you'd expect from Reba. She still thinks it's tough for women in Nashville: "You have to work about ten times harder," she says, but the key is "don't complain and bitch about it. Just go on with your work." As for her, she intends to keep on doing that.

"I'm going to be ninety years old," she says with a smile, "and I'll still be out there singing. They're going to have to drag me off with one of those old vaudeville hooks."

The Judds

HANK Williams. Tammy Wynette. Loretta Lynn.
Rags-to-riches stories are plentiful in country music, but so much of that success is accidental. Or gradual. Or the result of a manager or entertainer taking the star under their wings. Rarely does someone get to the top behind the kind of drive that propelled Naomi Judd.

Diana Ellen (Naomi) Judd was born on January 11, 1946, in Ashland, Kentucky, the daughter of a gas station operator. Her upbringing was comfortably middle-class, until she was seventeen. Then she met and fell in love with college student Michael Ciminella and became pregnant. At the behest of embarrassed educational authorities, Diana stopped going to school in January of 1964, when she was four months pregnant, taking her lessons in private and graduating alone. The couple eloped on the third of January, and Christina Claire (Wynonna) Ciminella was born on May 30.

Today, Naomi says, "We all make mistakes. I got married when I was seventeen. You can't top that one."

Wynonna adds—somewhat bitterly—"I was brought up with this kind of hanging over me," the fact that she was responsible for her mother losing her middle class paradise at such a young age.

In 1968, Michael was offered a job in the aerospace industry, and the Ciminellas moved from Kentucky to Los Angeles, where daughter Ashley was born. But while the move was a beginning of sorts, it was also an end. Within four years, the marriage was over.

Naomi says it probably would have ended much earlier, except for one thing: "I think it took getting away from Kentucky to give me the courage to get a divorce. I was so guilt-ridden, belonging to the church and not being happy with our marriage."

Michael didn't contest the divorce.

Shortly thereafter, he was transferred to Chicago, while his wife remained in Los Angeles in an effort to give their daughters some sense of continuity. In order to maintain their lifestyle, Diana went to work, holding a variety of jobs from managing a health food store to working as a secretary for the rocking Fifth Dimension to modeling, although she turned down several offers to appear nude in men's magazines.

"I used to get propositions from *Penthouse* and *Playboy* all the time," she says, but "I didn't even have to think twice about that." But not because she was necessarily opposed to the photographs, per se. She was worried what they might do to her reputation, locally. It was difficult enough being a beautiful single mother without having the reputation of a Pet or Playmate hanging over her. (As she was fond of saying later, anytime a man would mistake her as a bimbo because of her looks or accent, she'd say, "I'm divorced and I've been to the circus and I've seen the clowns. This ain't my first rodeo.")

One thing she did to establish her own identity was to go to court to change her name back to Judd. The name

Ciminella would be tough to give over the phone when ordering a pizza.

After a year on her own in California, she yearned for a more down-to-earth lifestyle and moved to Arizona to work at a hospital on an Apache reservation. But she left almost at once "because I couldn't subject my kids to their educational system. It was despicable."

(If you're wondering, by the way, if Naomi has ever heard the term "politically correct," it should be pointed out that what sound like slaps against Italians or Apaches aren't, really. She hates no one: she's simply a blunt, truthful lady.)

Instead, she drove home to her beloved Kentucky and settled in Morrill. There, Diana went to nursing school and got a job as a registered nurse. She says, "We lived in a house with no television, no telephone, and no newspaper. We just had our radio, and on Saturday nights we'd do the wash in our old Maytag wringing washer and listen to the *Grand Ole Opry*."

Those Saturday nights had a profound impact on young Christina. When Diana was at work, her eldest daughter would relieve the long hours of Ashley-sitting by emulating the *Opry* stars. She taught herself to play the guitar and, when her mother was home, they'd sing together, working out lovely harmonies.

Life wasn't all peace and euphony, however. Money was very tight, and Christina was extremely bitter about the divorce and about the responsibilities she had at home. She chowed-down on junk food, put on weight, was teased by the kids at school, and developed an extremely low self-image. She didn't do the cleaning or school work she was supposed to on her own, and she grew increasingly short-tempered and snotty.

Her mother says, "I couldn't get her to do *anything*. We were about to kill each other."

Wynonna admits, "I was a pretty rebellious kid. I al-

COUNTRY MUSIC BABYLON 193

ways had a feeling of insecurity. If it hadn't been for music, I would probably have been a real misfit."

Thinking that a less rural environment might enable Christina to have more friends and wondering if her daughter might even have a career in music, Diana got a job as a nurse at Williamson County Hospital and moved the girls to Nashville in 1979. Christina liked Franklin High School and *loved* the idea of being in Music City—and the possibility, however remote, that she might somehow get to sing professionally some day.

But there was still an enormous amount of tension in the household, and at times Christina considered committing suicide. Diana was upset about Christina's attitude, about how poor they were, and about her own rocky relationships with several boyfriends. She was distraught when one of them, Larry Strickland, "broke my heart," adding that when they split she "stayed up three days and nights, couldn't eat or sleep."

She worked over what would happen to her daughters if she were gone. Not physically, they could always go to live with their father, who was in Ocala, Florida now. She worried about their futures. If she had tried to instill any one idea in her girls, it was that women have to get out there and fight twice as hard to get their due. Neither Christina nor Ashley had quite learned that lesson yet, and she couldn't leave until they had.

Christina thought about ending it all on a number of occasions, though never stronger than when a bitter fight with her mother ended up with the girl leaving the house and staying with her father down in Florida for two months. One night, after having had several drinks, she was driving alone on a dark road. She floored the accelerator, going faster and faster until she was doing nearly ninety miles an hour. The only thing that caused the teenager to stop herself was a strange mix of ego and music. She wanted to sing. She wanted to be a big star.

She wanted to prove to her friends and family that she wasn't a loser, a "lard" as one of her classmates had taken to calling her. She braked the car and headed home. To mother.

"When I say country music saved us," Wynonna says today, "I'm not kidding."

To try and keep them together and happy, Diana bought a cheap cassette recorder and made some crude demos with Christina singing lead, she harmony. She presented these to several record executives with no luck. Naomi recalls two producers sitting behind their big cigars and saying, " 'Well, I'm booked today, but how 'bout coming away with me for the weekend and we'll discuss your music, honey.' " She says today, "Some day I'll write a book and burn them all in hell."

Then, in 1982, the duo got a chance by accident—literally. Diana Maher, the daughter of record producer Brent Maher, ended up in the hospital after a car crash. Diana took care of her, and when the girl recovered, the nurse asked her to give her father one of their tapes.

The girl said she would. When Diana didn't hear from Brent, she got fidgety and a little angry. She says, "I got dressed up and went to his studio. I said, 'Remember me, the one who brought your daughter her pain shots on time?' "

He said he did.

"Well," she told him, handing him another tape, "I'd like you to listen to this."

He promised he would and left it in a stack of tapes he planned to breeze through in the car. A few days later, he got around to popping the duo's tape in the player as he drove home. He recalls that he nearly drove his Mercedes into a ditch, so enthralled was he with Christina's strong, bluesy voice and her mother's sweeter tones. They had potential.

"I want to work with you," he told Diana as soon as

he could get to a phone. When Diana hung up the phone, she screamed with delight and gave her daughter the good news; then they hugged each other for the first time in months.

In March of 1982, Maher took them over to RCA for an audition. The duo sang a song Naomi had written over her break-up with the aforementioned singer, "Change of Heart". The label was as impressed as Maher and signed them, though Brent decided not to rush a record out. He recalls that because the singers "love everything from bluegrass to the Andrews Sisters . . . we worked for almost a year before we ever went in the studio, just trying to narrow it down."

They also did something else: changed their names. Again. "Naomi is from the Bible," says the former Diana, "and Wynonna means 'firstborn,' I think. We still have never figured this out." All she knew is that they sounded more exotic, and that they'd stand out in the minds of deejays and record buyers. Always thinking, that Naomi.

The Judds finally began recording in 1983. Their first single, "Had a Dream," went to number seventeen on the country charts; their second, "Mama He's Crazy," hit number one. The ascent was so quick, mother and daughter didn't even have time to make up. They were still fighting bitterly about nearly everything. Only when they began touring in support of their first album did they finally kiss and make up.

Manager Ken Stilts laughs today, "Wynonna just revolted at every turn, and Naomi was hard-headed. To be honest, there were times I thought it might be best if they didn't continue. I sent them onstage more than once with sunglasses on from crying."

"It was almost like tying two cats' tails together and throwing them over a clothesline," says Wynonna. "We didn't know what might happen." She pauses, then says that it turned out to be a good thing: "We were in each other's faces twenty-four hours a day. We *had* to work it out."

Hit followed hit, and in February of 1985 the Judds were nominated for the Best New Artist Grammy. The first time a country act was so-honored since 1969 when Jeannie C. Riley ("Harper Valley P.T.A.") crossed into the mainstream. They lost the award, but did win an award for Best Country Duo or Group. And the voters weren't just whistling Dixie: before the decade was through, they'd had a total of fourteen number one singles (the twelfth of which was "Change of Heart"), and their first six albums went platinum. Not a year went by that they didn't win an award or two from the Country Music Association. They copped three Grammy Awards. And best of all, they got to work with some of the greatest legends of music, most notably rockabilly pioneer Carl Perkins, who co-wrote and played guitar on their number one hit "Let Me Tell You About Love." For Naomi, who used to listen to Perkins' classic "Blue Suede Shoes" in 1956, it was one of the high points of her career.

Meanwhile, their personal lives had their ups and downs. Wynonna became engaged to musician Tony King, but after several years of conflicting schedules— he, touring with his group Matthews, Wright, and King —they decided to break it off.

"We just don't want to incorporate a marriage in between tours," she said at the time, then assured her fans that she wanted to get married *some* day. "To people in the South, especially," she says, "when you get to a certain age, if you're not married, something is wrong with you."

Naomi, however, finally straightened things out with former boyfriend Larry Strickland. The man over whom she was once despondent and whom she hadn't seen in a year-and-a-half was now "my own personal, custom-designed-for-Naomi-Judd Prince Charming." She said "I do" in May of 1989.

The next seven months were among the happiest in Naomi's life. Her marriage was ideal, the relationship with Wynonna couldn't be better, and Ashley was going great guns as a French major at the University of Kentucky. In fact, Ashley had spent the last few months of 1988 in France, which briefly caused her family a great deal of concern. On December 21, she missed her flight home by twenty minutes and boarded another plane. The Judds didn't know this, however, and spent eight awful hours not knowing whether she was alive or dead when the plane she was supposed to be on, Pan Am flight 103, exploded over Lockerbie, Scotland.

Naomi knew she had a lot to be thankful for, but that ended on January 1, 1990. After spending a restful night at home, she awoke feeling ill.

Six years before, when she and Wynonna were just getting their career under way, Naomi had felt worn down and a doctor told her she was suffering from cytomegalovirus—a largely untreatable but usually nonthreatening infection which may result in a fever or no symptoms at all. However, it's difficult to differentiate CMV from infectious mononucleosis and viral hepatitis. Her doctor told her, at the time, that all she needed was rest.

For the first few days of the new year, the lethargy and aches were more pronounced than ever before and retired nurse Naomi now had her doubts that it was CMV. She says, "I got my medical records and the results of a liver enzyme test" (which had been performed at the time). Somehow, her former doctor had missed the fact that there was liver damage. Together with her other symptoms, she knew that she might have hepatitis, not CMV.

Ashley happened to be home with a virus, and when Naomi took her to the doctor, she says, "I pulled a nurse back into an examining room and asked her to do some tests on me for hepatitis."

Several days later, the day before she was to begin the Judds' winter tour, Wynonna went along when Naomi went to the doctor. He didn't beat around the bush: "You're very ill," he said. "You have hepatitis."

Initially, Naomi's concern was not for herself but for Wynonna's career and her husband's health. Neither the doctor nor Naomi knew for certain how she had contracted the disease, though they suspected that during her nursing days, infected blood or unsanitary conditions had done the trick. However, he assured her that it wasn't contagious under normal circumstances, and tests subsequently confirmed that her husband was uninfected.

Both Wynonna and Larry were extremely supportive and understanding, though at times it was Naomi who had to be the strong one as family members would occasionally weep in her presence. She also felt awful for devoted manager Ken Stilts, whom she knew would feel "helpless" because he wouldn't be able to "fix this one for me" as he had so many troublesome business situations. She also felt terrible for all the people who worked for the Judds: "If the girls don't sing," she told *Us* Magazine, "the boys don't eat."

The tour was cancelled, though to keep from disappointing all of the fans of the Judds and to keep up a cash flow for their employees, Naomi agreed to do all of the larger venues, such as a sold-out ten thousand seat gig in Austin, Texas, on February 9, another at the Houston Astrodome on February 19, another a week later at the Hoosier Dome in Indianapolis, for 22,500 fans, and so on. The public was told that the schedule was being shortened because Naomi had been severely weakened by the flu and needed to rest up between concerts. So there wouldn't be ill-will among the promotors who'd arranged the other dates, a few were sworn to secrecy and told the truth: to a one, they were as understanding as could be.

Given Naomi's condition, there was a big difference between accepting the few engagements and actually seeing them through. Arriving at the airport in Austin for the first date, Naomi was so weak that she had to sit on the floor next to the gate to rest—hoping, all the while, that fans wouldn't recognize her and "come up and talk to me and I wouldn't be coherent. I ached, and I couldn't finish a sentence because I had no concentration."

She was able to get out of bed for the show, but had her driver stand on her side of the stage. "I told him my greatest fear was that I would pass out," but she also instructed him that "if he saw that I started to ramble or lose it . . . just to come and get me."

Wynonna says, "Seeing her helplessness was *horrible*."

Naomi made it through the concerts without arousing public suspicion that anything was wrong. However, she admits that there were times when her illness made her a bit reckless. For instance——

While sitting in her little bedroom at the back of her tour bus, the Juddmobile, which was taking the duo from Nashville to Indianapolis, she suddenly had an anxiety attack.

"I thought I was in my coffin and I was dying," Naomi says.

To prove to herself she wasn't dead, she ripped back the curtains of the window, but she couldn't see anything because they were frosted over. In a panic, she tore off her pajama top and pushed her chest against the window until the frost melted and she could look out.

"The next day," she says, "I had a good laugh . . .

because I thought what if some truck driver had looked over and seen more of Mama Judd than he expected to see?"

When the Judds finished up their commitments in March, Naomi decided to pay a visit to the Mayo Clinic. She'd been reading up on hepatitis, and had concluded from her symptoms—"things," she said, "I had not even thought to tell my doctor"—that what she had was not what they thought, but a potentially fatal form of the disease, chronic active hepatitis.

Keeping her unlucky streak alive, the four-day stay at the clinic confirmed her worst fears. Though there's no cure for the disease, the doctors put her on interfon, which helps control viral infections.

Some days were better than others, though the ones that Naomi remembers most vividly were those "when I couldn't get out of bed. I was in the fetal position in a dark room, unable to brush my teeth or anything."

Larry was constantly at her side, and both Wynonna and Ashley came at once whenever she needed them. However, Naomi was also ghoulishly pragmatic. Since Wynonna's marriage was off, and Ashley was constantly working—the stunning young woman had abandoned French to pursue an acting career—grandchildren were not in the cards for the near future. One day, Naomi decided to get in the car, go out, and buy loads of presents for them, just in case she didn't live to be a grandmother.

"It was a beautiful sunny day," she says, looking back on it, "but it was darker than a million midnights."

As if things weren't bad enough, on July 8, Naomi discovered a large lump in her right breast. Her doctor opted to remove it, but because of her impaired liver function they were unable to give her any medication other than "a pinch of lidocaine" (a local anesthetic) before she went under the knife.

For reasons unknown, no sooner had the surgery begun than Naomi's blood pressure began to plummet. The crash cart was rushed over—the cart containing everything a doctor might need to revive a patient in shock —and the operating room was plunged into what Naomi describes as "pandemonium." Meanwhile she says, "I'm lying there thinking, 'Boy, this just ain't my year.'" Quick work brought her blood pressure back to normal, and the doctors finished the procedure. Mercifully, the lump was benign.

Throughout the year, rumors circulated among reporters and fans about Naomi's health. Upset by the rumors, Naomi finally decided to go public with the truth and, on October 19, the singers held a press conference in Nashville. There, Naomi not only talked about the hepatitis that had made the year such a difficult one, but also announced that she and Wynonna were undertaking a final, extensive concert tour, after which she'd be retiring from performing and recording.

Fans were shocked and saddened. A few cynics complained that the two women simply couldn't get along, and that Wynonna was just as happy to go out on her own.

Wynonna called the suggestion ridiculous.

"Why would I *want* to go on my own?" she asked the *Los Angeles Times*. "I had it made. My life was so good the last few years that I felt like I had won the lottery. Most of the problems were the first two years, but the rumors continued."

Naomi husbanded her strength so she wouldn't have to cancel one date, fail to sign a single autograph, or otherwise disappoint a single fan on the tour. (The degree to which Naomi and Wynonna hated disappointing fans was made abundantly clear on August 27, 1988, when they were scheduled to appear at the Iowa State Fair and were also asked to perform for President Rea-

gan in San Diego that morning. Rather than cancel the
evening show, they raced back to Des Moines; incredibly, the show started just five minutes late.)

When the tour was just about over, Naomi was grate-
ful to her crew, to her fans, and to her God: "That I was
alive to finish the Farewell Tour," she told them later,
"meant everthing to me, to say goodbye with class and
dignity in every city."

Ironically, Naomi survived the grueling schedule just
fine, but it took its toll on Wynonna. For a full forty-
eight hours before their December 4, 1991 concert in
Murfreesboro, Tennessee—the last of the tour, it sold
out in seventeen minutes—Wynonna was so hoarse that
she couldn't speak. Naomi summoned a doctor from
Vanderbilt University, who couldn't find anything physically wrong with Wynonna. It was evidently an hysterical illness, and the two credit prayer and faith with
restoring the singer's voice to near-normal before the
performance.

The concert was filled with tears, ovations, and love,
and as much as it marked an end it also signified a beginning—that of Wynonna's solo career.

Throughout the tour, Wynonna had been working on
her debut album. "I'd come home from being on the
road with Mom just exhausted," she says, and "there
were days when I'd look at my producer like, 'If you
think you're going to make me sing today, I'm going to
start crying.' "

But she had to do it, mostly for herself. She says, "It's
always been Naomi and *isn't she cute and entertaining and
beautiful*. And then here's Wynonna, this kind of a kid,
kind of goofy." She had to win this battle to prove she
had what it takes and also to find out if people were "as
interested in Wynonna as they were in the Judds.

"It was death and rebirth," she says. "I didn't feel I
had any identity as Wynonna. I was in shock, and I

didn't feel I had any *right* to carry on without her; Mom had worked so hard, and I was just 'Naomi Judd's kid.' The guilt factor was pretty high because I didn't feel worthy." She laughs. "For eight years, I could never even find my *shoes*, so on the road she took care of everything."

Most of the work was for Wynonna's benefit, of course, but part of it was also for her mother. She didn't want to burden Naomi with the guilt that she'd been responsible for retiring *two* performers.

The worrying was for naught: the debut album, *Wynonna*, rocketed to the top of the record charts, helped along by a sell-out tour.

Naomi remembers, "Wynonna would call me every day (from the road) and say, 'Mommy, you're not in the room next to me, and I can't just push seven and your room number and talk to you instantly. I don't like this.' "

But Wynonna overcame that. Being alone, she says, has forced her "to strive to find the positive without feeling like something's been taken from me." And she *has* come into her own. In fact, even though her mother didn't quite agree with some of the soulful or rock-oriented selections she'd recorded, Wynonna came to realize they didn't *have* to agree. She reached a point where she was no longer "so worried about not pissing everybody off." She even did something her mother would *never* have allowed: she went bungee jumping—a big leap, literally and figuratively, for the singer.

However, both women know that while performing has been taken from Naomi, she's still here and intends to be here for quite some time. In the middle of 1992, she returned to the Mayo Clinic for tests; miraculously, her liver functions, though still below normal, were better than ever and it appeared that the disease was in remission, which Naomi says "is the most beautiful word in the world."

Naomi also *felt* better than she had for months, so much so that she accepted a part in Kenny Rogers' film *Rio Diablo*, which went before the cameras in the fall of 1992. Not once during the many back-to-back fourteen hour days did she fail to show up, bright-eyed and bushy-tailed, amazing the cast and crew. Ashley may have had a head start (co-starring on the TV series *Sisters* and *Star Trek: The Next Generation*), but "Mama Judd" loves the camera and vice versa. She says she'd love to act again.

Will the Judds ever perform together again? It seems likely, in fact, inevitable, for as Naomi told Robert Schuller on *The Hour of Power* TV show in October of 1992, not only was her illness "in full remission," but she will "always want to jump on the bus." And what Naomi wants, Naomi gets.

It's been an incredible ride for both women, but friends and fans alike can take this to the bank: the best is yet to come.

Lorrie Morgan and Keith Whitley

L ORRIE Morgan was born to sing.

For one thing, she was born Loretta Lynn Morgan, not planned, but a happy coincidence, since it was 1960 and the other Loretta Lynn had not yet made a name for herself.

For another thing, Lorrie was the daughter of silky-voiced country singer George Morgan, known as "the entertainer's entertainer," whose song "Candy Kisses" was the number one country hit in 1949. (He was also a great kidder, and the man who was responsible for starting the unofficial "Ugly List" which, each week, named the ten ugliest people on the *Grand Ole Opry* radiocast.)

As a little girl, Lorrie would stage performances in her home, charging her family admission to hear her sing. "I probably made twenty-five cents a show back then," she says, "which wasn't bad for a six-year-old."

With her father's help, she got the chance to charge the *public* to hear her in 1973, when she was thirteen and sang "Paper Roses" on the stage of the *Opry*. The audience gave the talented youngster a standing ovation, and Lorrie says, "From that point on, I said, 'This is for me.'"

She admits, however, that having a famous father was

a double-edged sword. "It was hard to get taken seriously," she says, because "I was always 'George's little girl.' I guess that's what happens when everybody knows you while you're growing up." As a result, when she turned pro, she says, "I was always getting doors slammed in my face. I was kind of like wallpaper in Nashville. Fresh new faces were coming into town, and those were the ones who were getting all the attention." However, lest she be regarded as bitter, she adds, "My dad was probably my greatest idol of all, and to be identified with him is about the biggest compliment anybody could give me."

When a heart attack claimed her father in 1975, Lorrie dealt with her grief by taking his band and going on tour, playing every venue they could in an effort to build a grassroots following. She eventually signed with Hickory Records and, in June of 1984, was made a member of the *Grand Ole Opry*—the youngest member in the history of that august organization.

By then, Lorrie had switched her label affiliation to MCA, and her smooth ride to the top was suddenly and cruelly derailed. MCA wanted to sell her as a "sophisticated" singer and asked her to sever her ties to the *Opry*. When she refused—politely, but adamantly—the label dropped her, and she was slapped with the reputation of being temperamental.

Her career stalled, an ill-advised marriage failed, and Lorrie had to provide for herself and her six-year-old daughter Morgan. She went back to touring on the club-and-honky-tonk circuit, sang at the *Opry* when she could, and cut demos for other record companies.

At one session in 1985, she met Kentucky-born singer Keith Whitley, a rising star who had been playing serious guitar from the age of six and was only fifteen when, in 1971, he released his first album (with friend Rickey Skaggs), *Cry from the Cross*.

Whitley toured with various bands until 1983 when he moved to Nashville, signed with RCA Records, and began his steady climb to the top, culminating with the number one country hit "Don't Close Your Eyes" in 1988. Other number one hits followed, including "When You Say Nothing At All" and "I'm No Stranger to the Rain."

Whitley was married when he met Lorrie, but he was entranced by her. When he found himself single less than a year later ("Lorrie had nothing to do with that," he said), he asked her to marry him. Keith and Lorrie tied the knot in November of 1986.

Whitley was being honest when he said that Lorrie had nothing to do with breaking up his marriage. The relationship had come apart because he was an alcoholic. The singer had nearly ruined his career and lost his life several times because of drink. He once said he "grew up with fast cars, motorcycles and drinkin'," laboring under the delusion that "in order to be successful . . . I had to emulate some of the people who had been idols of mine. I thought drinkin' was a part of it, but I found out the hard way that it's not."

For Whitley, "the hard way" was several brushes with death. When he was seventeen, he and a friend got drunk and went driving, at speeds of up to 120 miles an hour. Not surprisingly, they crashed; Whitley survived, but his friend did not.

When he was nineteen, he lost control of a car and ended up flying off a cliff into an icy river; luck was with him again, and he came away with just a broken collarbone.

Incredibly, none of this stopped him from drinking and, thanks to alcohol, Whitley's first two albums were recorded under dismal conditions. There were many times when he couldn't remember lyrics, slurred his words, and even went to sleep in the studio, right in the middle of a session. When it came time to cut his third record, Joe Galante of RCA recalls, "It just came down to the point of us having to say, 'Keith, get your life together or go find another home.' To his credit, he did go out and wrestle with the devil."

From the start, Lorrie was patient and compassionate about his problem, which wasn't exactly uncommon in the music business. Keith was a good man at heart, and she hoped that her love and the birth of their son Jesse in June of 1987 would help to get him on the wagon.

But Whitley wasn't able to stay on the wagon for very long. He stayed sober for the sessions or during concerts, but then would go out or go home, have a drink to relax, and find that he wasn't able to stop.

On May 9, 1989, just a few weeks after completing his new album, *I Wonder What You Think of Me*, Whitley started drinking sometime early in the morning. Lorrie wasn't home, and he phoned his mother around 9:00 A.M., bemoaning the fact that he was letting so many people down, people who really cared about him.

She told him that wasn't so. They were there for him. They wanted to help him.

Nonetheless, when he hung up the phone just before ten, he continued to drink for at least another hour.

Lorrie and the children weren't home when Whitley's brother-in-law stopped by at half-past-noon. He found the singer sprawled on the floor and called for an ambulance, but it was too late: the thirty-three-year-old was dead of alcohol poisoning. His blood alcohol level was .477, over four times the minimum level of intoxication in most states.

Lorrie was devastated, but she dealt with the loss in the same way she had when her father died: she plunged into her work, going back on tour a week after Keith's death. Not that that was any kind of escape, as many wags in Nashville charged. It was quite the opposite, in fact. Lorrie says that she and her road manager, Mike—who was a close friend of Keith's—"will often reminisce with me about him. And sometimes we just can't quit talkin'. It's strange how sometimes I need to do that, and other times I just can't."

Four months to the day after his death, Keith's posthumously released single "I Wonder What You Think of Me" hit number one, and a month after that Lorrie accepted an award given to Whitley by the Country Music Association for best single record of the year ("I'm No Stranger to the Rain"). She says she's a little bitter about the fact that he's more popular in death than he was in life, and she came up with a tribute of her own to her late husband, laying her vocals over his on " 'Til a Tear Becomes a Rose," a heartfelt and unforgettable duet that won her a slew of awards.

Even before " 'Til a Tear Becomes a Rose," Lorrie's career had begun to build up steam. She toured with Clint Black and record sales blossomed. Her 1989 album *Leave the Light On* is just shy of platinum, and her 1991 release *Something in Red* is gold and well on the way to sales of one million copies.

In March of 1991 she also began putting her personal life back together when she began dating Black's bus driver, Brad Thompson; the two were married in October of that year.

"With the type of career I'm in," she says, "I need somebody who is a constant in my life."

Her marriage was the high of 1991. The low that year was a visit to her doctor in which endometriosis—uterine cells growing elsewhere—was found "so I ended up needing a hysterectomy."

Lorrie's life is now back on track and her career is blooming, though neither she nor country fans will ever forget Whitley whose brilliant music, brief career, and sad end are all too common in Country Music Babylon.

Lynn Anderson

USUALLY, it's the guys who do time.

Paycheck. Cash. Merle Haggard. Prison's nothing new for country singers. In fact, in many circles it's considered a rite of passage, a badge of honor.

But when a lady singer goes to jail, even in these relatively enlightened times, that's news. Especially when it's a lady whose career was built, in part, on her image as a well-scrubbed, just-off-the-farm type.

Lynn Anderson was born in Grand Forks, North Dakota, on September 26, 1947. She's the daughter of Liz Anderson, a country singer and songwriter who had a modest career from 1964 to the early 1970s and wrote Haggard's smash "(All My Friends Are Gonna Be) Strangers."

Raised in Sacramento, where her father Casey sold used cars and wrote songs on the side, Lynn was only interested in horses during her formative years, winning one hundred–odd trophies over the years, including the title of California Horse Show Queen in 1966.

But Lynn also had a lovely voice, and when she was nineteen, at her parents' urging, she took on a different kind of challenge, entering and winning a singing contest being sponsored by a local TV show, *Country Cor-*

ners. After that she was hooked on music, and by the time she was twenty, the wholesome, sweet-voiced blonde was a regular on *The Lawrence Welk Show* in 1967–68, making her network TV's only country singer. After her stint with Welk, Lynn appeared on *The Ed Sullivan Show*, *The Dean Martin Show*, and other programs, and also got herself a contract with Chart Records where (talk about star treatment!) she also worked as a secretary. But that proved to be a smart move, because it not only helped to pay the bills, it helped get her albums into stores.

"I was taking orders for my own records," she smiles, "and if Handleman Distributing would call and order one thousand copies, I'd tell them they were selling like crazy. Usually, I sold some product that way."

But Lynn's recording career didn't chart until she married songwriter Glenn Sutton in May of 1969 and moved to Columbia Records the following year. Her first single there was her husband's "Stay There 'Til I Get There," which went to number three on the country charts. Then she cut Joe South's "(I Never Promised You A) Rose Garden." The song hadn't done anything for South, and Lynn recorded it only because she and her band had finished a recording session fifteen minutes early and, with nothing else on-hand, figured why not?

Why not indeed! "(I Never Promised You A) Rose Garden" was a number one hit for five weeks in December and January of 1970; it also went to number three on the pop charts and won Lynn a Grammy for best female vocalist.

Glenn wrote and produced Lynn's next number one smash, "You're My Man," which spent two weeks on top of the country charts in June of 1971 and earned her the Country Music Association award for female artist of the year. Lynn took two other Sutton songs to number one, though the singer admits "it caused a little friction"

when the talented, lovely, dark-haired Jody Miller had a
hit with Glenn's co-authored "There's a Party Goin'
On" the following year.

Truth is, that was the beginning of the end for the
Anderson-Sutton union, creatively and personally. In
1977, after ten years of marriage and one daughter, Lisa;
after increasingly vituperative creative differences; after
time apart as Glenn worked with other artists; and after
three years without Lynn having a hit single, the couple
divorced. Lynn says that their love hadn't so much died
as gone comatose; she saw no reason to live that way.

Later that year, while riding in a rodeo, Lynn found
love again in the person of super-rich Harold "Spook"
Stream III, of the powerful oil and ranch family, the
Louisiana Streams. The two were married on Valentine's
Day, 1978, and Lynn was back in the country top ten in
1979 with "Isn't It Always Love." After that, she and
Spook had a son, William, and a daughter, Melissa, and
Lynn retired to look after them. She says, "I had won
the awards and had a million-selling record, so I thought
it was a natural progression for me at that point to
change my priorities."

However, Lynn quickly found that she wasn't happy
amongst the Streams. Her own folks were easygoing
people, but her in-laws were far more uptight and didn't
approve of show business—and, implicitly, of her.
Morever, Spook's involvement with ranching and horses
kept him on the road constantly. She could've stayed
married to Glenn if she didn't want to see much of her
husband. And when Spook *was* home there was tension
and fighting about her retirement, which she regretted,
and what he perceived to be the duties of a southern
wife.

Lynn saw no point in living that way and, in 1981,
when Melissa was just six months old, Lynn left the family digs in Louisiana and returned to her 140 acre spread

in Nashville. She needed time to think, time to decide whether she wanted to get a divorce and return to singing. Spook made up her mind for her: two weeks after she left, he filed for divorce in Louisiana. Lynn first learned about it on the evening news, and says, "I couldn't believe it."

To avoid messy publicity that would have dirtied the Streams, they agreed that Lynn would retain custody of the children. Needing to earn a living, Lynn got back into music, recording background vocals for other singers, then scoring a top-ten duet with Gary Morris in 1984, "You're Welcome to Tonight." After that, she went label hopping and suffered a (to date) unbroken dry spell. She says she has had trouble reigniting her career because "There's a lot of time and expense that goes into making somebody a 'star,' and having the company put all that effort into me, just to have me walk away from it, they were understandably shy about putting all their guns behind me again."

However, Spook wasn't shy about using *his* guns—his legal guns. Deciding that his kids would be better off with him than with a singer, he initiated a custody suit that got ugly, real ugly. Lynn got so riled and so verbally abusive that Spook had to obtain a court order to keep her from abusing him in front of the children.

But keeping her feelings in check has never been one of Lynn's strong suits, and with thirteen-year-old William and eleven-year-old Melissa within earshot, she cursed out Spook again. She ended up serving a two-day sentence in a Nashville jail, in October of 1992, for violating the court order.

Okay, it wasn't *hard* time, but she had joined the ranks of country stars who, as Johnny Cash puts it, "Have sat and watched the iron bars rust."

But rather than let her weekend stay get her down, Lynn sang for the other inmates. David Warren, a spokesperson for Davidson County Sheriff Hank Hillin, says, "From what I was told, she was very entertaining."

As of this writing, the custody battle rages on, and Lynn is still trying to get her career back in gear. But she's in remarkably good humor, still trying to reignite her career. She says she has enjoyed the ups and can tolerate the downs: after all, as she points out, no one ever promised *her* a rose garden.

Kenny Rogers

KENNY Rogers recently said that it was "inevitable" that he get into country music: "Everyone with my surname, like Jimmy and Roy and David, seemed to be into it."

Well, it wasn't *quite* that cut-and-dried for Kenneth Donald Rogers, but it makes a nice, short, sound-bite of a story to tell when you're riding an elevator with a fan.

Born in Houston on August 21, 1938, the son of a fiddle-playing dock worker, Rogers didn't start out singing country. In high school, he and his band the Scholars were into that newfangled rock-and-roll.

"That was the mid-fifties," he says, "and not too many kids were forming bands—rock-and-roll wasn't exactly looked upon favorably in too many places. We caught some flak from folks about it."

But not enough to dissuade him. Over in Lubbock, Buddy Holly and his Crickets were also just starting out and fighting the same kind of prejudices, though Holly was fortunate enough to score a number one national hit, "That'll Be the Day," in 1957. That encouraged the Scholars, and their record, "That Crazy Feeling," went gold the following year. Rogers got to perform it on

American Bandstand, though the group was unable to follow with another hit, and disbanded.

After a semester at the University of Houston, Rogers joined a succession of groups, including the Bobby Doyle Trio, the Lively Ones, and the New Christy Minstrels. In 1967, he and three fellow Minstrels left to form the First Edition, which was signed by Warner's Reprise label. The group's "Just Dropped In (To See What Condition My Condition Was In)" was a top-five pop chart hit in early 1968, and in 1969 they followed it with the smash "Ruby, Don't Take Your Love To Town."

The group was renamed Kenny Rogers and the First Edition, but the hits dwindled, and in 1975, Rogers went off as a solo act. He signed with the Nashville wing of United Artists, and though his first album failed to make much of an impact, his second album's second single was a mammoth hit. Incredibly, the song almost wasn't cut! With just a quarter-of-an-hour of studio time left and thirty songs in the can, Rogers had wanted to lock the album up. But his producer, Larry Butler, encouraged him to learn and cut one more song, which two other artists had already turned down.

Butler says, "I ran the song down with the band, played it for them one time, we rehearsed it one time, we turned the machines on, and . . . we cut the song in fifteen minutes."

The song, "Lucille," made it onto the album, was released as a single in 1977, sold over a million copies, was a country and pop chart hit, won Rogers a Grammy and other awards, and put the big man with the beard over the top as a country *and* pop star. He followed it with another number one hit, "Daytime Friends," a song that Elvis had been slated to record, and then with the number one smash "Every Time Two Fools Collide," a duet with Dottie West—not what the industry expected from the fast-rising solo star.

But, says Rogers, "Anybody who's afraid to tamper with his image has a limited time in this business. Music is ever-changing and you have to go with it."

There was great demand for Rogers in Las Vegas, and he went, softening his country sound somewhat, allowing his gravelly voice to play across the musical spectrum. His popularity grew, along with his bank account. Before long, Rogers was earning a minimum of $100,000 a concert and doing one hundred-plus dates each year. And those ten million in earnings didn't even include record royalties and movie projects.

Like Dolly Parton before him, he was accused by some of his country fans as selling out. "Up to a certain point it was like a *Rocky* story," he says. "Then there was a certain backlash." But Rogers was pragmatic. He says though he has a fond place in his heart for his days with the Bobby Doyle Trio, when he was playing jazz in clubs for $125 a week, "I can't do that anymore." He says, "I have to make a certain amount of money to cover payroll, which has grown like mad."

Rogers was more successful establishing a singing career than he was settling into a comfortable personal life. His first two marriages, to high school girlfriends, lasted a year each; the first one produced a daughter who Rogers rarely saw, Carole Lynn, born in 1958. A third marriage lasted twelve years and produced a son, Kenneth II, born in 1964.

"The marriage problem was my fault," Rogers says. "I was so afraid of not being successful, professionally, that I sacrificed those relationships."

He was still with the First Edition when he met Marianne Gordon, an actress who had appeared in *Thoroughly Modern Millie* and *Rosemary's Baby* and had been a regular on TV's *Hee Haw* since 1971. Marianne was going through a divorce of her own when Rogers stopped by to visit a friend on the set in 1974. Kenny and Marianne began dating and married in October of 1977. They had a son, Christopher Cody, on December 4, 1981, who was born three weeks premature and overcame hyaline membrane disease, the same ailment that had claimed President and Mrs. Kennedy's son Patrick in 1963. As the new decade dawned, Rogers's home life finally seemed secure.

The singer continued to score massive chart successes, with songs such as "The Gambler" in 1978, which won a pair of Grammy Awards and inspired a series of made-for-TV movies starring Rogers; "Lady" in 1980, which became his first number one pop chart single and his fourth million-seller; and duets with pop star Sheena Easton ("We've Got Tonight"), Dolly Parton ("Islands in the Stream" and "Real Love"), and Ronnie Milsap ("Make No Mistake, She's Mine").

For a star of his stature, Rogers was surprisingly untouched by scandal. The divorces were behind him, his relationship with Marianne was stable, and no one really gave a hoot when the tabloids went into graphic detail about Rogers getting rid of his gut by undergoing liposuction. After everything that Michael Jackson had done to himself, Rogers's trendy cosmetic surgery seemed mild.

The truth is, Rogers is a friendly and generous guy, so what was there *to* say? It was hardly news when Marianne admitted that she didn't like it when he went at it hot and heavy on-screen with sexy Erin Gray in his theatrical motion picture debut, the flop *Six Pack* (1982). It didn't help his wife's feelings of insecurity when he admitted to *People* Magazine, "In order for it to *look* believable . . . there's *got* to be stimulation and motivation." However, he acknowledged that "that's potentially destructive at home," and decided that future projects would be Disney-clean.

"More than anything else in the world," he said of his

marriage, "I want this one to work out. It's just not fair to put it in jeopardy."

But was the gambler just talking through his ten-gallon hat? Possibly. Rogers's luck ran out in September of 1992 when one-time topless dancer Sue Ann Lenderman, a twenty-five-year-old advertising copywriter in Dallas, filed a lawsuit that told a startlingly kinky tale of a guy who didn't take his love to town, but to AT&T.

Sue Ann claimed that she was introduced to Rogers through a Dallas businessman whom she had met at a party. Sue Ann claimed that Rogers maintained a toll-free number which gave callers a recorded message. Only a select group of women had the number, and the contents of the message changed regularly, although according to Sue Ann, they were always sexual in nature. She claimed when he had a new message, he signaled his women via beepers he'd provided.

"The so-called messages were nothing more than filthy fantasies," Sue Ann says. "He's a sicko. Kenny's fantasies were revolting, humiliating and degrading."

After the women listened to them, Rogers allegedly called and, according to Sue Ann, the things the singer said during the live, follow-up conversations "were so despicable and disgusting I can't even bring myself to tell you about them. You wouldn't even be able to print the things he said to me."

Sue Ann says she endured several weeks of calls because Rogers and his friend are "very important people" and she feared he might put roadblocks in front of her advertising career. But when she finally did tell Rogers she wanted out, she says he continued to call. At that point, she claims, she was forced to see a psychologist because it was tough for her to trust people after what Rogers had done and because she claimed she had awful flashbacks whenever she saw the singer on TV.

Sue Ann says that by that time, she had no choice but

to tell Rogers that if he didn't leave her alone *and* pay her a sum of money, she was going to go public. Negotiations reportedly were held, but they fell through and Sue Ann went ahead with her lawsuit.

Rogers did not credibly refute the charges. He's not obliged to, of course; it's not like he's running for political office. He admitted to the press that he'd tried to get Sue Ann to go away without publicity, offering her what he called a "reasonable figure" for her troubles. But, he said, "she had the audacity to request one million dollars," at which point he told her where to go. Rogers added, "It seems obviously clear that she is doing this for the money. We feel this is a case of extortion and a countersuit will be filed in response to her lawsuit." He added, "I deeply regret this embarrassment to my family."

One of Rogers's attorneys, James Linn, says, "The whole thing is absurd," while another, James Rolfe, calls the suit "totally frivolous."

Of course, that's what lawyers are expected to say. The question is, are they correct?

Maybe.

Sue Ann was not exactly naive: she had been a topless dancer. And her charges of having suffered psychological damage, while not implausible, certainly give her the appearance of being a golddigging opportunist. Her attorney, Gary Richardson, says no, but then, that's what you'd expect *him* to say.

Unfortunately for Kenny, while Sue Ann's background made her a plaintiff of dubious merit, she wasn't alone. Once the former topless dancer had come forward, it was open season on Rogers and his libido.

On October 20, 1992, Lisa Applewhite, a twenty-six-year-old nursing student from Dallas, sued the star, alleging a sexual assault. According to Lisa's suit, she was introduced to Rogers by a mutual friend in September of

1990. An aspiring actress, Lisa was told that if she met the singer in his hotel, he'd help her get a part in a movie. Instead, she says, he pulled her "down next to him on the bed. Instantly he had his hands on me, grabbing my breasts." Wrenching free, she says she left the room.

However, Rogers reportedly phoned, apologized, and promised Lisa work if she'd phone his eight hundred number. She did, and says she "listened to the recording and it was filthy. I heard Kenny using my name and describing a sexual fantasy he had involving me, another girl and him."

She says that he called often—once, at the office where she worked. Disgusted, Lisa put the call on the intercom so everyone could hear him say, "Honey, I want you to sit in a chair and touch yourself while I talk to you."

After calling her once or twice a week for two months, Kenny stopped phoning, and Lisa put Rogers from her mind—until she read about Sue Ann's lawsuit. She says she decided, then, to come forward "to put a stop to this pervert."

Lisa's lawyer, Gary Richardson, adds, "We believe many other women will soon come forward with more shocking allegations about Mr. Rogers."

Richardson proved himself to be a prophet. A third lawsuit was filed against Rogers the following month, this one by thirty-two-year-old mother-of-two Lori Ann Walker. She says that she first met Kenny in September of 1990 and he invited her to a concert, sending a stretch limousine to collect her. She says that an eight-month-long affair followed and offers, as proof, a graphic description of the half-dollar sized hole below his navel where he was liposuctioned. What finally turned her off, she said, was the three-way sex Kenny reportedly enjoyed with her and a television personality. ("A pack of lies" is how the TV personality describes her alleged participation.)

When Lori tried to break the relationship off, she says Kenny threatened to make public her involvement in the three-ways. The pressure, says Lori, caused her to suffer, what her complaint describes as "extreme emotional distress," after which she filed her million-dollar-lawsuit claiming "mental pain and anguish."

As of this writing, the three cases (with more reportedly in the wings) are still making their way through the legal system. Kenny has filed a complete denial in each case.

Through it all, Marianne has stood by her husband and, when you get down to it, Kenny says that that's all that matters to him. Unfortunately, the messy confrontations *have* cast a pall over his career and good works. (Rogers has routinely given ten percent of his salary to charity and in 1982 he used one million dollars of his own money to kick off a program to feed the hungry.)

But, says Kenny with more than a touch of irony, "Good news doesn't always make good copy. All I can do is go on doin' my best, regardless."

True. And when all of this is said and done, the fact remains that it'll be the recorded music, and not the "sheet" music, for which Kenny Rogers is remembered.

Mac Davis

GROWING up in Lubbock, Texas, home of Buddy Holly and his Crickets, Mac Davis used to think that "it was sissy to sing." Part of that was due to his upbringing, his domineering father having made him join the church choir when he was ten. Part of it was the perception that there was something wrong with any guy who wouldn't rather work on cars or motorcycles or go cruising for chicks.

Then, one day in 1957, Mac happened to see one of the Crickets back in town after a tour. He was driving around in a new convertible that was jam-packed with girls. Mac did a quick about-face, deciding right then and there that singing was the career for him.

Born on January 21, 1942, Davis was a bright student who skipped two grades but had very low self-esteem because he was "the shortest, skinniest one in the class." When he was nine, his confidence suffered another blow: his parents divorced and he was left with his father, a religious fanatic who drove the boy to drink when he was thirteen.

"I figured drinking would be the meanest thing I could do," Mac says today, though by the time he was sixteen he'd found other bad things to do, such as hanging around "with the wrong crowd," stealing hubcaps, and selling bootleg alcohol.

Graduating from high school when he was fifteen, Mac moved in with his mother and her new husband in Atlanta. He spent a year at Emory University, after which his money ran out, and with the fervor of the converted, he formed a rock-and-roll band. He supported himself by working for the city probation department while playing gigs throughout the South—all the "high school sock hops and fraternity puke-outs."

Ultimately deciding that he "didn't want to be playing local dives for the rest of my life," he deep-sixed the band and became "responsible." He married Fran Cook, had a son, Scott, went to work as a promoter for Vee Jay records, then moved to Los Angeles to work for Liberty Records' publishing arm. But Fran wasn't happy there and left, taking Scott with her. Shortly thereafter, Mac met sixteen-year-old Sarah Barg, who lived in his building. They married in 1971, when she turned eighteen.

The Liberty job gave Mac access to record producers, and deciding that he could write better songs than the ones he was hearing, he began pitching tunes to them.

In 1967 Lou Rawls recorded Davis's "You're Good For Me," and Elvis Presley recorded his "In the Ghetto" and "Don't Cry Daddy." The hits kept coming: Kenny Rogers and the First Edition cut his "Something's Burning," Bobby Goldsboro had a hit with the autobiographical "Watching Scotty Grow," and the Statler Brothers sent his "I Believe in Music" into the stratosphere. He also wrote material for Glen Campbell, with whom he became good friends and a regular golfing buddy.

In 1971, with Sarah's encouragement, Mac began recording his own material, scoring a major hit the following year with "Baby Don't Get Hooked On Me."

Though his songs for Rogers, Campbell, Ray Price,

and others were country-slanted, his own recordings were very heavily country. Though tunes like "Dream Me Home," "Stop And Smell the Roses," and "One Hell of a Woman" were crossover hits in 1974, from 1975 on Mac was a permanent fixture on the country charts. He won the Academy of Country Music's Entertainer of the Year award; and from 1974 to 1976, he starred in the hour-long NBC variety series *The Mac Davis Show*, singing songs, talking about growing up in Texas, and showcasing new talent, country and otherwise. He also made movies, most notably *North Dallas Forty* in 1979.

And all the while, the boyishly handsome, oh-so-sincere Davis was suffering from what he'd started when he was a kid: he was spinning down the drain of alcoholism, and that was just for starters. In 1975, after five years of marriage, Sarah left him and took up with another man. But it wasn't just *any* man: it was Glen Campbell, whom she married in 1976.

Mac fumed. He says that when Glen and his second wife Billie were divorced the previous year, he lent Campbell an ear and a shoulder to cry on. "I guess he didn't have the same feeling for me," Mac says.

(Campbell denies that he stole Sarah from Mac, claiming that the marriage was already history when he started seeing Sarah. He also said—rather patronisingly —"Mac was my friend, and still is as far as I'm concerned, although I can understand how he might be bitter.")

Mac survived being "eaten alive by attorneys" after the break-up. He briefly dated Lorna Luft (Judy Garland's other daughter), who remembers him for his sense of humor and for his drinking. Then he began seeing twenty-two-year-old nurse Lise, who became the third Mrs. Davis. They had two children, Noah and Cody. Nor did he feel the least bit vindicated when the Campbell/Sarah marriage ended after four years, Sarah accusing Campbell of infidelity and Campbell accusing Sarah's mother of meddling in their affairs. (Campbell paid Sarah three million dollars and took up with hot young Tanya Tucker. That relationship also failed.) In fact, Mac says, after not having had any contact with his ex-wife for quite some time, he enjoyed talking with her.

"She's going through a real tough time now," he said at the time, "and I've seen her and talked to her. I remember how I felt when I went through it."

But this pillar of strength, Mr. Turn-the-Other-Cheek, was himself propped up by booze. He says, "I was never abusive or falling-down drunk—just basically sappy. I could never admit I had a problem."

But boy, did he. Mac went from a steady diet of beer as a teenager to "bourbon and Coke, then three-martini lunches. I was probably legally drunk every time I performed, but I didn't slur my words."

When Mac retired in 1989 to enjoy his new family, he was so chronically drunk that he was afraid to pick up his babies for fear he might drop them. His memories of his retirement are simple: "Blank nothingness."

Lise watched, in pain, for two years. Then, she says, she finally "told Mac I just couldn't watch him die." She finally convinced him to get help, and on November 16, 1991, he entered the Betty Ford Center to dry out.

When he emerged, he says he realized "I can never drink again or it will kill me." He also decided to un-retire himself and went to Broadway to replace Keith Carradine as the legendary humorist Will Rogers in *The Will Rogers Follies*. Apart from his formidable talents, he brought something else to the show; until his departure in February of 1993, after the cast had taken its bows, he stepped forward and said to the audience, "You're lookin' at a guy who could be drunk by four in the afternoon. I'm an Alcoholics Anonymous miracle and lucky to be here. Drive carefully."

Mac was back, all right, ready to record and act anew. Or, as he said after finding himself sober and truly happy for the first time in over thirty years, "The truth is, I think I've arrived for the first time."

Garth Brooks

"**T**HERE'S better songwriters than me," says Garth Brooks, "better singers, lots of better-lookin' guys, and I can't pick a guitar hardly at all."

True. But since his debut album was released in April of 1989, Garth Brooks has generated half a *billion* dollars in revenues, from record sales, concerts, and even a 900-GET GARTH number. His third album, *Ropin' the Wind*, was the first record in country music history to debut in the number one spot on the *pop* record charts, and his next, *The Chase*, was the first record in music history to be certified at sales of five million copies "out-of-the-box," in other words, skipping all the stages between gold and quintuple-platinum.

He's also generated controversy. On the one hand, there's his political activism, such as his outspoken (and justifiable) advocacy of gay rights.

"If I lose my career over this, I'll have passed something on," he says, but "a lot of ignorant people are in the spotlight, and they say traditional family values are a father, mother, 2.3 children, June and Ward out on the lawn. That's bullshit. Traditional family values are happiness and laughing your ass off with your children (whether) your parents are two people of the same sex. As long as those children are happy and they're providing input into this world, that's what traditional family values are."

On the other hand, there was also his long spell of voracious self-indulgence, which very nearly destroyed him.

Like the country and pop genres he straddles, Garth Brooks is nothing if not a man of contrasts, paradoxes, and extremes.

Born on February 7, 1962, the last of six children, Troyal Garth Brooks grew up in an Oklahoma household that was always filled with the sounds of Merle Haggard, Hank Williams, and other country stars. His father was an engineer with an oil company, and his mother, Colleen, had cut a country album and done some singing on TV before becoming a mother. It was she who bought Garth his first instrument, a banjo, which he taught himself to play. Later, he also taught himself to play the guitar.

Although he had wanted to be a country music singer since he was a young teenager, Garth went to college so he'd have something to fall on, besides his butt, if he failed. When he graduated in 1984, he headed to Nashville, armed with a demo tape, and naively expected to get a record deal. He failed.

"I came here thinking that country music needed me," he says today. "I didn't dream there would be a million other people thinking the same thing."

Returning to his parents' home, dejected but not defeated, Garth married his college sweetheart Sandy Mahl and began doing the clubs-and-bars circuit, learning more about music and about the business side of music.

"I got into a couple of situations where the money wasn't there at the end of the gig," he recalls, "and I had to either fight or get walked on." He tasted a little of both, but he grew up fast and never resented anything that was a learning experience.

Garth supplemented his income by writing songs, recording jingles for John Deere tractors and Lone Star Beer, among other companies. He also worked in a Nashville boot store, where he got to meet more of the music movers and shakers than he had while playing his music. Eventually, these contacts helped him get an audition with Capitol records, and in 1988, he signed with the label.

With Capitol's help, Garth and his band Stillwater got to perform in some of the hot clubs in the South, and he immediately began to build a reputation as a highly energized and charismatic performer. In fact, the seeds of both his success and his troubles were sown in the raw power he generated on the stage doing what he calls his "cowboy rock-and-roll." He says, "Beautiful women, women I thought were unreal, would walk up to me and say, 'Sign this.' Only there was nothing in their hands. So I just dove in and had a blast."

Women would ask Garth to sign their breasts even when Sandy was in the audience, and he says, "When Sandy gets mad, she counts to herself. One night this little gal was drunk and singing on the microphone, trying to get as close to me as she could, and I looked out there and Sandy was on three. I thought, 'Oh, god.'

"She didn't even get to five, she just stood up, and . . . grabbed her by the shoulders and threw her off the front of the stage and over the first table."

But Sandy wasn't always with Garth, and for the first year that he toured he did more than autograph bosoms that were proffered by fans. He slept with women left and right and partied into the night; country *had*, at last, achieved parity with headbanger rock-and-roll.

Meanwhile, someone (it's never been revealed who) phoned Sandy with names, dates, and other particulars of her husband's daliances. Garth was in Texas when his wife phoned. Distraught, she reached him at the airport, as he was about to head for his next gig, and confronted him with what she'd been told.

Caught totally off-guard, Garth stammered, "It ain't happenin'! You've been fed a bunch of lies!"

He knew that *that* was a lie, of course, but he didn't know what else to say. He calmed Sandy down and hung up, and as he headed for the next date he only hoped his wife believed him.

Boarding the plane proved to be a fateful event for Garth. He got onto "one of those little prop things" bound for Cape Girardeau, Missouri, and recalls that as soon as they were airborne, "it started throwin' us all over the place." Convinced that he was going to crash, Garth sat there and took stock of his life.

"I thought, if I died, what kind of partner would I have been?" Not a very good one, he decided, and as soon as the plane landed he says, "I ran, oh, I *ran* to a phone, and I poured my guts out to the woman, told her I'd lied."

Sandy's reaction was understandable. She told him she didn't know if she wanted to stay with him, and Garth hung up, utterly dejected. He thought of going home, but felt it would be best if both he and Sandy had time to think about what he'd told her.

That night, in concert, he started singing "If Tomorrow Never Comes." He stopped after the first line, told the band to stop, then looked out into the audience and said, "Man, sometimes the road is just pure hell on a marriage. If you don't mind, I'd like to start over."

Garth started the song over, but he knew—as did many members of the audience—that there was a double meaning to what he'd said. So did Mike Palmer, his drummer. During the number, Garth noticed that there were tears in Mike's eyes, tears for what his boss was going through.

After the concert was over, Garth headed offstage and says, "Everything got quiet, and I heard a voice (from the audience) shout: 'Go home and talk to her, Garth.' " He kept on walking—right to the nearest bus.

Garth remembers that ride home as being "the longest of my life." When he arrived, not even sure that Sandy would be there, he opened the door, saw her, and was moved to tears. He apologized over and over for what he'd done, begged for her forgiveness, and then they began to talk.

He says his wife was understandably "irate, as I would have been," but adds that while "I didn't deserve a second chance . . . I got one."

Sandy admits that she wasn't sure what to do when she saw him, but "realized there was definitely still love, because neither of us could imagine the one without the other."

Garth says, "It took a hell of a human being to forgive me. I had to promise I'd make this marriage work."

So far, with the help of his bandmates, he has. He says that whenever he starts to flirt, wittingly or not, one of them taps him on the shoulder and brings him back to reality.

He says that, much to his surprise and delight, his relationship with Sandy has changed as a result of their experience: "I'm not telling anybody, 'If you're not happy, go out and screw around because your wife will become a dynamo for you,' but I got to be honest with you, that's what happened for me."

But Garth is nothing if not a man of extremes, and when he repents he does so in a big, open, public way. His second album, *No Fences* (1990) contains the anti-adultery song "The Thunder Rolls," the video for which graphically shows a battered wife gun down her cheating husband—him.

"I enjoyed being the asshole," he says, "because it showed that the asshole doesn't win."

But the video was banned by The Nashville Network and Country Music Television, and Garth was angry and hurt by the ban. Still, despite the possibility that he might lose sales, he refused to edit or apologize for the video.

"Real life has brought me here," he said. "The video has already done in two days what I hoped it would do in its lifetime . . . making people aware of a situation which unfortunately exists in our society and causing them to discuss it, sometimes even heatedly."

The truth is, Garth was disgusted enough (and rich enough) to quit music right then and there. "I love all the VJs and crews at CMT and TNN," he said afterward. "It's the people in the ties in the upper offices that took it upon themselves to decide what people would see and what they wouldn't, and that really just flipped me out, and I don't want to deal with those people."

He was still mulling over the idea of retirement when near-tragedy struck; on a flight from Dallas to Los Angeles, twenty-six-year-old Sandy, four months pregnant, began bleeding and nearly miscarried. After a short stay in a Los Angeles hospital, with her husband never leaving her side, they returned to their Goodlettsville, Tennessee estate on Garth's tour bus; he cancelled $6 million worth of bookings to remain with her until the crisis had passed.

Their daughter Taylor (for James Taylor) Mayne (for the state in which she was conceived) Pearl (after Minnie Pearl) was born in July 1992, at which point Garth said, "The things . . . that I would have died for, that I would have traded my family for, are so unimportant. The things I thought were the bust-ass important things aren't. Bein' a dad seems to be a pretty full-time job. If you came up and said you were going to burn my barn and take all my horses, I'd say, 'Just don't take my daughter.' "

But as much as he wanted to just stay home with his wife and daughter, several factors kept him from retiring from music.

First, he'd built up a large organization, nearly three dozen strong, and he felt duty-bound to continue touring to keep his musicians, crew, managers, and assistants gainfully employed.

Second, he realized how much good he could do by remaining in the public eye—not just singing message songs, but also raising money for charity. To this end, in the fall of 1992 he headed a huge drive at his concerts to raise food and money for Feed the Children.

"When you've got the power to save lives," he said, "you don't think about hangin' it up."

Finally, he was surprised to find himself seriously energized by the sudden, mammoth, and unexpected popularity of Billy Ray Cyrus. The highly competitive Garth —a high school and college football and javelin star— had been complaining to friends and coworkers "about losing my edge," as he called it. But by the fall, he was determined not to let the young upstart become the king of country. At least, not without a fight.

"Once again I feel like the underdog," he grins. "It's new blood, a fresh breath. It's like, Yeah! I'm back in the fight . . . this is like the old days."

To make sure having a career and a family was really doable, he says he took his daughter on a "trial run" in his new baby-friendly tour bus. "As soon as the key was turned in the ignition, Taylor fell asleep." She was a born trooper. Garth was ready to roll.

Naturally, he needn't have worried about the Cyrus challenge: not only did *The Chase* quickly go quintuple-

platinum, but it looks to be the top-selling country recording ever.

Today, even though the Brookses travel together,
Garth gives himself more time at home between concert
dates. And unlike the old days, his wife doesn't have to
drag women off the stage anymore; there are security
people who do that for her. But even if they weren't
there, Garth says that one look at Sandy and Taylor are
enough to keep him true. He hopes.

"What I did was very, very wrong," he says. "I can't
even say I won't make the same mistake again, because I
don't know what tomorrow brings. But I do know I have
the rest of my life to love my wife, and that's what I must
do."

Like the characters in many of his songs, Garth says
he still has a lot of growing to do. But his heart's in the
right place and, with a little bit of luck, tomorrow won't
be more of the "Same Old Story."

Clint Black

COUNTRY heartthrob Clint Black and country superstar Garth Brooks were born just a few days apart in February of 1962. The debut albums of both artists were released in April of 1989, and both records went through the roof.

But that's about all the two men have in common. Garth's a round-faced Everyman from the South; Clint's a movie-star handsome glamor-guy from New Jersey. Garth has survived some rocky personal problems while his career has gone smoothly; Clint has had a relatively smooth personal life while his career has gone through the gauntlet.

Actually, Clint disputes the notion that he's "from" New Jersey. He says yes, he was born there, in Long Branch (as in the *Gunsmoke* saloon), but his parents moved Clint and his three older brothers to Katy, Texas, when he was just six months old, so he considers himself a Texan.

His brothers listened to country music constantly, and Clint became interested in it when he was still a young boy. With his parents' encouragement, he learned how to play the guitar, bass, and harmonica, and when he wasn't playing in his brother Kevin's band, he would go to a local park and serenade folks who were out for a walk or a picnic.

As a teenager, Clint held a wide range of jobs, from fishing guide to ironworker. But his heart was in music, and after his debut at the Benton Springs Club in Houston in 1981, Clint dropped out of high school and hit the road, convinced that he could make it, or at least, that he wouldn't be happy doing anything else.

(Today, Clint says that dropping out of high school was one of the biggest mistakes he ever made. "I don't want kids to say, 'Look, he's a high school dropout and he did fine,'" Clint says. "If a kid asked me today, I'd say, 'Stay in school, finish, do everything you can, learn as much as you can, you'll never regret it. I regretted it two years after I dropped out. My parents told me I would. Didn't take me long." He's got common sense, but feels so insecure about his lack of book-learning that he won't even take sides in political issues because "I don't know that much about government because I didn't pay attention.")

During one of his gigs in Houston in 1987, Clint found himself playing with Hayden Nicholas, a guitarist/songwriter, and the two of them hit it off. After the set, Clint told Hayden that what he wanted most of all was to make a good quality demo to send to the record companies. Hayden happened to have a modest studio in his garage, and the two recorded together. In May, the demo got into the hands of Bill Ham, the manager of blues-rock phenomenon ZZ Top, who then asked Clint over to hear him play. Ham liked the singer's soulful baritone and, as it happened, had been looking for a pure country act. He agreed to manage the young singer, and three months later Clint had a contract with RCA Records.

Clint was thrilled, of course, though he didn't know at

the time the heartache his contract with Ham would cause.

From the start, Clint has written his own material. He says, "Some people say you can't write until you've lied and been lied to, cheated and been cheated on (but) I don't believe that." He put together fifty songs for his debut album; these were whittled to nine and *Killin' Time* was released. The first single was "A Better Man," and thanks in part to a video which emphasized the singer's rugged good looks, it hit number one in June, five months after it was released. (When singer Buck Owens saw the video, he wasn't surprised that Clint was a hit, describing him as "the kind of guy you'd want to take home to meet your father if you could trust your mother.")

The second single, "Killin' Time," went to number one in October. By the time Clint was through, he'd placed five singles from the album in the number one spot—a record for a country debut—and the album went platinum. His second album, *Put Yourself in My Shoes*, was released in November of 1990; it went platinum in less than a month.

Who could ask for anything more? Clint could.

At a reception following a Houston New Year's Eve concert in 1990, Clint met Houston native, actress Lisa Hartman of *Knot's Landing* and *2000 Malibu Road*. The two hit it off and were married on October 20, 1991 on Black's 180 acre farm outside of Houston—to the sounds of female hearts breaking all over the country. The couple set up housekeeping in the Hollywood Hills, so she could be near the studios, though Clint hates the fact that because he's constantly on the road (he played over 130 cities in 1992) he can't always be with his wife.

"I don't like us being apart," he says, and admits liking even less the fact that the show that's kept them apart, *2000 Malibu Road*, has had "scenes of her getting beat

up. That really was hard for me to take." He's also sorry
that because of their two careers, "A family is not in the
plans for now." Both have said that they definitely want
children.

From the start, there were the to-be-expected tabloid
reports of unhappiness in the marriage, which Clint adamantly denies.

"We have to laugh at that," he says. "We're inseparable. I heard somewhere that we got into a fight in a
parking lot and stuff like that, you know. It couldn't be
further from the truth."

(Actually, what the report said was that they began
arguing in the Chalet Gourmet food store on Sunset
Boulevard, and the fight ended outside when Lisa kicked
her husband in the backside. Impartial eyewitnesses
swear it happened, though no one is sure whether they
were arguing or just fooling around.)

Clint says that he doesn't mind the tabloid stories as
much as their tendency to select the absolute worst photographs possible. "They'll take fourteen different pictures of you," he says, "but publish the one where you're
scratching your lip, and it looks like you're picking your
nose." He says he hasn't yet learned to do what Lisa
does: freeze into a Mona Lisa pose whenever photographers are around and hold it until they leave.

Except for the tabloid coverage, Clint's life was idyllic.
Unfortunately, it didn't stay that way for long.

When Clint was just starting out, he'd had no negoti-
ating leverage in his contract with Ham and, as a result,
gave him more money than he would have otherwise—
for example, most of the publishing royalties for his first
eight albums, and twenty percent of the concert grosses.

Fledgling songwriters or performers rarely have the
clout to keep from making rotten deals. Artists from Al
Jolson to Elvis Presley have strong-armed new songwriters looking for a break, and successful managers have

done likewise with untested new acts. But let Clint's be a lesson, kiddies, that the bed you make better be a comfy one because once you're in, it's damned difficult to get out.

The successful release of Clint's second album proved that he was no one-hit wonder, so he went to Ham and suggested that they reframe their deal. It didn't happen, and just over a year later, in January of 1992, Black up-and-quit, finding himself new representation. He said at the time, "It was shocking to discover that the financial aspects of my business relationship with Mr. Ham were grossly one-sided and served to advance Mr. Ham's personal interest at my expense, financially and professionally." He added that "since terminating my relationship with Mr. Ham, I am no longer subject to the total control and manipulation."

Ham was offended by the statement, shooting back that it "demeans Clint by asserting that I or anyone on my management team 'manipulated and controlled' him as if he were a child." Ham added that he resented public comments from Black that were a "thinly disguised, self-serving attempt to escalate a business dispute and degrade it into a personal smear campaign."

But Ham did more than fire off more words: he sued his former client for $110 million, citing breach of contract and loss of potential earnings. Black lobbed back a $6 million cross-complaint for fraud and breach of contract.

The lawsuits were the first negative, mainstream publicity that Clint had had, but they weren't the last.

Shortly before leaving Ham's firm, Clint hired his mother-in-law, Jonni Hartman, as his personal assistant. Soon after the split, he fired publicist Joe Dera and, for the sake of expedience, briefly replaced him with Jonni, who had previously done publicity for both Lisa and actor David Hasselhoff.

Dera sniffed, "I'm sure she'll do for Clint what she did for her daughter's career, or at the very least, David Hasselhoff." Touche, Joe. It was all starting to look like a replay of the Mike Tyson/Robin Givens/Ruth Roper triangle, in which the fighter's wife and mother-in-law were allegedly trying to get publicity and/or tuck away big pieces of his fortune.

Black was quick with the damage control, insisting that Jonni was "absolutely not" his new press agent or, as some people speculated, his new manager. "I guess it was a mistake," he said, to have her handle his publicity, however briefly.

Black's management consultant, Simon Renshaw, dismissed the speculation against Jonni as "just rubbish," and Clint himself said that he was "looking forward to the opportunity of addressing the attacks on both my name and professional reputation in the public forum of the courts."

Still, industryites openly speculated that Clint was being used, if not by Jonni then by Lisa, who made no secret of the fact that she wanted to be a singer as well as an actress.

As *The New York Post* reported on April 16, 1992, "Insiders say they won't be surprised if Lisa . . . starts recording and performing with her cowboy-hat–wearing hubby." Perhaps one label executive put it best when she said, "Remember when Sylvester Stallone tried to make a star out of Brigitte Nielsen? Obviously, Clint doesn't. Someone ought to tell him that you can't turn a silk purse into a sow's ear."

However, Clint was ripping mad about the accusations against Lisa and told an interviewer for *Modern Screen's Country Music Special* magazine, "A lot of the things they print about me and Lisa are very unfair. How can you get used to that?" He added that he couldn't "be bothered setting the record straight all the time." He left the matter this way: "Married life is great. It's the best life I know. She's wonderful." He also says it's sexist that while folks have charged that she's using him to get into music, how come no one's ever said he's using her to get into TV?

As it happens, says Clint, the two have "had a lot of things offered to us and we've considered them (but) it's very typical, too predictable and we don't want to do that." And though he'd love to work with Lisa in a movie or TV project, he says he doesn't want to stop making music in the studio or on the road.

Speaking of which——

Clint's third album was finished, but it was held up for months because of all the legal entanglements. Finally, said Clint, "the label and the former management and everybody (came) to an understanding that the album project needs to go on, and all these things can be sorted out in due time."

The Hard Way was finally released in July 1992 and quickly certified platinum, proving that the twenty-month layoff hadn't hurt Clint's marketability. He told *Country Fever* magazine, "My attitude is . . . if I dropped out of the picture for five years and came back with something good, it would be well-received." However, he admitted that he didn't intend to "push it five years just to find out."

Four years in the spotlight have certainly been a revelation for Clint, but all things considered, he's handled it with greater poise and good humor than most of his fellow singers. And the reason is simple.

"In the face of the adversities," he says, "I still maintain that nothing matters but the music." He adds from the heart, "You know, if I weren't getting paid, I'd probably still be fighting to do it."

Dwight Yoakam

AS it happens, despite the heat to which Clint and Lisa were subjected, they fared better than he-of-the-tight-ripped-jeans-and-eagle-like-stare, Dwight Yoakam, and his superfamous honey. Neither of them did anything wrong, mind you, but Yoakam didn't like the rules by which the paparazzi play, so he jumped ship.

But we get ahead of ourselves.

Yoakam was born on October 23, 1956, in Pike Floyd Holler, Kentucky, but raised in Columbus, Ohio, where his parents moved when he was a baby. They went back home on weekends, though, and Yoakam grew up to the music of the hills, especially of the local churches, where he sang.

From a very young age, Yoakam knew he wanted to be a singer, and after graduating from high school, he began hitting clubs with his own brand of honky tonk—pure, traditional, and Hank Williams-nasal. Much to his surprise, he found that the South didn't want him. In the late 1970s, the increasingly mainstream Nashville thought he was just too hillbilly.

As he later put it, disparagingly, "Their music always starts in offices and trickles down to the street." He says

—in a Bill Buckley style that's become a trademark— what music should *really* come from is "a spontaneous, metamorphic tradition (with) covert sociopolitical overtones."

Take that, Nashville.

Moving to Los Angeles, Yoakam drove a freight van during the day (it "gives you a lot of time to think," he says) and hit the clubs at night, making a name for himself by opening for hot bands like Los Lobos and X. After he garnered enough press to paper the Ozarks and sold a slew of his self-produced, self-financed 1985 album *Guitars, Cadillacs, Etc*, Nashville invited him back and he went—but on his own terms.

Hit records came quickly, including a cover of Johnny Horton's "Honky Tonk Man," which was a country top five in 1986, and a duet, "Streets of Bakersfield," which Dwight used to lure legendary Buck Owens out of retirement. It went to number one in October of 1988. Yoakam's first solo number one was "I Sang Dixie," which reached the top spot the following February.

But if Yoakam has been able to make his own kind of music, life on top has bummed him out in another way.

Yoakam is a fiercely private kind of guy (he gave *Us* Magazine an interview in 1992, snottily answering most questions with "You figure it out" or "You'd rather not know"), and he made a *big* mistake in December of 1991, when he began dating highly visible actress Sharon Stone, in the wake of her *Basic Instinct* success.

Stone was a hot mainstream item, and though they were able to keep the relationship a secret for four months, when Yoakam went with her to that most public of events, the Oscars, the cat was out of the bag.

After that, photographers followed the couple everywhere: to dinner, to the movies, to concerts, to visit friends. That didn't sit well with Yoakam, and when Sharon wanted to go to the Country Music Awards ceremony, he said no. He didn't even want to go himself. When she went anyway, alone, that was the end of the relationship.

Yoakam may never win any awards for compromise, but you've got to give him credit for sticking to his guns, which, like his music, hat, and tight blue jeans, is a country tradition.

Eddie Rabbitt

A lot of country stars sing about pain, but not all of them have lived it. *Really* lived it.

Eddie Rabbitt has.

A lot of country stars have come to their careers in unusual ways, but they tend to have one thing in common: they're usually from the South, or maybe the Southwest.

Eddie Rabbitt isn't.

About the only thing Rabbitt has in common with the bulk of his colleagues is that he started with a dream and realized it.

Born in Brooklyn, New York, on November 27, 1944, Rabbitt was raised in New Jersey, not exactly a mecca for future country stars. He says he had two jobs as a kid: because of his name he was always "giving or taking bloody noses," or he was busy playing the guitar, which he first learned to do as a Boy Scout. He fell in love with the instrument and with country music. Rabbitt says that his passion isn't as strange as it might sound; his father, who had come to the U.S. with his wife Mae in 1924 and worked at an oil refinery in Newark, New Jersey, played the fiddle or accordion at clubs in Manhattan on nights and weekends.

Besides, Rabbitt says, "I'm Irish. Country music is Irish music. Appalachian music was brought over by the Scotch and the Irish."

Rabbitt went with his father whenever he could, and his mother remembers, "He was never one for school. His head was too full of music."

That's putting it mildly. Rabbitt bought records and every fan magazine he could find, and sat around memorizing facts, lyrics, and even the running times of songs.

Dropping out of school at fifteen, he got himself arrested for driving without a license, spent four days in jail, and decided to go back to school and graduate.

"I wanted to be somebody," he says, "and I decided the best way to start was by finishing something I'd begun."

But a high school degree didn't help much with his chosen profession. After graduating, he worked days as an attendant at a mental institution, soda jerk, fruit picker, and truck driver, trying to save money. By night, he played at any club that would have him, which was a useful if humiliating experience. Boos and catcalls taught him first-hand the kinds of music working people did and didn't respond to.

When he was twenty, he cut a record, "Six Nites & Seven Days" on 20th Century Fox's label; it flopped. He knew it wasn't his fault alone. Fox had done nothing to market it. Still, he felt as though he'd blown it and resolved to get more experience before going back into a recording studio.

He got that experience performing on WRGB Radio in Albany, New York, from 1967 to 1968, after which he hit Wheeling, West Virginia, appearing on WWVA. Signed by Columbia, he cut more flop singles, including "Bottles" and "I Just Don't Care Any More."

At this point, Rabbitt might have concluded that he was in the wrong business, save for one thing. In 1967,

Grand Ole Opry star Roy Drusky recorded his "Workin' My Way Up From the Bottom," and Bobby Lewis scored a top twenty hit with his "Love Me and Make it All Better." These small triumphs made Rabbitt realize that, at the time, "Singers were a dime a dozen. But there weren't a lot of good songs." Songwriting was where he'd stake his claim.

In 1968, with one thousand dollars in his pocket and a trunkful of songs, he drove to Nashville. His car literally died the minute he arrived, and taking an apartment, he spent nearly two years making the rounds and trying to peddle his songs without much success. Then, unexpectedly, Rabbitt batted one out of the park: Elvis Presley heard and recorded the young composer's "Kentucky Rain," which snared the King his fiftieth gold record and earned Eddie an instant reputation as a hitmaker.

Presley cut two more Rabbitt songs, Mel Street got to the top ten with the sadly appropriate "Livin' On Borrowed Time," and in 1974, Eddie had another big success as the author of Ronnie Milsap's first number one hit, "Pure Love." Willie Nelson, Roy Clark, and others also recorded his songs.

Thanks to his newfound fame and some impressive local performances, Eddie landed a recording contract with Electra in 1974, and hit the charts on his own with "You Get To Me." The next two singles ("Forgive and Forget" and "I Should Have Married You") went even higher, making the country top twenty. In April of 1976, "Drinkin' My Baby (Off My Mind)" gave the singer his first number one hit.

Rabbitt's career had finally been launched, and his personal life was also cooking. He went to a party in 1971, and says, "I saw this little thing about five feet tall, with long, black, beautiful hair and a real pretty face. She looked like an angel to me." They began dating, and in 1976—as soon as Rabbitt felt secure in his career—he married medical technician Janine Girardi. (He did it on his birthday, explaining to *People* Magazine, "I can't remember dates, so I thought I'd make it easy on myself.")

The couple had a daughter, Dimelza, born in 1981.

Professionally, there seemed nowhere the hot young star's talent couldn't take him. Single after single went to the top of the country charts, and he scored big-to-huge crossover hits including "I Can't Help Myself," "You Don't Love Me Anymore," "I Just Want to Love You," "Every Which Way But Loose" (from the Clint Eastwood picture of the same name), and "Step By Step" (which went to number five on the pop charts in 1981 *and* was the first country video ever broadcast on MTV).

Then the roof fell in on Rabbitt with the birth of son Timmy in 1983.

Timmy had been born with an extremely rare birth defect, biliary artresia, which attacks the liver and destroys the body's ability to deal with waste products.

Without a liver transplant, there was no hope for Timmy to lead a long or normal life. From the day he was born, the boy was forced to live on waste processing machines, first in Franklin, Tennessee's Williamson County Hospital, and then in famed Vanderbilt University Hospital in Nashville.

Rabbitt immediately put his career in a drawer and spent five or six days of every week, for two years, at his son's bedside.

"Maybe it's the chauvinistic Irish in me," Rabbitt said. "I felt like I had to be there if I'm any kind of man."

His wife told *People* Magazine, "We made a family affair of it. Dimelza loved playing with him."

"He was beautiful," says his dad. "He became the hospital mascot."

In an effort to keep his band together, and to help pay the nearly half-million dollars in medical expenses, Rabbitt fulfilled whatever concert dates and recording obligations he could, such as cutting the sadly ironic "The Best Year of My Life," which went to number one. But he admits, "With some of those projects, I just wasn't into it."

He stopped writing, unable and unwilling to put his sorrow into words. He also let his own health go by the wayside. He stopped running his two miles a day and working out with weights and started eating, packing on fifty-five pounds.

The boy's health was more or less stable over this two year period, but Rabbitt maintained that "existing on machines is not life. We'd all sit and cry together on Timmy's bed."

The Rabbitts and Timmy's doctors all agreed that a transplant was preferable. Unfortunately, donor organs are never plentiful, and the Rabbitts had no choice but to wait for a suitable liver to become available.

Finally, in July of 1985, with the frustration and pressure at its peak, Rabbitt took his wife and daughter on a brief vacation to Florida. No sooner did they get there than the doctors phoned. A liver had been found, and Timmy would have to be in Minneapolis in less than a day to receive it.

From his hotel, Rabbitt made the appropriate arrangements, and the family flew to the hospital to be at Timmy's bedside. They arrived after the surgery, and Rabbitt says tearfully, "Timmy wasn't awake. He was in a kind of coma from which he never came out."

After all the waiting, the boy's body had rejected the transplant; the machines which had managed to keep him alive on a barely functioning liver simply couldn't compensate for a rejected one.

When Timmy died, Rabbitt stayed at home, despite the urging of his colleagues to go back to work—not just for his own state of mind but for his future. Rabbitt says, "I was told, 'They (the public) forget you real fast these days,' and I said, 'Well, that's just too bad. This is where I need to be right now.' "

Slowly, with the help of his wife and daughter, Rabbitt got back into emotional and physical shape. He and Janine had another son, Tommy, in 1986, and Rabbitt says, "The new guy in the house kind of brought sunshine back in our lives."

With the sunshine returned, Rabbitt finally got back to work. But inside, he was still hurting bad. With the exception of the duet "Both to Each Other (Friends & Lovers)," which he recorded with Juice Newton and which went to number one in October of 1986, his songs were mired in the darker side of life. The death of a child, he says, "Takes the cockiness out of your walk," and he says he had no choice but to "weave the pain and suffering through my songs."

He had a few hits, but it wasn't until 1988 that he found his lighter muse and chart success again, going to the top with "I Wanna Dance With You."

One of the things that had helped Rabbit find his more optimistic side again was becoming honorary chairperson of the American Council on Transplantation, which provides information and help for both would-be donors and recipients. He recorded radio and TV spots, saying, "If there's anything I can do, I want to do it."

Actually, he learned that there was a great deal he could do for *many* causes. He worked on behalf of a local "Say No To Drugs" project in Nashville, then became involved with the National Safe Kids Campaign, after learning that more kids die in preventable accidents than from childhood diseases.

He had the enthusiasm and energy of any convert and, after a few years, he had decided that there was still another great problem facing our kids: MTV. Describing the music cable channel as "soft pornography," he said that "music should soothe the wild beast in us, not turn us into wild beasts." Rabbitt became an advocate of labeling albums with parental advisory stickers, which he says "is only to protect children and people who may not want to buy something pornographic." (The operative phrase is "may not want to buy." Kids who want it are going to get it, whether or not it's labeled. And keep in mind that the labeling is terribly subjective. Some folks don't make a distinction between Prince and Bobby Brown: they think all of it should be burned. Moreover, pundits in the 1950s argued that rock-and-roll and violent TV shows were corrupting the youth of America, yet that generation grew up flashing peace signs at passersby and making music in the Summer of Love. ["Sure they did," says Bones Howe, who produced Elvis Presley and the Association, among others. "They were stoned beyond belief."])

Nonetheless, Rabbitt takes some pride in the fact that country music has been in the forefront of positive change.

"You don't hear as many of those drinking-type songs anymore," he told *Country America* magazine. "You don't hear as much of the cheating thing. Country music is dealing with relationships now in a not-so-silly way. Nothing country music could do surpasses what's going on in the rap end and some of the rock music of today."

Though talk like that is bound to alienate many people, Rabbitt doesn't care. In fact, he goes even further. "I have a feeling," he says, "that the movies and television and the records that seem to be very popular today are causing a disease to settle into America." One, he says, that needs a transplant of wholesome values and positive role models.

While some people feel that Rabbitt has gone overboard in his criticism, he's been shaped by events that most people can't even begin to appreciate, and he insists his social stance isn't reactionary, just "old-fashionedness. I really do feel that, as artists, we have a responsibility to the people who listen to our music, especially the kids."

Whatever you think of Rabbitt's views, it's no surprise that Rabbitt the reformer is as determined as Rabbitt the performer.

After all, the kid *is* from Jersey.

Doug Stone

I T doesn't always take years of drug and/or alcohol abuse to fell a star. Sometimes, the body rebels on its own, as when we lost fifty-year-old George Morgan in 1975 and fifty-seven-year-old superstar Marty Robbins in 1982, both victims of heart attacks. Roger Miller, at fifty-six, succumbed to cancer.

Sometimes, though, the stars—and their fans—are lucky. Roy Acuff survived for a decade after his heart attack, and Tammy Wynette has come through nearly a score of operations. And luck was surely with young Doug Stone as he had his brush with death.

Born Doug Brooks on June 19, 1956, the Atlanta, Georgia native was introduced to music by his mother, who was a singer with the Country Rhythm Playboys. He took guitar and singing lessons, and in 1964, he was allowed to join his mother onstage, playing drums for the band, despite the fact that he was only seven and, he says, "the next oldest guy in the band was thirty-four."

His parents were divorced four years later, and twelve-year-old Doug lived with his father. "We were dirt poor," Stone says, and they kept moving from place to place. The singer recalls that one house was so drafty "the wind would roll the rug up off the floor," while another, which had a tin roof, was struck by lightning one day "and it lit that sucker up like a million camera flashes going off at once."

Living with his father, Doug taught himself how to play the piano, bass, and drums. Falling passionately and hopelessly in love with music, he dropped out of school when he was sixteen and hit the road, singing in bars, clubs, and even hotel lounges.

But it was a hard life for the young man and the young woman he'd married, and after ten years, despairing that he'd never make it big, he returned to Georgia to work in the diesel-engine repair shop his dad had set up. He also split from his wife, who moved away with their two children, young Daniel and Michelle. He married his second wife Carie in 1984, and they had a daughter Kala and a son Chanse.

Doug kept his toe in the musical water by performing at a VFW lodge in nearby Newnan, where—as ever, when you least expect it—he was noticed by Phyllis Bennett, an up-and-coming manager.

"It's fate," says Stone, with some amazement. "In this business, I found out, it's eighty percent luck and twenty percent talent."

Phyllis introduced Doug to a producer who liked what he heard and gave the singer a recording contract. The only catch in the deal: the label wanted Doug to change his name so he wouldn't be confused with that other Brooks. Doug selected Stone, inspired by a song he'd written called "Heart of Stone."

His first single, "I'd Be Better Off (In a Pine Box)" was released in 1989, went top-five the following spring, and was nominated for a Grammy. It was followed by other hits including "Fourteen Minutes Old" and the number one hit "A Jukebox With a Country Song." His debut album, *Doug Stone*, made it to number twelve on the country chart and also went gold.

At the time, he explained the popularity of his music by telling an interviewer, "I've had a lot of experience in my life, and I think that helps my songs." However, he couldn't have imagined the experience that lay ahead.

Maintaining a backbreaking touring schedule for a full three years after the release of the first single, Doug first began feeling numb in his left arm during the winter of 1992. He went to the doctor and tests were performed, but nothing insidious was found. Just a little worn down, was all.

Since the numbness was nothing serious, there was no reason not to continue performing concerts or a lifestyle that included no exercise, lots of greasy food, and as many cigarettes as American tobacco farmers could produce.

By May, it was time to pay the piper. In Prineville, Oregon, as Doug sang with one of his idols, Kenny Rogers, he began to feel sharp pains in his chest.

"I knew something was wrong," he told *Country America* magazine. "But like an idiot, I never once thought to get off. I thought, 'These people paid their money. I'm going to give them a show—even if I die doing it.' "

He came close. Each stab nearly brought him to his knees, but he refused to leave the stage. Only when the show was done, did he arrange to catch the next plane to Nashville, where he checked himself into the Centennial Medical Center.

A fresh series of tests were performed, and this time doctors found the problem: four major arteries were ninety to ninety-nine percent blocked and his heart was on the verge of shutting down.

As soon as he was told, Stone turned to the surgeon and said, "Slice away, Doc." Stone says, "I just figured that it's like having a flat tire on your car. I had a flat, and if it didn't get fixed, I was going nowhere."

Quadruple bypass surgery was performed, and Stone's life was saved. But even that couldn't keep Doug down for long. Just six weeks later he was back on his feet, moving into his new home in Nashville, appearing at Fan Fair in Nashville, and undertaking a limited concert schedule.

He also cut out the smokes, changed his eating habits, and got himself into the treadmill-and-rowing-machine habit. As he puts it, "My daddy always taught me: You get up and do something about your situation. You don't sit around feeling sorry for yourself."

Stone is the first to admit how lucky he was to have survived. In an interview he gave shortly after his surgery, he said that while he draws on his own experiences for his music, the title of his debut single is *not* about him. "I'm not quitting until the fans say I'm through."

Clearly, that won't be for quite some time. His second album, *From the Heart*, landed in the country chart top twenty, and also went gold.

And maybe somewhere, Marty and George are smiling. . . .

Travis Tritt

TO say that Travis Tritt doesn't play by the rules is an understatement.

He refuses to wear the obligatory hat. In fact, in 1992, he and hillbilly rocker Marty Stuart teamed for the No Hats tour, which packed in the hatless nationwide. Even a few hats went to see what all the rockin' was about.

And get this. After years of chowing down on sausage sandwiches, he found out that what he really liked was sushi. Raw fish and veggies from Japan are not the kind of foodstuffs typically found backstage on the country circuit.

Then there's his social life. After two failed marriages, he's taken to dating the kind of women that turn heads. For the past few years, he's won the paparazzi's unofficial award for the star with the hottest date at the Country Music Association awards show.

Finally, and most significant of all, there's his breaking of the Country Commandment never to dis other artists. Although he was not only out of line but dead wrong in his judgment, did Travis Tritt care whether or not people approved? Not on your life.

"When we give honest opinions or talk about things

in an honest and open manner, society tends to penalize us for that," he says. "I think that's wrong. I was always raised to tell the truth, no matter what. Even if it does get you in trouble from time to time, I think people respect you if you say honestly what you really believe and back it up."

Naturally, Travis's truth may be another person's falsehood, but no matter. His strong sense of right and wrong are reflected in his music, and that makes him, in his words, "Somebody who moves people emotionally, that says something to them specially."

Born in Marietta, Georgia, on February 9, 1963, Travis sang in the children's choir of his church and fell in love with music—and the spotlight. He recalls, "We got a standing ovation, and I remember thinking, 'Boy, I like this!' "

At the age of eight, he taught himself to play the guitar, remembering, "I was really into it, and adamant about learning." Within six years, he was writing songs.

When he graduated from high school, his parents tried to discourage him from pursuing a musical career. He bowed to their wishes and went to work on a loading dock. By the time he'd married his first wife, he was in management at the truck company. But music was still his first love, and he put together a band that rehearsed at his house during the evenings.

Taking a new job at an air conditioning and heating company, Travis talked music. He composed during breaks. He listened to music while he worked. Finally, his boss took him aside and suggested that he follow his heart.

"He had been a rock 'n' roller," says Tritt, "and at one time had the opportunity to lay everything aside and go play music—and he didn't do it. He's very successful financially, but he kicks himself every day for not pursuing his dream." Tritt says that after talking things over with the fellow, he realized, "I didn't want to wind up sitting on a porch when I'm old and wondering if I could have done it."

Tritt held onto his job, but cranked up his nightly endeavors, playing solo at clubs, weddings, parties, and anyplace that would have him in and around the Atlanta area. The operative word is "played," since Tritt says he did "whatever I had to do to get the audience's attention —jumping on tables, kicking things over. I got fired a lot, but I got a reputation that attracted attention."

Tritt's wife discovered that she didn't like musicians' hours or their antics. Tritt admits, "I started to drink too much both on- and off-stage. I did real stupid things, like drinking all night and then getting in a car and driving." When Tritt quit his day job six months later to do music full time, his wife also discovered that she didn't like the insecurity of an unsteady paycheck. The relationship ended before their second anniversary.

Meanwhile, Tritt's father—horrified by what he regarded as his son's irresponsibility—refused to speak to him.

Travis kept on making music, and in 1984 he met country-loving bartender, Jodi Barnett, who became his manager, and the following year, his second wife. Jodi aggressively promoted her husband and helped him to link up with record promoter Danny Davenport, who had connections at Warner Brothers Records.

Travis used Davenport's home studio to record material over a two year period, after which Davenport brought it to Warner Brothers. The songs made their way up the food chain until, in 1988, the label finally offered Tritt a contract, but with a caveat: to avoid confusion with Randy Travis, they wanted Tritt to change his name. He refused, and the label decided not to press the issue. He also eschewed a country trademark—the ever present hat—feeling that it detracted from the music. Again, Warner decided not to make a federal case out of it. If the music worked, his name and looks wouldn't matter. If it didn't, they wouldn't help.

Turns out that Tritt didn't need anything but his voice and songs, which he describes as being "for the everyday, ordinary working person." His first album, *Country Club*, came out in 1990 and went gold; within a year, it was platinum, then double platinum. His second album, *It's All About To Change*, went double platinum even faster.

Unfortunately, Tritt's good fortune earned him more gold than he bargained for. Jodi was hurt when she found herself replaced by professional managers, and when her husband ended up on the road 280 days a year, she knew that things wouldn't be getting better real soon . . . especially when he told the press how much he enjoyed performing and looking out at the women ("It's better than hairy legged ol' guys," he said). Jodi returned her wedding band and split.

However, some good did come from the split. Jodi's departure inspired him to write his signature tune, "Here's a Quarter, Call Someone Who Cares." Tritt says, "Sometimes, I joke that I'm gonna go out and get married and divorced again so I can come up with the next album."

(Though perhaps Jodi got the last word. While singing the song in Bristol, Tennessee, Tritt was hit hard on the forehead by a quarter thrown from someone in the audience. Though he says he tried to perform with "blood dripping down my eyebrows (I) started getting pretty dizzy," and the rest of the performance had to be cancelled so he could receive medical attention.)

Things were going great guns for Tritt through 1991, despite the fact that his controversial song "Bible Belt" raised a few eyebrows for telling the sordid tale of a "looker" from Atlanta who seduces a preacher. Then, the next year, his tongue dug him a deep hole when he shared his bizarre thoughts on hot country hunk Billy Ray Cyrus.

In June of 1992, at Nashville's big Fan Fair, he told an Associated Press reporter that he thought Cyrus "degrades" country music because he'd reduced it to nothing more than "an ass-wiggling contest." He also trashed Cyrus's megahit "Achy Breaky Heart," complaining that the song doesn't "make much of a statement."

Though Tritt is a phenomenal talent, his comments were stupid and uninformed. The early songs of Elvis and the Beatles didn't always have much to say and, besides, a number of songs on Cyrus's album *do* make statements and have nothing to do with "ass-wiggling," songs such as "Some Gave All" and "Could've Been Me."

But right or wrong, Travis's remarks were unparalleled in the gentlemanly world of country music. While a few radio stations and artists rushed to his defense—without necessarily echoing his opinions—many others boycotted Tritt's music out of protest. A few people in Music City went so far as to suggest that Tritt's comments were jealousy, pure and simple. Before Billy Ray Cyrus came along, Tritt and Garth were the dominant country forces in the top-forty region of the pop music charts.

Outspoken musical outlaw Waylon Jennings put in his unasked-for two cents, comparing Cyrus to fifties quasi-rocker Fabian. "Fabian couldn't sing. He was a wonderful guy, a good-looking guy. Billy Ray, he's not a good singer, but he don't need to be if you look that good." (Waylon was also *way* off the mark; see the entry on

Billy Ray Cyrus for comments about an a cappella show-stopper of his.)

Cyrus remained somewhat above the fray, stating in his quiet, gentlemanly way, "I don't make my music for Travis Tritt or anybody else. I make my music for myself and my fans." He added, "From what I've seen on the road, there's an awful lot of 'Achy Breaky Heart' fans out there. The people of the world have made their decision, and that's all that matters to me."

At Alabama's June Jam concert, performing a few hours before Tritt, Cyrus told the adoring throng, "I don't care what anybody else says. From the bottom of my 'Achy Breaky Heart' I love all of you."

When it was his turn to perform, Tritt wisely retreated just a bit from his untenable position, telling the crowd (that Cyrus had worked to a frenzy), "If anything I have said hurt Billy Ray Cyrus or his family, I apologize," he said. "But I don't apologize for my opinion." Rather absurdly turning it into a First Amendment issue, Tritt's spokeswoman Nancy Russell added that opinions are "what this country is all about." (No argument, but some of us still remember how foolish host Dean Martin looked when he made a face after the Rolling Stones's American TV debut on *Hollywood Palace*. Whose records outsold whose?)

For his part, Garth Brooks laughed off the controversy when asked, saying that in his own case, "chunk" is more appropriate than hunk.

When the brouhaha had died down a bit, Travis was somewhat bitter, telling the press, "I think people definitely don't want to hear honesty." Of course, Tritt was equating honesty with truth, which it certainly was not. When the maverick began his no-hat style of "country music with a rock-and-roll attitude," there were plenty of folks who thought *he* was way off-base. There's room for everyone.

What's really bugging Tritt is more than the fact that a Billy Ray Cyrus concert looks and sounds more like a rock show than it does a country show. He's annoyed at how country music heroes are also coming and going as fast as rock stars traditionally have done. There's too much money to be made and lost in country these days. Dead and buried is the era when a label would stick by a slow-selling but promising artist, or a veteran who's selling below par.

"Look how fast it is," Tritt complains. "Randy Travis would be the first one to tell you, less than four years ago he was the Garth Brooks of our age now. During that time period, he could not lose. Now he's virtually ignored by every major award show in the country. One day you're in, the next day you're out."

Hank Williams Jr. agrees: "It's a pretty quick turnover business now."

Ironically, it was Tritt who found himself on the receiving end of a snub in September of 1992 when he was banned from *The Tonight Show* because he refused to cancel an appearance on the rival *The Arsenio Hall Show*. It wasn't Tritt's fault: he simply got caught in a power struggle between the two shows.

To his credit, Tritt laughed the whole thing off. "Even a bad night of music," he said, "beats the best day you'll ever have in the heating and air-conditioning business." In short order, though, the negative publicity threatened to damage *The Tonight Show* and helped to get the producer fired, and Travis was invited back. The producer denies banning Tritt, saying she was just adjusting her schedule during a difficult week.

So Travis Tritt keeps on trucking, making his own kind of music and his own kind of rules. (Ditto pal Marty Stuart who, when he was inducted into the *Grand Ole Opry* in November of 1992, said, "I'd like to sing you old farts a song." Like Travis, Marty ended up backpedaling later and apologizing, saying he was nervous.)

As Tritt forges ahead, two things are certain: he's going to be around for a while, and like a stick poked into a hornet's nest, he's going to keep stirring things up.

Billy Ray Cyrus

A framed note hangs on Billy Ray Cyrus's bedroom wall. It says, "Sorry if I stammered when I met you, but I'm just like other girls, just a little older (ha)." It's signed Dolly Parton, a usually unflappable lady who's gotten smoochy on screen with the likes of Sylvester Stallone and Burt Reynolds. But her knees shook and her palms sweated when she met Billy Ray, and she's not alone.

There has never been a country star like Billy Ray Cyrus, a charismatic six-footer who sold over four million albums in four months, which boils down to roughly twenty-five thousand records a *day*. And that's in the U.S. alone. In December, his album *Some Gave All* was number one in Australia, and its hit single "Achy Breaky Heart" was number one in Spain.

Dolly's reaction may be typical, but soft-spoken and scrupulously polite Cyrus is as self-effacing and charming as can be.

"I *love* to hear women screaming over me," he says, "but I don't consider myself a hunk. The album wouldn't have been number one all this time if people were buying it solely on the hunk stuff."

True. "Achy Breaky Heart" has been called "rockasilly" music, but his blue-eyed soul is solid stuff. He's got a voice reminiscent of David Clayton Thomas and Bruce Springsteen, and in his stage show he effortlessly moves from ballads to hard-driving rock with no problem. But a build like Schwarzenegger's doesn't hurt either, and Billy Ray's physique is well-displayed by the singer's habit of cutting the sleeves and collar off his shirt, something he's done ever since he was in high school.

"Am I showing off?" he laughs. "Naw . . . that's just the way I'm comfortable. I did it even when I was a shy little misfit of a kid."

A shy *misfit*? Billy Ray?

He says that as a young teenager, "My ears stuck out, my eyes were too big, and my hair was always in a butch cut." He remembers that once, when he was in the first grade, a gang of older kids surrounded him, pulled their ear lobes out and ahead, and reduced him to tears with their laughter.

But today, confidence and fame have brought their share of problems and criticism as well.

His detractors ask, will he be country's answer to Vanilla Ice, vanishing after one album? Will other women claim that he's fathered their children? Will there be other professional lawsuits, other tribulations to give him achy breaky heartache in his personal life?

"I'm sure there will," he says with resignation. "Man, I'll probably die with lawsuits hangin' over me, with all those thunderstorms and stuff cracklin' around my head. But you know, I'll just continue making' my music and lovin' my fans and the rest of it—it don't matter. I'll live with it."

Born in Flatwoods, Kentucky, on August 25, 1961, Cyrus was first exposed to music when he was four years old and singing gospel songs in and out of church.

"My dad had a gospel group called the Crownsmen

Quartet," he says, "and for as far back as I can remember, my mama would ask my dad if I could get up and sing 'Swing Low, Sweet Chariot.' She liked to hear me sing, and that happened to be the one song I knew all the words to."

The experience wasn't, however, a pleasant one. He recalls: "I didn't have many teeth at the time, and sometimes my tongue would get stuck between them. It horrified me."

But there were also warm, pleasant memories associated with music, his mother playing piano, his grandmother playing organ, his father playing fiddle, and the three of them jamming "real high energy stuff—cool, cool stuff." Those memories would return at a key time in Billy Ray's life.

He mucked through school, a quiet loner who was so shy he "wouldn't even get up to dance at the school dances because I was nervous." He liked listening to country and popular music, he loved baseball, and those were his life. As he entered his teenage years, he found another interest: working out. Exercise helped to alleviate his frustrations and build his self-confidence. By doing five hundred pushups a day and various iron pumping exercises, he hoped he might even put enough muscle on his frame to become a professional baseball player.

"I wanted to be one ever since I was three years old, old enough to hold a glove and throw a ball. I wanted to grow up to be Johnny Bench, who was my hero, and I *was* a really good catcher. I hoped that building myself up would help my game."

After graduating from high school, Billy Ray went to Georgetown College in Kentucky, where he pursued his dream. But there's a big difference between "really good" and "world class," and after three years of college, he only had offers from a few minor league teams to join them after graduation.

Profoundly disappointed, and realizing he might never make the grade, the twenty-year-old wasn't sure what to do about his future when he was rescued by an inner voice, a voice that remembered the happy times he'd had and the sense of belonging he'd felt when his parents used to make music.

He says, "The voice told me to pick up a guitar, form a band, and sing. I realized that I wasn't just set here by accident. I was to use my life for something good, for something positive. I felt very strongly at that moment that music was to be my chosen thing."

Now, Billy Ray hadn't played the guitar before, but he bought one, got together bandmates that same day, and began teaching himself how to play. He quickly fell in love with the instrument and with singing. He gave himself and his band, Sly Dog, a year to build a local name for itself or give it up; he achieved his goal, landing a steady gig at the Sand Bar in Ironton, Ohio one week before the year was out.

For the next two years, Cyrus and Sly Dog played local clubs and bars, honing their musical abilities and getting audience feedback. They began making demos, which Cyrus dutifully took to Nashville; he went through the phone book and called everyone who made records, but says, "I never got to play anybody anything. I never got in."

In 1984, a fire destroyed the band's equipment, and taking that as an omen—and fed up with the Nashville scene—Billy Ray moved to Los Angeles where he worked as a car salesman by day and played with various California bands by night as he tried to catch a break in the West Coast music industry.

For nearly three years, he succeeded at doing nothing

except selling cars, which given his smooth style, piercing gaze, and down-home credibility, is not surprising.

However, he says he "got really depressed because I lost everything I came to California for. That was to get a record contract and pursue my music."

In 1986, he gave up on Hollywood and returned to Flatwoods, feeling it was "important to get back to my roots." It was also important to get away from a woman he'd fallen in love with out there, one who was "wanting me to quit the music business and sell cars." He says he remembers thinking, "How could anyone love me if that's what they want me to do with my life?" (Actually, Cyrus had a number of girlfriends during this period, one of whom, Charlotte Stephens, says he wrote his song "Someday, Somewhere, Somehow" for her in 1985.)

The week that Billy Ray returned to Flatwoods, he met Cindy Smith, who worked as a sales rep for Philip Morris, and they married shortly thereafter in nearby Gatlinburg.

The singer and Sly Dog reunited, bought a barely-functioning bread truck to get around in, and landed a five-nights-a-week gig at the Tagtime Lounge in Huntington, West Virginia. Cyrus got better, wrote stacks of songs, made more demos, and began returning to Nashville virtually every week; in 1989 alone, he made forty-two trips to Tennessee.

"That's a six-hour drive each way," he points out. "I'd drive Sunday night, get to Nashville on Monday morning, then just get to a public phone, look in the phone book, and call whoever would see me. I'd go see the janitor—anyone—that would let me play 'em my tape."

But things also began to break in his favor that year. Country superstar and *Grand Ole Opry* legend Del Reeves heard Cyrus, recorded a song he'd written, "It Ain't Over 'Til It's Over," signed him to a contract in

January of 1988, and introduced him to a manager, Jack McFadden. With McFadden's help, the singer was chosen to be the opening act for Reba McEntire, which brought him to the attention of Harold Shedd of Mercury Records. The label signed him, and Cyrus began working on his first album, which consisted of six of his own or co-written songs, and four tunes by other composers, though Billy Ray says, "The songs on the album that I haven't written are all songs that I can truly relate to."

One of the non-Cyrus songs he cut—in fact, the last song selected for the album—was a tune that, like the singer himself, had been rejected by just about every label and artist in town. However, Cyrus recalls that the first time he heard it, he "immediately fell in love with it. It hit me like a hit record does."

Cyrus was right, and his first time at bat, the former college baseball player hit one of the world's great musical homers.

"Don't Tell My Heart" was written by Don Von Tress, inspired by the line "Aching, Breaking Heart" from George Jones's 1962 song. It's an infectious song lasting under three and a half minutes and, before recording it, the singer tried it out for local audiences. They loved it, and returnees would cry out for "that achy breaky song," thus giving the song a new title.

Sadly, it was Cyrus's fame that cost him his home life. "My personal life," he grins, "was a mess, and still is. It started to be a mess back then."

Cindy divorced her husband in October of 1991, long before he joined the ranks of the super-famous. She'd divorced him not because she didn't love him, but because she couldn't compete with his music. Not only was he never around, but even when the two were together women were *constantly* flinging themselves at Cyrus. As far back as 1990, Cyrus was being followed by a band of groupies known as the Cheerleaders, who came to every show he gave (and some of those ladies *are* stunning).

One of the Cheerleaders was especially hot for Cyrus, and one night, when he was performing at a bar, she decided to get Cindy out of the picture by maiming her. Using a Bic lighter, the woman set fire to Cindy's hair, which according to an eyewitness, "went up like a torch because she wore so much hairspray." Cindy would have been seriously hurt if another fan hadn't "thoughtfully" doused it with a pitcher of beer. Cindy hardly ever went to one of her husband's shows again after that.

Sitting home alone each night, she became more and more fed up with the lifestyle until one night in the spring—when he didn't come home—she packed up all his belongings and set them on the porch, then fell asleep on the couch. When he finally returned from his gig at 4:30 in the morning, she said, "I think you're getting way too cocky." He moved out and she filed for divorce. (And he was inspired to write the song "Wher'm I Gonna Live," which would become his third hit single; he gave Cindy half the songwriting credit, and royalties, for the tune.)

Billy Ray says one aspect of the breakup is amusing to him now. The fact that because he was on the road, he hadn't been able to contact his lawyer to find out when the divorce was final. "So," he says, "I called home to find out from Cindy. When the answering machine came on, instead of my voice, it was hers. I knew, then, it was over."

He also realized, then, how valid Cindy's complaint really was. He'd called home so infrequently that he couldn't even remember his own phone number.

However, he says today that not only didn't he blame Cindy for what she did, he still adores her.

"I don't think that true love ever really goes away," he says softly. "There's a part of me that will always love

Cindy and will always miss the things that we went through and the things that we did and the things that we shared. Most importantly of all, as far as Cindy goes, I can only hope that her life is just full of happiness and prosperity and that all of her dreams come true. And that when she looks back on Billy Ray Cyrus, I just hope she'll be able to say that I was a good-hearted man—but *just* a man. Just a dude."

For her part, she says that he really is "the kindest person offstage, very different from his onstage person. He's very soft-spoken, the most polite man you would ever meet." She adds, "We're really better friends now than ever."

Before the single of "Achy Breaky Heart" was released, it was supported by a highly energized video *and* a "how-to-dance-the-Achy-Breaky" video created by choreographer Melanie Greenwood of Nashville. It was sent to thirty country dance clubs and caught on. The day after the video was first shown on Country Music Television, Billy Ray says, "I went to a McDonald's to eat and I was mobbed.

"That was the day my teeter went to totter."

Before long, the network was airing the video every four hours, which was unprecedented; according to Country Music Television's program manager, "My grandma's seventy-nine, and even *she* wants him."

The video made the single an out-of-the-box smash hit when it was released on April 6, and it sold nearly a half-million copies in a month. Numbers like that are rare for a rock-and-roll hit, and were virtually unheard-of for a country single.

As a result of its popularity, Cyrus's first album, *Some Gave All*, not only went straight to the top of the country music charts when it was released on May 24, but it debuted at number four on the pop music charts, the highest first-week-showing of any debut album in pop chart history. It went to number one the next week and stayed there for seventeen weeks, longer than the debut album of any artist in music history.

(The album took its name from a saying common among Vietnam veterans, one of whom told him, "All gave some, but some gave all." That inspired Cyrus to write the song of the same name, which he describes as "an anthem for a time that had no anthem. I love 'Achy Breaky Heart,' but 'Some Gave All' is my very special song.")

Some Gave All sold over five million copies before the year was through—quintuple platinum—and that was just in the U.S. By the time his album *It Won't Be the Last* was released in 1993, the first record had sold some fifteen million copies worldwide. Not bad for a thirty-one-year-old who couldn't get himself an audition just three years before, and was making calls from a pay phone because he couldn't afford to stay in a hotel room.

But fame was not without its price, as Cyrus quickly learned.

On September 23, 1992, he ended up on the receiving end of separate lawsuits filed by Del Reeves and his wife, Ellen. Del's suit claimed that, according to the agreement they'd signed, he was entitled to eight percent of the retail price of every record Cyrus sold, and fifteen percent of his gross earnings as a recording artist—lucrative concerts included. Ellen's suit said that she'd paid $2,200 for the recording of two singles and a five-song demo tape, in return for which she was supposed to receive two-and-one-half percent of his gross earnings from all musical endeavors for a period of one year after he signed with a major label.

Jack McFadden scoffed at the first of the suits, insisting, "The only thing Del Reeves had to do with his record contract was introduce him to me. I'm the one who got the contract."

As for the second, a member of Billy Ray's team says, "That's a helluva interest payment on two grand. The lady oughta lighten up."

Cyrus himself rolled with the blows and considered the suits the price of fame and of doing business. What really hurt him, though, were the many personal missiles he suddenly found himself ducking, from his suddenly open-to-scrutiny private life to the backlash he experienced from country stars and members of the press.

The barrage began when Cyrus began wiggling his butt on TV and in concert. In the same way Elvis was hounded and dogged by his "Pelvis" epithet, Billy Ray's twitches were nicknamed the Cyrus Virus.

Cyrus acknowledged, "I just get into the music and do what comes naturally. But I'll tell you this—I not only admire Mr. Presley, but I sure am learning a little bit of what he went through."

Disc jockeys and reporters threw what were initially lighthearted barbs at the singer, and a parody song, "Achy Breaky Butt," received a bit of airplay on country stations. Things didn't turn ugly until June, when Travis Tritt (see page 258) became a self-appointed music critic and started sniping at the singer.

Cyrus didn't pay much attention to Tritt, though one of his staff members said, "I call the guy Mr. Twitt. He's just jealous 'cause his records don't sell what Billy Ray sells, and when he gets up in the mornin' and looks in the mirror, he don't see what Billy Ray sees."

The Cyrus backlash reached its peak in September, when it was announced that after one album and one hit single, he was being inducted into the Country Music Hall of Fame. What outraged many people was that at the same ceremony on October 1, another singer was being inducted: Patti Page. Unlike Cyrus, who had one hit album and two number one singles to his credit ("Could've Been Me" followed "Achy Breaky Heart" to the top of the charts), Ms. Page's career covered five decades and 160 singles. And, unlike Cyrus, because she was no longer under contract to a label, she was obliged to pony up $2,000 for her star on the Walk of Fame in Nashville.

However, Irving Waugh, the seventy-nine-year-old producer of the Country Music Association Awards show, defended the induction of Cyrus by stating that he is "pretty unusual in country music" and, though a new-comer, had done a lot for the field. He added that as long as someone can sing, there isn't anything wrong "with being a hunk, or gracefully exuding sensuality."

Ah . . . but that *was* the big question. *Could* Cyrus really sing? How much had electronics helped him in the studio? Well, in the summer he added a song to his act that made a believer of anyone who heard it. In front of a huge U.S. flag, he sang—a cappella—"The Star Spangled Banner." Anyone who's tried to sing the national anthem at ball games knows it's a killer, but not only did Billy Ray hit the notes clean and strong and without an instrument accompanying him, but he gave the anthem its most stirring interpretation since Whitney Houston reduced a nation-at-war to tears when she sang it at the 1991 Super Bowl. Even more amazing: crowds of ten or fifteen thousand screaming fans, stirred to a frenzy by "These Boots Are Made For Walkin' " fell stone-quiet as he sang.

But the trashing of Billy Ray Cyrus wasn't limited to criticism of his musical abilities. As soon as he became a public figure, his private life went down the tubes. He says he didn't mind that, though he *was* disturbed about the affect his fame had on his ex-wife and mother.

"That was the hardest part," he says, "the assaults on the privacy of my mother and my ex-wife. Billy Ray Cy-rus signed a contract opening his life up to the entire world. My mom didn't. Neither did Cindy. And they've had to be real security conscious because of me, which is sort of a shame."

However, even though they'd split, Cyrus generously paid for a security system in Cindy's home when his own fame made her the target of reporters, paparazzi, and fans looking for Cyrus memorabilia.

A third front opened up against Billy Ray on April 8, just two days after his single was released and became a smash. That was the day twenty-three-year-old Kristen Luckey, with whom Cyrus had had a romantic liaison, gave birth to a boy, Christopher Cody Cyrus. The two first met about the time Cindy filed for divorce, while Kristen was waitressing at The Doll House in Myrtle Beach, South Carolina, and singing at a nearby place called Cowboys.

Billy Ray said that yes, the child was his, conceived "after my ex-wife filed for divorce. I was a hurtin' person and this lady was my friend." He agreed to pay child support and more, saying, "His mother and I are friends. I respect her, she respects me, and we created a beautiful baby together. I love this baby son.

"I've been making sure that he has a nice bank account. So anything his mom decides he needs, they got the money to go get it. He's livin' good. The only thing I worry about is I'd like for him to be able to go out and play like all the other little boys. I don't want him to have to live in the shadow of Billy Ray Cyrus."

Then, in September, a twenty-five-year-old Kentucky woman, Leticia "Tish" Finley, who had appeared in the "Achy Breaky Heart" video, came forward and claimed to be pregnant with Cyrus's child.

McFadden told the press, "Billy Ray knows the young lady," and said that "if it is proven to be his child, I know he'll stand up to his obligations."

As of early 1993, Billy Ray has not confirmed that he is the child's father, though Billy Ray says if he is the dad, "I wouldn't be ashamed. I'm sure I wouldn't be the first man to have two babies." However, he says that he won't be having any more casual liaisons in the future. "I'm tryin' to be as intelligent (*read: careful*) as I can be, as far as that's concerned. I'm really at this point where friendship is my most valuable commodity. If I can find somebody that can just have a conversation with me about the ozone layer or about Somalia or about the life of Thomas Edison, or anything, that's very valuable to me. I'm takin' time these days to read people's vibes." (A knack, by the way, which serves as a joke in his show. He calls himself "a human vibe reader," which, quite intentionally, sounds like something very different when run through his eastern Kentucky accent.)

As if all of this weren't enough, there were allegations first made by Nashville's music publication *Entertainment Express* and picked up by TV's *Hard Copy* that claimed Cyrus's onstage moves were the result of his having been a Chippendale's dancer in California. The claim was that he'd taken the job for several months to help pay the bills while he was out there. He didn't own up to it because he already felt his grinding moves were detracting from his music. Cancelled checks were rumored to exist, but no one produced any.

These days, he just shakes his head when the subject comes up.

"They can research this Chippendale's thing to the root, to the very core, and they will not find one ounce, one second, one iota of proof or truth in it. And the reason is, because I was never one of them. It just absolutely has no substance to it. And you know—I'm not putting it down. It's a legitimate way of making a living. It wouldn't have made me a bad guy even if I had done it. I just never did, is all."

More than the charges themselves, he resented the fact that *Hard Copy* had gone to his mother's house "in the wee, wee hours of the morning, bangin' on the door. And when my poor mom opened the door, they shoved a camera in her face. She almost had a stroke over it. That ain't right."

Still, he's been able to keep his equilibrium thanks to something his father once told him: "Know where you're going, always be aware of where you're at, and most of all, never forget where you come from." And that's no small feat with the press watching every move you make and women heaving their underwear on stage each night, sometimes, with the women still in them. (Security personnel escort them offstage, often kicking and screaming, Billy Ray frequently yelling at the guards, "Be gentle! She ain't gonna kill nobody!")

Living comfortably but not ostentatiously in a log cabin on five acres in Franklin, Tennessee—with a pool and two lakes—Cyrus says, "I'll tell you what the great thing is about all this. I don't do this for money. I ain't had a day off since it all started, but I don't mind. I'm sure there will never be a day that I go out and sit on the beach and stretch my feet out and say, 'Ah. Today is smooth.' That's why when I go out on stage, and I have that two hours to make my music and be with the audience, I'm truly happy. It's the only time and place on the planet that I can find true peace of mind.

"And you know somethin'?" he says. "I'm lucky to have that. Bad things happen to everyone, so even with the bad things, I'm a lucky man. I think if you asked Johnny Cash or Willie Nelson or anybody else, for all the troubles they've had, I think they'd all say the same thing: All of us who have ever made music are fortunate. We're truly blessed."

Naomi Judd and her daughter Wynonna shocked the world when they announced they'd be ending their seven-year career together. Despite her spirited performances at dozens of sold-out concerts, Naomi's battle with a life-threatening disease was forcing her into retirement—leaving Wynonna to carry on the family tradition. But this was not the first time Naomi had fought the odds and won....

Here is an honest, in-depth look at the lives of Naomi and Wynonna Judd—the early years of struggle, the superstar years as the queens of country music, and their heart-rending personal tragedies. For their millions of devoted fans, THE JUDDS is a rare glimpse into the lives of two remarkable women.

the Judds

The Unauthorized Biography

BOB MILLARD

With a hillbilly twang, he sang racy honky-tonk songs
next to tender gospel ballads, and his wide-brimmed hat
was his symbol. From his dirt-poor childhood with a
domineering mother, he was driven to drugs by a crippling
spinal disease and into despair by two failed marriages.
A man of down-home faith, his salvation lay in music, the
bottle, and women. Now, including never-before-
published material on the controversial emergence of
Williams' daughter, this is the rags-to-riches story of the
first "Cadillac Cowboy." It is a tale as triumphant and as
tragic as the immortal songs he crafted before his untimely
death at age twenty-nine.

Your Cheatin' Heart
A BIOGRAPHY OF HANK WILLIAMS

CHET FLIPPO

"Flippo has managed to put flesh and blood on the
sturdy bones of the Williams legend." —*People*